Forgiveness

A Philosophical Exploration

Nearly everyone has wronged another. Who among us has not longed to be forgiven? Nearly everyone has suffered the bitter injustice of wrongdoing. Who has not struggled to forgive? Charles L. Griswold has written the first comprehensive philosophical book on forgiveness in both its interpersonal and political contexts, as well as its relation to reconciliation. Having examined the place of forgiveness in ancient philosophy and in modern thought, he discusses what forgiveness is, what conditions the parties to it must meet, its relation to revenge and hatred, when it is permissible and whether it is obligatory, and why it is a virtue. He considers "the unforgivable," as well as perplexing notions such as self-forgiveness, forgiving on behalf of others, and unilateral forgiveness, while also illuminating the associated phenomena of pardon, mercy, amnesty, excuse, compassion, and apology. Griswold argues that forgiveness (unlike apology) is inappropriate in politics and analyzes the nature and limits of political apology with reference to historical examples (including Truth and Reconciliation Commissions). The book concludes with an examination of the relation between memory, narrative, and truth. The backdrop to the whole discussion is our inextinguishable aspiration for reconciliation in the face of an irredeemably imperfect world.

Charles L. Griswold is Professor of Philosophy at Boston University. He has been awarded Fellowships from the Stanford Humanities Center, the National Endowment for the Humanities, the Woodrow Wilson International Center for Scholars, and the National Humanities Center. Winner of the American Philosophical Association's F. J. Matchette Award, he is the author and editor of several books, most recently *Adam Smith and the Virtues of Enlightenment.*

Forgiveness

A Philosophical Exploration

CHARLES L. GRISWOLD

Boston University

CAMBRIDGE UNIVERSITY PRESS
Cambridge, New York, Melbourne, Madrid, Cape Town, Singapore, São Paulo, Delhi

Cambridge University Press
32 Avenue of the Americas, New York, NY 10013-2473, USA

www.cambridge.org
Information on this title: www.cambridge.org/9780521878821

First published 2007

Printed in the United States of America

A catalog record for this publication is available from the British Library.

Library of Congress Cataloging in Publication Data

Griswold, Charles L., 1951–
Forgiveness : a philosophical exploration / Charles L. Griswold, Jr.
   p.   cm.
Includes bibliographical references and index.
ISBN 978-0-521-87882-1 (hardback) – ISBN 978-0-521-70351-2 (pbk.)
1. Forgiveness.   I. Title.
BJ1476.G75   2007
179′.9–dc22   2007003936

ISBN   978-0-521-87882-1 hardback
ISBN   978-0-521-70351-2 paperback

To Lisa and Caroline

After such knowledge, what forgiveness?
T. S. Eliot

Contents

Acknowledgments

The bulk of this book was written while I was a Fellow at the Stanford Humanities Center during the 2004–2005 academic year. I am deeply grateful for the Marta Sutton Weeks Fellowship awarded me by the Center, as well as a Boston University sabbatical for the same year. The Center truly provided the perfect working environment.

For helpful comments or conversation about the ideas and arguments of this book, I thank Lanier Anderson, Margaret Anderson, Keith Baker, Sandra Barnes, Heike Berhend, John Bender, Christopher Bobonich, Rémi Brague, Michael Bratman, Susanna Braund, Richard Carrington, Lorraine Daston, Remy Debes, Steve Feierman, Eckart Forster, John Freccero, Aaron Garrett, Hester Gelber, Peter Goldie, Jeffrey Henderson, Pamela Hieronymi, Walter Hopp, Brad Inwood, Laurent Jaffro, Simon Keller, Nan Keohane, Barnabas Malnay, Richard Martin, Christine McBride, Mark McPherran, Adam Morton, Josh Ober, John Perry, Robert Pippin, Linda Plano, Christopher Ricks, Amelie Rorty, Lisa Rubinstein, Steve Scully, David Sedley, Tamar Shapiro, James Sheehan, John Silber, Ken Taylor, Howard Wettstein, Elie Wiesel, Ken Winkler, and Allen Wood. I am forever grateful to Stephen Darwall, Ed Delattre, Steve Griswold, David Konstan, and David Roochnik for their comments on large swaths of the manuscript and for discussion about the effort as a whole. Lanier Anderson, Stephen Darwall, Alasdair MacIntyre, Jonathan Lear, Robert Pippin, and Howard Wettstein supported my project at crucial stages, and I am much in their debt. I also thank the Press' reviewers for their extraordinarily useful queries and comments.

Discussions with my Boston University students in two seminars on the "reconciliation with imperfection" theme were very helpful during the early stages of this project, as were those with the participants in my seminar at the University of Paris 1 (Sorbonne) in May 2004. Audiences at Boston University, Harvard University, Stanford University, St. John's College, the University of Arizona, and the University of California (Riverside), offered valuable criticisms and suggestions. A conference on "Memory, Narrative, and Forgiveness: Reflection on Ten Years of South Africa's Truth and Reconciliation Commission," held in Cape Town in November 2006, was stimulating and enlightening. I am grateful for the responses to my presentation, and for the opportunity to participate in presentations by Desmond Tutu and Pumla Gobodo-Madikizela.

I am pleased to thank Collin Anthony and Jennifer Page for their efficient assistance in collecting and organizing many of the secondary sources on which I have drawn. The Boston University Humanities Foundation generously supported Lauren Freeman's expert compilation of the index; I am grateful on both counts. I also thank my editor at Cambridge University Press, Beatrice Rehl, who was wonderfully supportive and efficient throughout the entire process, and Jennifer Carey for her patient copyediting. Leslie Griswold Carrington and Sarah Fisher were especially helpful with respect to the choice of cover image, and Peter Hawkins inspired the phrasing of the subtitle. Oxford University Press granted permission for quotation from its edition of Adam Smith's *Theory of Moral Sentiments.*

I can scarcely repay, and shall never forget, the support and encouragement given me by family and dear friends as I pushed through to completion of this book.

To Katie: we are testimony to the benefits of mutual forgiveness. For your honesty, steady sense of what really matters, and trust through so many seemingly impassable junctures, thank you. May our friendship continually deepen.

To my daughters Caroline and Lisa: you know the meaning of the phrase of the ancient tragedians, *pathei mathos.* For your depth of soul, brilliance of mind, exemplary generosity of spirit, and forgivingness – not to mention for those wonderful discussions as we made our way up and down invented alpine paths – I am forever grateful. I dedicate this book to you with love and admiration. *Pas à pas on va loin.*

On the façade of beloved Chalet Killarney it is also written: *Je lève mes yeux vers les montagnes, d'où me viendra le secours.* This book was twice revised from start to finish at the Chalet. The sublimity of the Swiss Alps and the tranquillity of high meadows helped me gain clarity about the sense in which forgiveness is an appropriate response to the wrongs that plague human life in every valley of our troubled Earth.

I have frequently placed epigraphs at the start of chapters and sections. These are not necessarily meant to encapsulate the main point of the discussion in question. At times they offer a counterpoint or question to what I have to say, and in this and other ways are meant to enrich the discussion. The epigraph to the book as a whole is taken from T. S. Eliot's "Gerontion," *The Complete Poems and Plays* (New York: Harcourt Brace Jovanovich, 1962), p. 22.

Prologue

Nearly everyone has wronged another. Who among us has not longed to be forgiven? Nearly everyone has suffered the bitter injustice of wrongdoing. Who has not struggled to forgive? Revenge impulsively surges in response to wrong, and becomes perversely delicious to those possessed by it. Personal and national credos anchor themselves in tales of unfairness and the glories of retaliation. Oceans of blood and mountains of bones are their testament. Homer's Achilles captured the agony of our predicament incomparably well:

why, I wish that strife would vanish away from among gods and mortals, and gall, which makes a man grow angry for all his great mind, that gall of anger that swarms like smoke inside of a man's heart and becomes a thing sweeter to him by far than the dripping of honey.[1]

How often have we dreamed of the reconciliation that forgiveness promises, even while tempted by the sweetness of vengeful rage?

Forgiveness is of intense concern to us in ordinary life, both as individuals and as communities. Not surprisingly, the discussions of forgiveness, apology, and reconciliation in theology, literature, political science, sociology, and psychology are innumerable. In a development of great importance, Truth and Reconciliation Commissions have been forging powerful new approaches to age-old conflicts. Ground-breaking work in conflict resolution, international law, the theory of reparations, and political theory pays ever more attention to forgiveness and the related

[1] *Iliad* 18.107–110; Achilles is reflecting on his furious resentment of Agamemnon. Trans. R. Lattimore (Chicago: University of Chicago Press, 1961). All further citations from the *Iliad* advert to this translation.

concepts of pardon, excuse, mercy, pity, apology, and reconciliation.[2] Surprisingly, philosophy has hitherto played a relatively minor (albeit ongoing and increasingly vocal) part in the debates about the meaning of this cluster of concepts. Yet every position taken in theory or practice with regard to these notions assumes that it has understood them accurately. The implicit claim of this book is that these topics are of genuine philosophical interest, and benefit from philosophical examination. My explicit claim is to have provided a defensible analysis of forgiveness in both its interpersonal and political dimensions. Consequently, forgiveness, political apology, and reconciliation are my central themes.

What is forgiveness? A moment's reflection reveals that forgiveness is a surprisingly complex and elusive notion. It is easier to say what it is not, than what it is. Forgiveness is not simply a matter of finding a therapeutic way to "deal with" injury, pain, or anger – even though it does *somehow* involve overcoming the anger one feels in response to injury. If it were just a name for a *modus vivendi* that rendered us insensible to the wrongs that inevitably visit human life, then hypnosis or amnesia or taking a pill might count as forgiveness. Our intuitions are so far from any such view that we count the capacity to forgive – in the right way and under the right circumstances – as part and parcel of a praiseworthy character. We justly blame a person who is unable to forgive, when forgiveness is warranted, and judge that person as hard-hearted. The person who finds all wrongs unforgivable seems imprisoned by the past, unable to grow, confined by the harsh bonds of resentment. He or she might also strike us as rather too proud, even arrogant, and as frozen in an uncompromising attitude. At the same time, someone who habitually forgives unilaterally and in a blink of an eye strikes us as spineless. One should protest injury, and feel the gravity of what is morally serious. Given that wrong-doing is pervasive in human affairs, the question as to whether (and how) to forgive presents itself continuously, and with it, the question as to how the idea should be understood. The daily fact of wrong-doing requires us to answer the question whether, when, and how to forgive.

---

[2] The bibliography to the present book lists all of the relevant recent philosophical work, including on political forgiveness, apology, pardon, and related concepts such as mercy and pity, that I have been able to find. The bibliography includes some works that are more psychological or theological in character, but does not aspire to completeness in respect of them. See www.brandonhamber.com/resources_forgiveness.htm, www.forgiving.org, www.forgivenessweb.com/RdgRm/Bibliography.html, www.learningtoforgive.com, and the "Kentucky Forgiveness Collective" at http://www.uky.edu/~ldesh2/forgive.htm for a sample of the non-philosophical literature, with links to more of the same. I regret that M. Walker's *Moral Repair* (Cambridge: Cambridge University Press, 2006), came into my hands just as this book was going to press.

It may seem at the outset that the dream of reconciliation, both political and private, cannot be fulfilled through forgiveness because forgiveness and its political analogues aspire to something impossible: knowingly to undo what has been done. The stubborn, sometimes infuriating metaphysical fact that the past cannot be changed would seem to leave us with a small range of options, all of which are modulations of forgetfulness, avoidance, rationalization, or pragmatic acceptance. Yet forgiveness claims not to fall among those alternatives; it is a quite different response to what Hanna Arendt aptly called "the predicament of irreversibility."³ Because a central purpose of this book is to work out a defensible conception of forgiveness as it pertains to the interpersonal as well as political realms, I also seek to explain the sense in which it undoes what was done.

One reason philosophers have shied away from giving the topic its due, or from counting forgiveness as a virtue at all, may concern its religious overtones. While it is true that in the Western tradition forgiveness came to prominence in Judaic and Christian thought, I see no reason why we should be bound by its historical genealogy.⁴ There is nothing in the concept itself that requires a religious framework, even though it may be thought through within such a framework. The question as to the conceptual relation between a religious and a non-religious view of the subject is interesting in its own right. In the present book I offer an analysis of forgiveness as a secular virtue (that is, as not dependent on any notion of the divine), although I will also make reference to theological discussions as appropriate, both by way of contrast and because the touchstone of modern philosophical discussion of the topic is to be found in Bishop Butler. Let me sketch the strategy I will pursue as well as some orienting distinctions and questions.

A fundamental thesis of this book is that forgiveness is a concept that comes with conditions attached. It is governed by norms. Forgiveness has not been given, or received, simply because one believes or feels that it has been. Uttering (even to myself, whether about another or about

---

³ As she writes: "the possible redemption from the predicament of irreversibility – of being unable to undo what one has done though one did not, and could not, have known what he was doing – is the faculty of forgiving." *The Human Condition* (Chicago: University of Chicago Press, 1958), p. 237. This is well put, except for the clause freeing the agent of responsibility.

⁴ Arendt overstates the point when she writes that "the discoverer of the role of forgiveness in the realm of human affairs was Jesus of Nazareth." The historical genealogy of the notion is much more complex. But her next sentence is on the mark: "The fact that he made this discovery in a religious context and articulated it in religious language is no reason to take it any less seriously in a strictly secular sense." *The Human Condition*, p. 238.

myself) "I forgive you" does not mean I have in fact done so, regardless of the level of subjective conviction. So too "I am forgiven." Any number of thought experiments confirm this point, as, for example, that already mentioned: if a victim of injury has pretty much forgotten what took place, we would not accept the inference that all is therefore forgiven.

One of my central themes is forgiveness understood as a moral relation between two individuals, one of whom has wronged the other, and who (at least in the ideal) are capable of communicating with each other. In this ideal context, forgiveness requires reciprocity between injurer and injured. I shall reserve the term *forgiveness* for this interpersonal moral relation.[5] All parties to the discussion about forgiveness agree, so far as I can tell, that this is a legitimate context for the use of the term; and most take it as its paradigm sense, as shall I. This implies a controversial position about "forgiveness" in the political context, which I will defend in detail.

There are modulations of forgiveness that lack one or more of the features of the model case. These notions include (i) forgiving wrongs done to others (including victims no longer living), i.e., "third-party forgiveness"; (ii) forgiving the dead or unrepentant; (iii) self-forgiveness; (iv) God's forgiveness; and perhaps even (v) forgiving God. These seem best understood as departures from and conceptually dependent upon the paradigm. For example, in (iii) the forgiver cannot easily be said to resent the candidate for forgiveness, or to expect contrition and amends tendered by the injuring party, if the injury for which one is forgiving oneself is an injury one has done oneself. In (iv) the party from whom one requests forgiveness (God) may be conceived as immune to injury; which raises the puzzling possibility that (iv) is a case of third-party forgiveness (we ask God to forgive us the wrongs we have done to *others,* and thus on behalf of others).[6] In these non-paradigmatic cases, special problems arise due to the absence of one of the features of forgiveness.

Further, it is an important claim of this book that cases (i) through (iii) are *lacking* or imperfect relative to the paradigm, in the sense that were it possible for all of the conditions pertaining to the paradigm to be fulfilled, we would wish for them to be so. We nonetheless speak of forgiveness in these non-paradigmatic situations, and it would be arbitrary

---

[5] I do not assume, however, that the parties involved in the scene of forgiveness had any personal relation to each other prior to the events that initiate the question of forgiveness.

[6] A point trenchantly put by J. Gingell, "Forgiveness and Power," *Analysis* 34 (1974): 180–183. See also M. Lewis, "On Forgiveness," *Philosophical Quarterly* 30 (1980): 236–245.

to rule them illegitimate a priori. Our task is to understand the notion and its conceptual structure, not to revolutionize it. In what follows, I will discuss the first three of the non-paradigmatic cases I have mentioned, in the order given. Because my approach to the topic is secular I will not venture into the issues surrounding forgiveness of God.

Forgiveness and its modulations do not exhaust the meanings of the term, and for the sake of clarity it is essential to distinguish five of these other meanings. The first of them will receive considerable attention here, as it is one of my central themes. The other four are not my subject, but are easily and often confused with it. Forgiveness and the five other senses of forgiveness may usefully be thought of as bearing a Wittgensteinian "family resemblance" to one another.[7] These siblings of forgiveness are:

1. *Political apology*: apology offered in a political context. This notion encompasses a cluster of phenomena, including apology (understood as the acknowledgment of fault and a request for the acceptance thereof) offered by the appropriate state official for wrongs committed by the state. Possibly the apology may be offered to the state. The exchange may or may not be accompanied by reparations. Such "state apologies" are becoming an established part of the political landscape. As well, political apology may take place when previously conflicting groups within the community (or within an envisioned, hoped-for community), as well as individuals within those groups, are publicly called upon to forgive one another in the name of civic reconciliation. The relevant institutions or organizations include corporations, churches, and other civic associations. In some contexts, political apology may shade into invitations to or encouragement of forgiveness, in which case it is tempting to speak of political forgiveness, always in relation to some political entity. Perhaps the most famous recent argument for the political role of forgiveness was articulated by Archbishop Desmond Tutu. He did so in the context, of course, of the transition from apartheid to a democratic state in South Africa, through his

---

7 Wittgenstein remarks that understanding the different meanings of a term is a matter of grasping "a complicated network of similarities overlapping and criss-crossing: sometimes overall similarities, sometimes similarities of detail." *Philosophical Investigations*, 3rd ed., trans. G. E. M. Anscombe (Oxford: Blackwell's, 2001, par. 66). I should add that there are yet other senses of "forgive," as when one says "forgive me" after having accidentally bumped into someone; there it just means "excuse me." These relatively trivial senses are not my focus here.

writings, and his position as chair of the Truth and Reconciliation Commission.[8] Chapter 4 is devoted to political apology.

2. *Economic forgiveness*: the forgiveness of debts. We also speak of "pardoning" a debt; the debtor is released from the obligation of repayment.

3. *Political pardon*: this encompasses a cluster of phenomena, including prominently the pardon that a duly recognized member of a non-judicial branch of government may grant (in the American system, an "executive pardon" issued by the President or a Governor); the granting of amnesty;[9] the decision by the victorious state or its leader not to punish the defeated, for any of a number of reasons including strategic or political advantage, or from a sense of humanity (this last easily shades into "mercy").[10] Executive pardon

---

[8] See D. Tutu, *No Future without Forgiveness* (New York: Random House, 1999). As already noted, the Truth and Reconciliation Commission (hereafter, "TRC") also included a committee that granted amnesty, but I am not here referring to that part of the process. For some of the historical background, see D. Shea, *The South African Truth Commission: The Politics of Reconciliation* (Washington, DC: United States Institute of Peace Press, 2000). The discussion of the political role of forgiveness is terminologically unsettled and confusing for that reason among others. As the title of Digeser's *Political Forgiveness* suggests, elements of what I am calling political pardon and political apology have been seen as species of forgiveness. Digeser writes that "political forgiveness is not about clearing the victim's heart of resentment. Rather, it entails clearing a debt that the transgressor or debtor owes to the victim or the creditor. . . . Political forgiveness can be understood as an action that forgives a debt, reconciles the past, and invites the restoration of the civil and moral equality of transgressors and their victims or the restoration of a relationship between creditors and debtors to the status quo ante" (p. 28). In Ch. 4, I explain my choice of terminology and my objections to Digeser's approach.

[9] The amnesty can be extended individual by individual, as was the case recently in South Africa under the auspices of the Amnesty Committee of the TRC; or to an entire group, as, for example, to the defeated Athenian oligarchs and their supporters in 403 BCE (the amnesty included the provision that no mention could be made in a court of law that a person had collaborated with the oligarchy). There are numerous contemporary examples of amnesty being granted to classes of people, often wrong-doers and their collaborators who are no longer in power. In the context of debates about illegal immigration, by contrast, amnesty has come to mean something like immunity from prosecution, or pardon.

[10] For example, Julius Caesar famously granted "clemency" (*clementia Caesaris*) to some he conquered in war. Whether or not he did so for political reasons, this species of pardon is certainly to be distinguished from forgiveness in the sense discussed in the present chapter. See Seneca, *De Clementia* 2.3, for his definitions thereof, and his defense of the view that *clementia* is a virtue. He sees clemency as leniency in the administration of due punishment, and distinguishes it from pity as well as pardon (i.e., pardon of a judicial nature).

may amount to a grant of immunity, without necessarily implying guilt or that a set punishment is suspended.[11]

4. *Judicial pardon*: the exercise of mercy or clemency by a court of law in the penalty phase of a trial, in view of extenuating circumstances, such as the suffering already undergone by the guilty party, or of similar sorts of reasons. Normally this would come to obviating the expected, or already determined, punishment. As in (3), the pardoner must have recognized standing to issue the pardon, and the pardoned has, at least in some cases of (3) and in all of (4), committed offences as defined by the law of the land.

Neither in (3) nor in (4) is the individual *forgiven* for his or her wrong-doing. Normally, in those cases, the pardoner will not be the person who was injured, or at least not have been intentionally singled out to be wronged. In none of (2), (3), or (4) is there a necessary tie to any particular sentiment; in particular, pardon does not require the giving up of resentment.[12]

5. *Metaphysical forgiveness*: this may be characterized as the effort to give up *ressentiment* caused by the manifold imperfections of the world. It comes to forgiving the world for being the sort of place that brings with it a spectrum of natural and moral evils, from death, illness, physical decay, and the unstoppable flow of the future into the past, to our limited control over fortune, to the brute fact of the all too familiar range of wrongs people do to each other and to themselves.[13] I use "ressentiment" here because its connotations are broader than "resentment," including as it does malice, desire for revenge, envy (admittedly not apt to this context), but also anxiety, suspicion, the holding of a grudge, a hatred of whatever or whoever one feels has called one's standing into question, a

---

[11] President Ford's executive pardon of President Nixon led to a debate about whether pardon implies guilt. See K. D. Moore, *Pardons: Justice, Mercy, and the Public Interest* (Oxford: Oxford University Press, 1989), pp. 193–196; and P. E. Digeser's *Political Forgiveness* (Ithaca: Cornell, 2001), pp. 125–130.

[12] Further, "I pardon you," in both (3) and (4), is a performative utterance, as is pointed out by R. S. Downie, "Forgiveness," *Philosophical Quarterly* 15 (1965), p. 132.

[13] D. Konstan refers to this as "existential resentment"; see his "Ressentiment Ancien et Ressentiment Moderne," in P. Ansart, ed., *Le ressentiment* (Brussels: Bruylant, 2002), p. 266. He there cites M. Scheler and R. Solomon as carving out a place for this type of resentment.

feeling of powerlessness, a loss of self-respect, and (especially as Nietzsche describes it) a generalized sense that the world is unfair. It suggests frustrated and repressed anger. This sense of the term seems to have been coined by Nietzsche. I do not, however, want to saddle "metaphysical resentment" with all of the connotations of Nietzschean "ressentiment." Perhaps what Nietzsche himself called the "spirit of revenge" (*Zarathustra*, Part II, "On Revenge") is closer to the target. Forgiveness is an intriguing candidate for curing the "spirit of revenge," because it allows for a certain willing of the past through re-interpretation and re-framing. Giving up metaphysical ressentiment could mean many things other than forgiveness. One would be the "happiness" in the recognition of the absurd that Camus attributes to Sisyphus.[14]

To repeat, the last four of these siblings of forgiveness are not the primary focus of this book. I devote a chapter to the first of my list of five – political apology – because it is naturally confused with giving and receiving of forgiveness, because understanding clearly why that is both a conceptual and political mistake is so helpful to grasping the character of forgiveness, and because it joins with forgiveness in aiming at reconciliation (albeit of a different sort).

A moment's reflection on the nature of forgiveness raises multiple questions, including these:

- Is forgiveness (or, the disposition to forgive) a virtue?
- Is the wrong-doer or the deed the focus of forgiveness?
- What, if anything, ought the candidate for forgiveness say or do or feel to warrant forgiveness, and what the victim truly to forgive?
- Are you morally obligated to forgive when the offender has taken the appropriate steps, or is forgiveness a "gift"?
- How is forgiveness related to apology, mercy, pity, compassion, excuse, contrition, and condonation?
- How is it related to justice (especially retributive justice, and the issue of punishment)?

---

[14] Editions of the French dictionaries of the Académie Française from the seventeenth century on define "ressentiment" primarily as what we would call resentment (see http://www.lib.uchicago.edu/efts/ARTFL/projects/encyc/). For the citation from *Thus Spoke Zarathustra*, Part II, "On Revenge," see p. 252 of the W. Kaufman trans. in his *The Portable Nietzsche* (New York: Penguin, 1976). I return to Nietzsche in Ch. 1. For the reference to Camus see his *The Myth of Sisyphus*, trans. J. O'Brien (New York: Random House, 1955), p. 91.

- Is there such a thing as "the unforgivable"?
- Is forgiveness necessary to moral and spiritual growth, and to what ideals does it aspire?
- How is forgiveness related to reconciliation?
- Can one person forgive (or ask for forgiveness) on behalf of another?
- Can one forgive (or be forgiven by) the dead, or forgive the unrepentant?
- How is self-forgiveness to be understood?
- Does forgiveness have a political role to play?

In the course of this book I shall offer answers to these much disputed questions, among others.

I begin Chapter 1 by discussing a number of classical perfectionist views in which forgiveness has little or no place. (I also comment very briefly on a contrasting modern perfectionist view, that of Nietzsche.) My objective is in part to disentangle forgiveness from various notions with which it has long been clustered, such as "excuse" and "pardon," to begin to draw its connections to other notions intuitively connected with it (such as sympathy, the recognition of common humanity and fallibility, and the lowering of anger), and to better understand the conditions under which forgiveness is a virtue. I seek to show that a certain type of perfectionist outlook – a well-established and perpetually attractive one – is inhospitable to seeing forgiveness as a virtue. I sketch the ways in which forgiveness does meet criteria of virtue theory as classically understood. The attempt is to understand forgiveness against the backdrop of perfectionist and non-perfectionist moral theory, and to argue that it is at home in a certain kind of non-perfectionist theory.

We habitually think of forgiveness in relation to the emotion of resentment. Is this justified? What is resentment, how does it differ from hatred and other forms of anger, in what way is it cognitive, and how are we to understand its infamously retributive tendency? What are we to make of its famous propensity to tell a justificatory story about itself? How are forgiveness, revenge, and the administration of justice related? These and related questions are also taken up in Chapter 1 by means of an examination of a seminal eighteenth-century analysis. We owe the linkage of forgiveness and resentment to Bishop Joseph Butler's acute and seminal sermons, and they set the stage for all subsequent discussions of the topic (even though, as I shall show, one of his key points is regularly misquoted in a revealing way). Understanding the merits as well as shortcomings of his analyses of resentment and forgiveness is extremely helpful to working out a theory of forgiveness. Butler begins both his sermons by noting the imperfection of the world and implicitly, the problem of reconciliation with it. This brief examination of several of the most important philosophers in the ancient tradition, and of two moderns (Butler and Nietzsche), serves the purposes of conceptual clarification and of determining the geography, as it were, of our topic.

In Chapter 2, I build on the results and set out a theory of forgiveness. I analyze the "paradigm case" in which injured and injuring parties are both present as well as willing and able to communicate with each other. I also discuss the criteria or norms that each party must meet if forgiveness is to be fully expressed, as well as the question as to whether forgiveness is "conditional," supererogatory, and analogous to the canceling of a debt. The related issues of self-respect, regret, the "moral monster," the relevance of notions of shared humanity, pity, and sympathy (with Homer's masterful depiction of Achilles' encounter with Priam as touchstone), the reasons for which giving and receiving forgiveness is desirable, the vexed question of "the unforgivable," are examined in detail. Because the offender and victim develop narratives as part of requesting and granting forgiveness – narratives of self as well as of the relationship of self to other – I sketch the basics of a theory of narrative and show how it illuminates forgiveness. I examine the ideals underlying the narrative, and conclude by returning to the broader issue of the relation between forgiveness, the aspiration to perfection, and reconciliation.

Both paradigmatic and non-paradigmatic species of forgiveness depend on the capacity for sympathy in something like the sense of putting oneself in the situation of another, and seeing things from that perspective. They also depend on our capacity to correct for distorted perspective, by adopting something like the standpoint of "the moral community" or (in Adam Smith's phrase) the "impartial spectator." An entire book could easily be written on those topics alone, and my discussion of them in Chapter 2 is strictly limited by my present purpose.

In Chapter 3, I also turn to the three non-standard or non-paradigmatic cases of forgiveness already mentioned, viz. third-party forgiveness (forgiving or asking for forgiveness on behalf of another), forgiveness of the dead and unrepentant, and self-forgiveness. Each presents puzzles of its own – beginning with whether they count as instances of forgiveness at all. I argue that they can, but imperfectly. It is not inappropriate that a virtue that responds to certain imperfections of human life – above all, our all too well-established propensity to injure one another – itself reflects something of the context from which it arises. We very often find ourselves called upon to forgive when the offender is unwilling or unable to take appropriate steps to qualify for forgiveness (the obverse also takes place). I work out the structure and criteria for such cases, and end with a discussion of the role of "moral luck" in forgiveness.

Forgiveness has become a major political topic in recent decades, as already mentioned, thanks in good part to the remarkable work of the South African Truth and Reconciliation Commission and its chair, Archbishop Desmond Tutu. Apology and reparations too are very widely discussed, offered, and demanded not just by political entities but also by or from corporations and other institutions. Forgiveness is touted as indispensable to reconciliation in the context of both civic strife and international conflict. Ought it to be? I offer a controversial answer to the question in Chapter 4, and argue that apology (and its acceptance) rather than forgiveness should play the envisioned role. They differ in structure and criteria, though they also overlap in some ways, as is natural to concepts bearing a "family resemblance" to one another. Some of the same issues arise at this political level as did at the interpersonal level, in particular the problem of that which cannot be apologized for (the analogue of "the unforgivable"), the structure of the narrative and nature of the ideals underlying political apology, and the relation of apology to reconciliation.

I have developed the analysis of political apology in good part through reflection on examples, as this is the clearest and most persuasive way to draw distinctions and make the argument, given the role that perception of the particulars (to borrow Aristotle's thought) plays here. Some of the cases are of successful apologies (such as that of the U.S. government for the internment of Japanese-Americans during World War II), some of failed apology or of avoidance of apology where it is due. Some cases I examine – in particular, traditional rituals of reconciliation in Uganda, for example – seem to blur the line between apology and forgiveness. In yet other instances, reparations seem to function as the moral equivalent of repentance, further complicating the question as to the lines between questions of justice, apology, and forgiveness. The relevant distinctions embedded in social practices are surprisingly subtle, as reflection on the particulars shows, but important to clarify.

The sheer pervasiveness of the language of apology and forgiveness today suggests that we have developed what might be called a culture of apology and forgiveness. There are benefits as well as serious risks inherent in such a culture. The former are as routinely proclaimed as the latter are overlooked. I examine them both.

As was true with respect to interpersonal forgiveness, the backdrop of political apology is a picture of the imperfection of the political and social world. Political apology attempts to respond to that imperfection in ways that allow for emendation but make no promise of comprehensive improvement of the picture as such. Its aim on any particular occasion is quite specific and localized, and its ideals encourage the possibility of that sort of patchwork improvement. To one attempting either to flee the imperfections of the socio-political world, or to emend those imperfections in some comprehensive way, political apology as I have defined it would seem either irrelevant or unacceptably accommodating.

One of the contentions of this book is that successful forgiveness and political apology depend on truth telling and that, more broadly, we are better off responding to wrong-doing with recognition of the truth rather than with evasion. Truth telling is one of the ideals underpinning both forgiveness and apology, and it is an implicit thesis of the book that reconciliation is furthered by truth telling and, as apposite, forgiveness or political apology (or both). Especially at the political level, however, truth telling in the relevant circumstances is normally partial or shaded, if it occurs at all. Because the narrative in which the truth is told (or partially told, as the case may be) is by definition backward looking in part, the issue becomes how we should remember the past. At the same time, the narrative is forward looking in that it is inevitably meant to influence future perspective and perhaps action. In the concluding chapter, I examine a revealingly imperfect recent example of political memory and truth telling, namely the Vietnam Veterans Memorial in Washington, DC. It is currently the best known and most visited memorial in the United States, and quite possibly its most discussed and debated such memorial as well. One of the striking features of this brilliant and subtle work is that, without quite saying so, it offers reconciliation without apology and thus avoids taking a stand on the moral essence of the matter. In that crucial respect it is a counter-example to much of what is implied by this book, and thereby offers another occasion for examining the relation between our key notions. I argue that the Memorial sidesteps confrontation with the whole truth, compromising its success as memory and narrative, along with the depth of the reconciliation it makes possible. The Memorial thereby makes an indirect case for the political importance of full and honest confrontation with injury and wrong.

"Reconciliation" can of course be understood in a number of quite different ways. It may mean resigned acceptance, perhaps in the light of the futility of protest, and this may in turn offer sad consolation (as when one says "I am reconciled to my fate, there being nothing I can do to avoid it"). Or it may simply mean acceptance and an agreement to cease hostilities, as when two warring nations reconcile in the sense of establishing a truce: hatred may subsist, but forcible intervention in each others' affairs stops. In a quite different register, "reconciliation" may carry a strong sense of affirmation, as when previously antagonistic partners find a way to rebuild and even flourish together. As is sometimes pointed out, the very term suggests (though it does not require) a narrative in which the two parties begin as friends, become estranged, and become friends again – the basic pattern being one of unity, division, and reunification.[15] Still further along the spectrum, reconciliation may connote joyful endorsement. If that came to deluding oneself into the cheery view that the world is simply wonderful without qualification, or to a Panglossian attitude that manages to explain evil away, then joyful reconciliation would amount to a kind of moral blindness that flees from rather than appropriately responds to the relevant features of the world. True reconciliation, however, does not close its eyes to, or simply avoid, that which creates the challenge to which it is a response.

A common thread through all these senses of reconciliation is the fact of either natural or moral evil (or at least, wrong or badness – I shall sometimes simplify here and below, and speak of "evil" *tout court*, without assigning any added significance to the word). Given that the omnipresence of evil is one way in which the human world is imperfect, a standing challenge is to understand whether and how it is possible to be reconciled to evil. Forgiveness is a prime candidate in part because it does not reduce either to resigned acceptance or to deluded avoidance. But to say this is simply to restate the question: how can one accept fully that moral evil has been done and yet see its perpetrator in a way that counts as "reconciliation" in a sense that simultaneously forswears revenge, aspires to give up resentment, and incorporates the injury suffered into a narrative of self that allows the victim and even the offender to flourish? This is not primarily a psychological question, though there is an unavoidable affective dimension to forgiveness, but rather both an analytical question (one that seeks a definition specifying what it would mean to forgive, and so to succeed or fail at doing so) and an ethical question (one that seeks

---

[15] I refer to M. O. Hardimon's *Hegel's Social Philosophy: The Project of Reconciliation* (Cambridge: Cambridge University Press, 1994), p. 85. The senses of "perfection" and the ways they have functioned in moral and political philosophy are many as well; for an excellent study, see J. Passmore's *The Perfectibility of Man*, 3rd ed. Rpt. (Indianapolis: Liberty Press, 2000).

to articulate the reasons for which one ought or ought not forgive, or in a political context, accept an apology). The answer is not the magic key to reconciliation with imperfection – there is no magic key to so multi-faceted a problem – but it would nonetheless be desirable to have a good answer. We shall not likely achieve the stance of what Nietzsche called, in a compelling and complex passage praising affirmation of the world as we have it, a "Yes-sayer."[16] And yet when arrived at through forgiveness or apology, interpersonal or political reconciliation confronts what is the case, without blindness or evasion, insists that wrong-doing be addressed appropriately, and affirms the value of moral repair. Affirmation in something like Nietzsche's sense must join hands with protest against evil, if the former is to have any content, and if evil is not to destroy perpetrator and victim alike.

---

[16] "I want to learn more and more to see as beautiful what is necessary in things; then I shall be one of those who makes things beautiful. *Amor fati*: let that be my love henceforth! I do not want to wage war against what is ugly. I do not want to accuse; I do not even want to accuse those who accuse. *Looking away* shall be my only negation. And all in all and on the whole: some day I wish to be only a Yes-sayer." F. Nietzsche, *The Gay Science*, trans. W. Kaufmann (New York: Random House, 1974), par. 276, p. 223.

1

Forgiveness Ancient and Modern

Ancient pagan notions of forgiveness are a vast and poorly studied topic.[1] That such notions existed is more than merely probable. The vocabulary for them was in place, along with a cluster of related notions – pardon, mercy, pity, compassion, apology, debt relief, excuse, among others – as was a sophisticated understanding of the emotions (in particular, retributive anger) to which forgiveness somehow responds. Similarly, the ends that forgiveness proposes, such as reconciliation, peace, and certainly the forswearing of revenge, were well understood. I very much doubt that there existed a single view on any of these topics (something like "the ancient pagan view"), though establishing that point would require a careful and comprehensive study of ancient literature, law court speeches and jurisprudence, the writings of the historians and physicians, and of course the philosophical texts. As is true in respect of other ideas, it would not surprise if the philosophers rejected or modified common views about forgiveness and related notions. Nonetheless, such notions did circulate in pre-Christian pagan thought and culture (counting here the Roman as well as Greek), contrary to common wisdom.

---

[1] Some help concerning their role in the Western tradition (to which my discussion is limited) may be found in K. Metzler, *Die griechische Begriff des Verzeihens: Untersuch am Wortstamm syngnome von den ersten Belegen bis zum vierten Jahrhundert n. Chr.* (Wissenschaftliche Untersuchungen zum Neuen Testament, Zweite Reihe, 44; Tübingen: J. C. B. Mohr, 1991); and J. Krašovec's *Reward, Punishment, and Forgiveness: the Thinking and Beliefs of Ancient Israel in the Light of Greek and Modern Views* (Supplements to Vetus Testamentum 78; Leiden: Brill, 1999). I am grateful to Chris Bobonich, Brad Inwood, David Konstan, David Roochnik, and David Sedley for discussion of the issues examined in this chapter.

Another vast territory stretches between them and Bishop Butler's influential eighteenth-century account, examined in the second section of this chapter. I doubt that there existed a single view about our topics during that long period – Christian "forgiveness" too has an interesting conceptual history. Because my focus in this chapter is not primarily historical, however, and because the conceptual framework assumed here is secular, I offer only the briefest of observations about "the Christian tradition" of thought about my topics.

It is surprising and illuminating that forgiveness is not seen as a virtue by the ancient Greek philosophers. Understanding why helps to explain something about the conceptual context in which it becomes a virtue (or the expression of a virtue), as well as what it would mean to think of it in that way, and it is a chief aim of the following section to offer that explanation. I also attempt to delineate differences between forgiveness, excuse, and pardon, and to begin setting out the connection between forgiveness and anger. I argue that the perfectionism of ancient philosophical ethics, along with views about human dignity, provide the backdrop against which the ancient philosophical view of forgiveness is conceived. Limited in focus as it is, my discussion of ancient and modern forgiveness attempts to articulate the complex conceptual landscape in which forgiveness is located, thereby contributing significantly to the project of setting out a theory of forgiveness.

[i] PARDON, EXCUSE, AND FORGIVENESS IN ANCIENT PHILOSOPHY: THE STANDPOINT OF PERFECTION

> From you let me have
> much compassion (*sungnômosunên*) now for what I do.
> You see how little compassion (*agnômosunê*) the Gods
> have shown in all that's happened; they
> who are called our fathers, who begot us,
> can look upon such suffering.
> No one can foresee what is to come.
> What is here now is pitiful for us
> and shameful for the Gods;
> but of all men it is hardest for him
> who is the victim of this disaster.
>   Sophocles, *The Women of Trachis*, 1264–1274[2]

---

[2] Trans. M. Jameson, in *Sophocles II*, ed. D. Grene and R. Lattimore. Chicago: University of Chicago Press, 1969.

The vocabulary of forgiveness, and certainly of political and judicial pardon, was known to Plato, Aristotle, and their contemporaries as well as successors. The Greek term typically used is *sungnômê* or a cognate.[3] The rarity of the relevant use of the term by ancient philosophers, then, is not due the unavailability of the word. The verbal form of *sungnômê* is "sungignôskô," meaning to think with, agree with, consent, acknowledge, recognize, excuse, pardon, have fellow-feeling or compassion with (as in the quotation from Sophocles with which this section begins). The etymology of the term suggests cognitivist connotations. Similarly, we talk of "being understood," where this means that one's interlocutor has entered into one's situation, grasped it sympathetically from one's own perspective, seen why one has acted or reacted as one has, and made allowances (this could mean anything from forgiving to pardoning to excusing). The range of meanings of *sungnômê* – from sympathize, to forbear, forgive or pardon, excuse or make allowance for – is fascinating, and anticipates several of my questions about the connections between these notions.

We find appeals to "sungnômê" among the law court speeches of various ancient rhetoricians. Consider Isocrates 16.12–13 and Andocides 1.57, 2.6–7, where the defendant appeals for pardon by reminding the

---

[3] By contrast, the verb used in the Lord's Prayer in Matthew 6:12 is *aphiêmi*, whose meanings include to acquit (in a legal sense), release, send away, cancel a debt, excuse. The 1611 King James version translated "and forgive [*aphes*] us our debts, as we forgive our debtors." So too in Luke 11.2.4 (where the King James translates "and forgive [*aphes*] us our sins, for we also forgive everyone who is indebted to us"); 23.34 ("Father forgive [*aphes*] them, for they do not know what they do"). Wyclif's fourteenth-century translation of the Bible renders the term as "forgiveness." Yet the Liddell, Scott, and Jones *Greek-English Lexicon* (Oxford: Clarendon Press, 1968) does not list "forgive" as one of the meanings of *aphiêmi* (though it does for the noun *aphesis*). The Latin vulgate used "dimitto," meaning at base to release from, discharge, send away, with a primary context of forgiving a debt; and in Matthew, "sin" is "debita;" so too Luke 23.34, "Pater, dimitte illis; non enim sciunt quid faciunt." (I am grateful to Hester Gelber for bringing my attention to the Latin, and for conversation about the complex meanings of pardon, forgiveness, and mercy in Medieval philosophy and culture.) For some discussion of the Biblical notions of forgiveness see A. Margalit's *The Ethics of Memory* (Cambridge: Harvard University Press, 2002), ch. 6. He notes on p. 188 that the Hebrew Bible uses two notions of forgiveness, one as "blotting out the sin" and the other as "covering it up" (disregarding but not forgetting). Only God can "forgive and forget," that is, blot out the sin, remove it from the book of life, so to speak. See also D. W. Shriver, Jr., *An Ethic for Enemies: Forgiveness in Politics* (Oxford: Oxford University Press, 1995), ch. 1 and 2; and *Dimensions of Forgiveness*, ed. W. Worthington, Jr. (Philadelphia: Templeton Foundation Press, 1998, Part I ("Forgiveness in Religion")). For a monumental scholarly examination, see J. Krašovec's *Reward, Punishment, and Forgiveness*. Krašovec does not tackle the Gospels, and about 700 pages of his 800-page text are devoted to the Hebrew sources. As will become evident in Chapter 2, my own view of forgiveness combines elements of "sungnômê" and "aphiêmi."

jury of shared human shortcomings.⁴ Something similar goes on in tragic appeals based on an analogous situation, such as in Euripides' *Iphiginia in Tauris* 1401–2, where Electra, in praying to Artemis that she sympathize with Electra's love for her brother Orestes, reminds Artemis of her love for her own brother Apollo; all of which is meant to elicit "forgiveness" ("sungnômê") for Electra.⁵

In the *Nicomachean Ethics*, Aristotle uses the term mainly in two connections. The first concerns the nature of voluntary action in Book III. When the agent's deeds are caused by external force or are undertaken in ignorance of the relevant facts, the person is neither simply culpable nor praiseworthy. Sometimes, maybe often, there are mixed actions, as when someone is "forced" to throw the cargo off the ship in order to prevent it from sinking. When the external force is extreme, and people commit one of these "qualified willing" acts and, we proceed from this thought: "there is pardon (*sungnômê*), whenever someone does a wrong action because of conditions of a sort that overstrain human nature, and that no one would endure" (1110a24–26).⁶

---

⁴ See also Andocides I.141, where the term means "sympathy." For another interesting example of a court room use of the term, see Lysias 31, where as D. Konstan notes, *sungnômê* "is not pardon or acquittal; it is more like a shared attitude." *Pity Transformed* (London: Duckworth, 2001), p. 39. I would maintain that this case is still rather like the Isocrates and Andocides passages in meaning something like "excuse"; but agree that all three assume the innocence of the plaintiff (it is not an appeal to mercy). See also Lysias 1.3 and 10.2.

⁵ Consider Sophocles *Electra* 257 and Euripides *Ion* 1440, where the term means excuse or pardon but could be understood as "forgive." See also J. de Romilly, "Indulgence et Pardon dans la Tragédie Grecque," in her *Tragedies Grecques au Fil des Ans* (Paris: Les Belles Lettres, 1995), pp. 62–77. At Thucydides 3.40, in the course of the Mytilenean debate, Cleon advocates that no hope should be extended that the rebels will "be excused (*xuggnômên*) on the plea that their error was human"; they acted intentionally, and "it is that which is unintentional which is excusable (*xuggnômon*)." Trans. C. F. Smith, in *Thucydides* 4 vols, vol. II (Cambridge: Harvard University Press, 1988). The family resemblance of the notions of excuse, pardon, and forgiveness is indicated by the fact that P. Woodruff translates here "pardon" (*Thucydides: On Justice, Power, and Human Nature* [Indianapolis, In: Hackett, 1993], p. 70), while R. Warner chooses "forgive" (*Thucydides: History of the Peloponnesian War* [New York: Penguin, 1987], p. 216). When we come to "xungnômês" at 3.44, Smith and Warner both have "forgiveness," and Woodruff "pardon." Thucydides pretty clearly means "excuse" or "pardon" rather than "forgiveness" in the sense I will specify. However, it is interesting and relevant that he ties *sungnômê* to a fault with which one can sympathize, and whose expression is unintentional. Compare Herodotus VI. 86, where the term should be translated "forgiveness."

⁶ I am using T. H. Irwin's translation of the *NE* (Indianapolis: Hackett, 1999), 2ⁿᵈ ed; unless otherwise noted, all further references to Aristotle advert to that translation of the *NE*. I note that at *Rhetoric* 1384b3, "suggnômonikos" has the sense of being inclined to make allowance, to be indulgent.

At 1111a1–2, Aristotle remarks with respect to the ignorance condition that it is ignorance of particulars (not the universal) that makes an action involuntary. Such cases of involuntariness "allow both pity and pardon." We read later in Book V, 1136a5–9 that

some involuntary actions are to be pardoned, and some are not. For when someone's error is not only committed in ignorance, but also caused by ignorance, it is to be pardoned. But if, though committed in ignorance, it is caused not by ignorance but by some feeling that is neither natural nor human, and not by ignorance, it is not to be pardoned.

Thus far, *sungnômê* means something like excusing, and Aristotle is setting out conditions for permissible excusing (cf. 1109b32). Because it is a matter of excusing or pardoning rather than forgiveness, it is perfectly proper for it to be tendered by someone who was not injured by the behavior in question. Indeed that is one of the indications that we are in the presence of pardon rather than forgiveness.

The second connection in which Aristotle uses the term concerns his treatment of *akrasia* in Book VII. Aristotle is arguing that akrasia caused by *thumos* (emotion), which reflects a partial listening to logos, is less shameful than that caused by *epithumia* (appetite). He adds: "it is more pardonable (*sungnômê*) to follow natural desires, since it is also more pardonable to follow those natural appetites that are common to everyone and to the extent that they are common" (1149b4–6).[7] So we can pardon someone who has unfortunately given into a desire that is natural and common, that is, one that we can recognize in ourselves too. Presumably this requires a degree of self-knowledge, the ability to put oneself in another's place by imagination (admittedly this is debatable), and the recognition of shared humanity. These three elements were also implicit in the passages from the orators and Euripides mentioned above, and their connection with forgiveness is indeed intuitive, a point to which I will return below. At 1150b5–12 we read:

It is similar with continence and incontinence also. For it is not surprising if someone is overcome by strong and excessive pleasures or pains; indeed, this is pardonable, provided he struggles against them – like Theodectes' Philoctetes

---

[7] Cf. 1146a2–5, where in the discussion of incontinence Aristotle remarks that if a person has belief but not knowledge, and is in some doubt, "we will pardon failure to abide by these beliefs against strong appetites. In fact, however, we do not pardon vice, or any other blameworthy condition [and incontinence is one of these]." See D. Roochnik, "Aristotle's Account of the Vicious: a Forgivable Inconsistency." *History of Philosophy Quarterly*, 24(2007): 207–220.

bitten by the snake, or Carcinus' Cercyon in the *Alope*, and like those who are
trying to restrain their laughter and burst out laughing all at once, as happened
to Xenophantus.

In this second context (that concerning incontinence and intem-
perance), *sungnômê* seems somewhat ambiguously positioned between
excuse and forgiveness. The incontinent action is not simply involuntary
due to ignorance or external force (indeed, Aristotle rules that he acts
willingly, 1152a15); on the other hand, it seems that even a person not
injured by the agent's incontinence may offer *sungnômê*. Aristotle says
nothing about the identity of the wronged party, so it does not seem to
be the case that the wronged party alone grants *sungnômê*. Indeed, nobody
but the agent himself may have been harmed by the incontinence. Consequently it seems best to interpret this as a matter of excuse and pardon
rather than of forgiveness. Given the ambiguities, however, we may also
grant that this passage is evidence that the idea of "forgiveness" was hov-
ering in the air.

Irwin translates the term throughout as "pardon," with one exception,
viz., 1143a19–24, where "Aristotle plays on the etymological connection
with *gnômê*; 'consideration' is needed" (Irwin, p. 341).[8] This chapter
in Book VI in which Aristotle describes "consideration" occurs in the
context of the discussion of the intellectual (rather than moral) virtues,
and makes it clear that it is the virtue of taking all things into account:
"considerateness is the correct consideration that judges what is decent;
and correct consideration judges what is true." The considerate judge
takes into account the particulars of the situation, and does not, as Irwin
points out, simply apply the rule inflexibly.

Interestingly, for present purposes, in running through the moral
virtues Aristotle discusses the mean with respect to anger: to be angry "at
the right things and toward the right people, and also in the right way,
at the right time, and for the right length of time, is praised" (1125b31–
32). Hitherto this "mean" condition has been nameless, so Aristotle calls it
"mildness" (*praotês*, which might also be translated "calmness"; cf. *Rhetoric*,
bk. II.3). But mildness immediately comes in for mild chiding, as it errs
more "in the direction of deficiency, since the mild person is ready to

---

[8] In the Glossary to his translation, Irwin defends his translation of "sungnômê" by "pardon"
as follows: "it is the exercise of judgment and consideration that finds circumstances (as
we say, 'special considerations') in an action that exempt the agent from the blame *usually*
attached to that type of action" (p. 341). I take this as confirmation that Aristotle has in
mind here excuse rather than what I am calling forgiveness.

pardon (*sungnômê*), not eager to exact a penalty" (1126a1–3). Being too mild and pardoning is "slavish," for such a person fails to defend himself and his own. The excess of anger is irascibility. Once again, the mild person's fault is his tendency to excuse or to let the offender off the hook too quickly, and this is linked to the former's tendency to give up his anger too quickly. At the same time, the anger in question is, for Aristotle, directed toward an individual (it is "personal"), and thus resembles what we would call "resentment." The connection between pardoning and giving up (personal) anger captures an intuition to be explored below.

Aristotle's analysis of the conditions under which one would excuse (in that sense, pardon) someone is perceptive. But how is excusing, so understood, to be differentiated from forgiving? The question is surprisingly complex, but at a minimum we may say that to excuse is not to hold the agent responsible, even while his or her action is recognized as wrong. In one sense or another, the agent is judged to have acted involuntarily (for Aristotle, then, excusing would seem to mean not taking a wrong act as a sign of the agent's inherent viciousness). This being accepted, and abstracting from such considerations as negligence on the part of the wrong-doer, it would be inappropriate for the wronged party to hold onto her resentment against the wrong-doer. This is a case of what one author calls "exculpatory" excuses, as distinguished from "mitigating" excuses.[9] To forgive someone, by contrast, assumes their responsibility for the wrong-doing indeed, what distinguishes forgiveness is in part that it represents a change in the moral relation between wrong-doer and wronged that accepts the fact that wrong was indeed done, and done (in some sense) voluntarily. The difficulties arise in part because of the sheer complexity of the concept of voluntary action. One could argue that there are always mitigating excuses, that wrong-doing is never just voluntary; there is always a story about how one ended up doing the evil deed. This is perhaps why people hold that *tout comprendre c'est tout pardonner*. Granting the complexity of the just-mentioned issues however, the common saying is mistaken, if "pardoner" means "forgive."

Why is it that Aristotle nowhere praises forgiveness (as distinguished from pardoning and excusing) as a virtue? The core answer lies in the

---

[9] T. Govier, *Forgiveness and Revenge* (New York: Routledge, 2002), pp. 55–56. For an illuminating and precise discussion of excuses, see J. L. Austin's "A Plea for Excuses," in his *Philosophical Papers*, 2nd ed., ed. J. O. Urmson and G. J. Warnock (Oxford: Oxford University Press, 1970), pp. 175–204.

character of his perfectionist ethical scheme, for it is one that seeks to articulate and recommend the character of the man – and in Aristotle, it is a man – of complete virtue.[10] The gentleman possessing the perfection of moral virtue – the *megalopsuchos* – certainly has no need (by his own lights, anyhow) for being forgiven, because by definition he is morally perfect (and in any case, his pride would not allow him to recognize himself as in need of forgiveness). He also would seem unforgiving of others, for three reasons. First, he has no interest in sympathetically grasping the situation and faults of non-virtuous persons – they are of little account to him. Second, he would judge himself immune to being injured by them morally (with a problematic qualification to be mentioned in a moment), though of course he could be harmed (say, by being murdered). He would seem to be above resenting the actions of *hoi polloi* (and by definition, another *megalopsuchos* would not injure someone of the same stature). Hence Aristotle's comment that the *megalopsuchos* or magnanimous man

cannot let anyone else, except a friend, determine his life. For that would be slavish; and this is why all flatterers are servile and inferior people (*tapeinoi*) are flatterers. He is not prone to marvel (*thaumastikos*), since he finds nothing great; or to remember evils, since it is proper to a magnanimous person not to nurse memories, especially not of evils, but to overlook them. . . . He does not speak evil even of his enemies, except [when he responds to their] wanton aggression. He especially avoids laments or entreaties about necessities or small matters, since these attitudes are proper to someone who takes these things seriously. (1124b31–1125a5, 8–10)

The magnanimous person is "self-sufficient" (*autarkos*; 1125a12). The problematic qualification to all of this is that the polis could deny him something he does very much wish for, viz. warranted honor. But the denial of that honor would not, one assumes, elicit from the *megalopsuchos* resentment or forgiveness so much as contempt, even if it also elicits

[10] In *Perfectionism* (Oxford: Oxford University Press, 1993), T. Hurka says of a "perfectionist" moral outlook that "this moral theory starts from an account of the good human life, or the intrinsically desirable life," and that its "distinguishing ideal is that of *human perfection*" (p. 3). Hurka distinguishes between the "narrow" (and traditional) version of the view, according to which the good life "develops these properties [of human nature] to a high degree or realizes what is central to human nature" (p. 3), from the "broader" view that focuses instead on excellence (p. 4). Rawls states that for a perfectionist we are to "maximize the achievement of human excellence in art, science, and culture" (quoted by Hurka as an example of the "broad" view; p. 4). The philosophers I am discussing in this chapter all see their ideals as excellences of human nature, set a high (to very high) bar for that excellence, and correspondingly (I am arguing) end up without a place for forgiveness in their moral outlook.

anger.[11] It is worth recalling Aristotle's comment that "it is difficult to be truly magnanimous, since it is not possible without being fine and good" (1124a3–4); the paradigm of moral virtue sets a *very* high standard. In painting the magnanimous man, Aristotle is not simply reproducing the pathology of the run of the mill aristocratic gentleman.

The third reason why forgiveness is not part of the magnanimous person's outlook is implicit in the hierarchical value scheme that is part and parcel of this perfectionist outlook, and comes across in the dismissiveness that characterizes the attitude of the *megalopsuchos* toward "inferior people." Non-magnanimous victims of wrong-doing do not seem to have any standing to be treated otherwise, or at the very least, their being wronged just does not command the magnanimous person's moral concern. Differently put, the idea of the inherent dignity of persons seems missing from this perfectionist – or as we might also say, keeping in mind the etymology – aristocratic scheme. The non-perfectionist scheme within which forgiveness has its place recognizes the reciprocal moral claims and demands that people have standing to make of one another.[12]

There is even less place for *sungnômê* in the supremely worthwhile theoretical life as Aristotle describes it, because that life abstracts as far as possible from involvement with other human beings (except, perhaps, those friends engaged in the same study of the divine; *NE* 1177a33-b1). The perfect theorizer is god, and Aristotle's god manifests no concern whatever for anything or anybody but himself qua thinking about himself. Strictly speaking he (or, it) can neither be said to *act* nor to have emotions; god neither forgives nor requires forgiveness. For Aristotle,

---

[11] Did the Greeks have our idea of "resentment," including of "class resentment" and "existential resentment"? For discussion, see D. Konstan's "Ressentiment ancien et ressentiment moderne;" and W. V. Harris, *Restraining Rage: the Ideology of Anger Control in Classical Antiquity* (Cambridge, MA: Harvard University Press, 2001), ch. 8 (esp. pp. 187–197). Konstan does allow that, in spite of semantic ambiguities and the relevance of social context to determining who may be the proper object of resentment, Aristotle in particular does recognize something closely resembling our concept of resentment. And the first word of the *Iliad* certainly carries, as the context makes clear, the sense of "deliberate anger" as defined by Bishop Butler (see below). See also Konstan's illuminating chapter on anger in *The Emotions of the Ancient Greeks* (Toronto: University of Toronto Press, 2006), ch. 2.

[12] I am grateful to Stephen Darwall for some of the phrasing here, and for urging me to emphasize this point with respect to the ancient philosophers. For an account of the idea human dignity involves a standing to demand certain forms of treatment, see Darwall's *The Second-Person Standpoint: Morality, Respect, and Accountability* (Cambridge, MA: Harvard University Press, 2006).

god leads the life of the mind, and is therefore the paradigm of perfection. Consequently, we would live god's life fully, were we able.

The situation is even starker in the case of Plato, who barely mentions forgiveness (or even pardon) as a virtue at all. The word "sungnômê" in something like the sense of forgiveness certainly presents itself in Plato, but as in Aristotle, it is not put to any serious ethical work.[13] His perfectionist ethics is more extreme than Aristotle's in its thesis that *no* harm can come to a good person. Consider Socrates' defiant statement to the jury of his peers:

> Be sure that if you kill the sort of man I say I am, you will not harm me more than yourselves. Neither Meletus nor Anytus can harm me in any way; he could not harm me, for I do not think it is permitted that a better man be harmed by a worse; certainly he might kill me, or perhaps banish or disfranchise me, which he and maybe others think to be great harm, but I do not think so. I think he is doing himself much greater harm doing what he is doing now, attempting to have a man executed unjustly. (*Apol.* 30c7-d6)

Presumably a person who cannot be harmed, thanks to the armature that virtue furnishes, has nothing for which to forgive the wrong-doer;

---

[13] *Sungnômê* or a cognate is used by Echecrates at *Pho.* 88c8 to mean that he sympathizes with Phaedo's plight given the failure of the arguments; at *Symp.* 218b4 Alcibiades says that his auditors "will understand and forgive" (trans. Nehamas and Woodruff) his drunken remarks about Socrates; at *Phr.* 233c4, Lysias's non-lover claims he will "forgive" (meaning excuse) the lover for the latter's unintentional errors; at *Rep.* 391e4 it means excuse (so Grube translates it) and at 472a2 "sympathy" (Socrates is saying they will sympathize with his delaying tactics when they hear the next proposition, viz. that philosophers should rule). At *Laws* 757e1 the Stranger speaks of "toleration" (*suggnômon*), as T. Saunders translates, of a shortfall from perfect justice (but perhaps "lenience" would translate the term better); so too at 921a3-4, of a cheating workman who counts on the "indulgence" of his god (similarly 906d1; cf. 731d7, for an interesting reference to [falsely] pardoning oneself due to self-love). See also *Laws* 770c4 (where the term means something like "sympathetic" or in agreement with our way of thinking); 863d4 (showing understanding of wrong-doers because of their ignorance); 866a4 (the granting of pardon, immunity from prosecution); 924d2 (excuse); 925e8 and 926a1 (a citizen is to forgive the lawgiver for inconveniencing the individual while promoting the common good, and the lawgiver to forgive individuals for their inability to carry out some orders). These last two references may mean excuse rather than forgiveness – the sense is ambiguous. At *Euthydemus* 306c Socrates says that we "ought to forgive them [the pretenders to philosophy] their ambition and not feel angry" (trans. Sprague). The connection there between forgiving (that does seem to be the right translation) and surrendering anger is noteworthy. All of the translations of Plato cited in this chapter are to be found in J. M. Cooper and D. S. Hutchinson (eds.), *Plato: Complete Works* (Indianapolis: Hackett Press, 1997). Socrates nowhere recommends that others forgive wrongs; indeed he predicts that "vengeance will come" upon those who voted to execute him (*Apol.* 39 c–d), evidently at the hands of his followers. As Mark McPherran has pointed out to me, Plato's eschatological myths too leave little or no room for forgiveness in the afterlife (though see *Pho.* 114b).

and such a person would not, by definition, injure others (as Socrates explicitly says of himself at *Apol.* 37b2–3; and at 37a6–7, he claims that he never willingly does harm). As Socrates resolutely argues in the *Gorgias*, "doing what's unjust is more to be guarded against than suffering it" (527b4–5); properly speaking, though, he does not suffer it either (he is treated unjustly, and yet in the sense that counts for him, he is not injured by injustice). Insofar as one is successful as a philosopher, as a virtuous person, one is not vulnerable to others; the transcending of mutual vulnerability seems to go hand in hand with the dismissal of the idea of inherent equal dignity, an idea nowhere defended or even proclaimed in the Platonic dialogues. In the *Apology* Socrates exhibits a certain contempt for his accuser Meletus, but no resentment or even anger; and he explicitly declares that he is not angry either with the jury for convicting him or with his accusers (*Apol.* 35e1–36a1, 41d6–7). In the *Gorgias* he seems irritated with Callicles (*Gorg.* 511b1–5 and context), and passionately intent on working out the argument, but not resentful, injured, or wounded. And nowhere else in the Platonic corpus is he portrayed as coming even that close to anger. Socrates apparently has no need to forswear resentment or to struggle with the impulse to take revenge.[14]

To this we may add that the Platonically perfected soul has as far as possible escaped the cares and vicissitudes of this world. The successful life of theorizing simply is not focused on others (except possibly other fellow travelers, and then only secondarily). As Socrates puts it in the *Phaedo*:

The lovers of learning know that when philosophy gets hold of their soul, it is imprisoned in and clinging to the body, and that it is forced to examine other things through it as through a cage and not by itself, and that it wallows in very kind of ignorance. Philosophy sees that the worst feature of this imprisonment is that it is due to desires, so that the prisoner himself is contributing to his own incarceration most of all. . . . Philosophy then persuades the soul to withdraw from the senses in so far as it is not compelled to use them and bids the soul to gather itself together by itself, to trust only itself and whatever reality, existing by itself, the soul by itself understands, and not to consider as true whatever it examines

---

[14] In the *Protagoras*, to be sure, Socrates seems at times exasperated with Protagoras, and the central drama of the dialogue consists in their inability to communicate; on which see my "Relying on Your Own Voice: an Unsettled Rivalry of Moral Ideals in Plato's *Protagoras*," *Review of Metaphysics* 53 (1999): 533–557. Note that at the end of the dialogue Socrates invites Protagoras to continue the conversation. I add that the view repeatedly expressed in Plato's dialogues that nobody does wrong willingly (*Prot.* 345e, *Tim.* 86d-e, 87b, *Laws* 731c-d, 860d-861b, *Apol.* 37a) provides further explanation of the absence of forgiveness as a virtue in the non-ideal world populated by non-Sages who are injured and respond with anger. The appropriate response would be excuse or pardon.

by other means, for this is different in different circumstances and is sensible and
visible, whereas what the soul itself sees is intelligible and invisible.... The soul
of the philosopher achieves a calm from such emotions; it follows reason and
ever stays with it contemplating the true, the divine, which is not the object of
opinion. Nurtured by this, it believes that one should live in this manner as long
as one is alive and, after death, arrive at what is akin and of the same kind, and
escape from human evils. (82d9–83b4, 84a7-b3)

As in Aristotle, the related notion of "sympathy" plays little ethical role
in Plato.[15] Indeed, we might add – to anticipate another of our themes –
that reconciliation between individuals who have injured one another
also plays little role in their ethical outlooks, even though the concept
of "reconciliation" is not absent from the philosophical vocabularies in
question.[16]

   The story with respect to forgiveness is, not surprisingly, generally
similar in the Stoics. The Stoics are certainly interested in the issues of
common humanity and faultiness. But in true Socratic spirit, the Stoic

---

[15] *Sympatheia* can match the sense of "sympathy" as "fellow feeling." It occurs about ten
   times in Aristotle (whose range of definition is pretty well illustrated by the essay on
   "Sympathy" [*Problems* vii]) and regularly in later philosophers. Aristotle does not use
   the term in the ethical or political works in the sense at stake (mostly it is used in a
   physical or musical context, e.g., *Politics* 1340a13). A detailed discussion of the issues of
   empathy (or sympathy in the sense I am using it), the recognition of shared humanity,
   and forgiveness in Aristotle would have to take into account both Aristotle's discussion
   in the *N.E.* of friendship, and in the *Poetics* of the spectator's engagement with drama.
   I do not believe however that the central point I am making here would be affected.
   Aristotle does, of course, attempt to articulate the notion of shared humanity, in the
   sense of a theory of human nature; and he recognizes the idea of a "philanthropos"
   (*NE* 1155a20). As to Plato, a qualification: in *Rep.* X (605d4) Socrates speaks of the
   audience as "sumpaschontes" with a character's emotions represented by Homer or a
   tragedian. This bears an interesting resemblance to "sympathy" in the sense of putting
   yourself in the shoes of another. However, Plato seems to think that the poets produce
   fellow-feeling rather indiscriminately by means of a kind of verbal enchantment, and in
   a way that is harmful. Nonetheless, he does not give the notion (let alone something
   like putting yourself in the situation of another) a central place in his ethics, and in
   that respect is at one with Aristotle. The development of the idea in Stoicism is a whole
   other topic. E.g., consider Marcus Aurelius, *Meditations* 8.61, where we are told that one
   must "enter into the governing mind of every man and allow every other to enter into
   your own."
[16] There is serviceable Greek for "reconciliation," viz. "diallagê" (and much more rarely,
   "katallagê"). It is usually used in a political context (reconciling with one's enemies)
   rather than a personal one, though in the *Symp.* Aristophanes explicitly recommends
   the virtues of wholeness and "reconciliation" with god (193b4); see also *Symp.* 213d7,
   Rep. 470e2–471a4, *Laws* 628b8. Aristotle quotes a relevant proverb at *Rhet.* 1418b35.
   "Katallagê" is used once by Plato (*Rep.* 566e6), and once by Aristotle (*Rhet.* 1418b37).
   In this meaning as "reconciliation" the terms are mainly post-classical, appearing earlier
   only very infrequently in historians and orators in the context of treaties between warring
   factions or *poleis*.

Sage is pictured as invulnerable to injury, and consequently would never judge it appropriate for him to forgive. The Sage would certainly not feel resentment. This is not to say that it is impossible to act wrongly toward a Sage, that is, to act in a way that calls for condemnation and perhaps judicial response (whose purpose – as in Plato – would be (re)education and emendation of character). But as for Plato's Socrates, one cannot wrong the Sage in the sense that counts (at least according to the Sage). Further, the Sage's judgment about what response to wrong-doing is warranted takes everything into account and is complete. Forgiveness ends up being understood as a kind of pardon, and in particular as the clemency or mercy that may be offered once all considerations of justice are in (or more precisely: the judgment as to what is just and right response to the wrong-doer already factors in any warrant for leniency). Finally, the Sage would do no harm and thus not be in need of forgiveness.[17]

We find fundamentally the same indifference to forgiveness in Epicurean philosophy. In fact, Epicurus and Lucretius scarcely mention or allude to forgiveness (in my paradigm sense of forgiveness), let alone count it as a virtue. The perfected soul – the one that as Epicureans we are attempting to understand and to become – cannot be injured, does no injury, and presumably surrounds itself with fellow travelers so far as is possible.[18] Epicurus tells us in the *Letter to Herodotus* (77) that the Sage

---

[17] However, on the theme of *iniuria* and the Sage see Seneca's *De Constantia Sapientis*, esp. ch. 5, and *De Clementia* bk. 2.7, where Seneca argues that the wise man will not grant forgiveness, i.e., pardon – because that would obviate deserved punishment and the Sage never does wrong – but may exercise mercy (*clementia*), which orients itself by what is "equitable." See also Stobaeus *Eclogae* II 7.11d, Wachsmuth 2.95.24–96.9 = SVF 3.640; trans. in B. Inwood and L. P. Gerson, *Hellenistic Philosophy* 2nd ed. (Indianapolis: Hackett, 1997), pp. 220–221, where forgiveness is grouped with *epieikeia* – the disposition to release a malefactor from merited punishment. Or again, cf. Diogenes Laertius 7.123: the Sages "do no harm: for they harm neither others nor themselves. But they are not prone to pity and forgive (*sungnômên*) no one." Along with *epieikeia* (equity), pity and forgiveness are rejected because they mitigate or negate the punishment that is due (the DL text is in Inwood-Gerson, p. 200). There seem to be variations in Stoic views about equity, mercy, and pardon; and differences between them and Plato and Aristotle on the same topics. Seneca also comments in *De Ira* (II.10) that "to avoid anger with individuals, you must forgive the whole group, you must pardon the human race." In *Seneca: Moral and Political Essays*, ed. and trans. J. M. Cooper and J. F. Procopé (Cambridge: Cambridge University Press, 1995), p. 49 (all further references to *De Ira* advert to this edition). Useful here is T. J. Saunders, "*Epieikeia*: Plato and the Controversial Virtue of the Greeks," in *Plato's Laws and its Historical Significance*, ed. F. L. Lisi (Sankt Augustin: Academia Verlag, 2001), pp. 65–93; and more generally M. Nussbaum, "Equity and Mercy," in *Literature and Legal Problem Solving*, ed. P. J. Heald (Durham, NC: Carolina Academic Press, 1998), pp. 15–54. I am indebted to Brad Inwood for his guidance with respect to Seneca and the Stoics.

[18] H. Usener lists a single occurrence of "sungnômê" in the Epicurean works (Ep. Fr. 16). *Glossarium Epicureum*, edendum curaverunt M. Gigante et W. Schmid (Rome:

will, as one commentator puts it, "avoid being in any condition of weakness or need towards his fellow humans; in this way, he will manage to avoid both anger and gratitude." For them as quite probably for Lucretius, the gods rightly conceived are (our pictures) of the ideal – tranquil, self-sufficient, and unafflicted by emotions such as anger or resentment. They neither do nor suffer wrong, and have no concern for the human. They are perfect. The successful Epicurean too creates protective walls around himself, and from within his fortified "templa serena" gazes out safely at a suffering world (*De Rerum Natura* II.7–8).[19]

We may conclude that forgiveness (as distinct from pardon, mercy, lenience, compassion, and excuse) is not a virtue within these perfectionist ethical schemes. The perfected person is nearly or totally immune from mistakes in judgment; there is nothing of the past for him or her to undo, reframe, or accommodate, at least so far as the past is connected with perfected agency. The character type on whom such theories are focused, and which they hold up as the moral exemplar, is perfect or like-the-perfect, and thereby rises quite distinctly above the merely human. Forgiveness is more appropriate to an outlook that emphasizes the notion of a common and irremediably finite and fallible human nature, and thus highlights the virtues that improve as well as reconcile but do not aim to "perfect" in the sense we have been examining. Forgiveness is a virtue against the background of a narrative about human nature and its aspirations that accepts imperfection as our lot (in a religious view, our lot absent divine grace, and in a secular view, our lot unalterably). Our interdependence as social and sympathizing creatures; our embodiment and our affective character; our vulnerability to each other; our mortality; our standing to demand respectful treatment from one another, as befits creatures of equal dignity, and our obligations to one another; the pervasiveness of suffering – most often unmerited where it is intentionally inflicted – and of pain, violence, and injustice: these are part and parcel of that imperfection. In short, the context is that of creatures

Edizioni dell'Ateneo & Bizzarri, 1977), p. 615. Similarly, consider the Epicurean works by Philodemus; in his *Peri parrhêsias, sungnômê* – which the Konstan edition translates as "pardon" – occurs only in Fr. 20.6 and Col. Xb.3. See *Philodemus On Frank Criticism: Introduction, Translation and Notes*, by D. Konstan, D. Clay, C. Glad, J. Thom, and J. Ware (Atlanta: Scholars Press, 1998), pp. 38, 124.

[19] The commentator is M. Nussbaum; see her "'By Words not Arms': Lucretius on Gentleness in an Unsafe World," in *The Poetics of Therapy*, ed. M. Nussbaum (Edmonton, Canada: Academic Printing & Publishing, 1990), p. 53. Nussbaum briefly discusses the debates as to whether or not the Epicureans understand the gods as human projections, and as to the sense in which (projections or not) we are to model ourselves on them.

such as ourselves, inescapably rooted in a world that is, so to speak, fractured and threatening. Forgiveness is responsive to the demands of a world so understood, and in a way that helps to enable its possessor to live a good life.

Contemporary discussions of forgiveness often mention the views put forward by another advocate of a perfectionist moral outlook. Different though Nietzsche's conception of the ideal may be from the thinkers mentioned above, he too denies that forgiveness is a virtue in ways that resonate with theirs. For him, the reactive feeling of *ressentiment* is tied to the "slave revolt in morality," which revolt "gives birth to values" including pity, benevolence, and prudence.[20] He writes:

> For the *ressentiment* of the noble human being, when it appears in him, runs its course and exhausts itself in an immediate reaction, therefore it does not *poison* – on the other hand it does not appear at all in countless cases where it is unavoidable in all the weak and powerless. To be unable for any length of time to take his enemies, his accidents, his *misdeeds* themselves seriously – that is the sign of strong, full natures in which there is an excess of formative, reconstructive, healing power that also makes one forget (a good example of this from the modern world is Mirabeau, who had no memory for insults and base deeds committed against him and who was only unable to forgive because he – forgot.).[21]

As in the classical perfectionist outlooks I have mentioned, forgiveness is not a virtue because the perfected soul is by definition almost, or entirely, immune from receiving injury, or from doing injury. Nietzsche also sees forgiveness as part of a moral system that must be rejected *in toto*, for it is a system in which the weak and ignoble are empowered, control is

---

[20] I take the term "reactive feeling" from P. F. Strawson, *Freedom and Resentment* (New York: Methuen, 1980), p. 6; resentment and gratitude are among his examples of reactive feelings or attitudes.

[21] *On the Genealogy of Morality*, trans. M. Clark and A. J. Swensen (Indianapolis: Hackett, 1998), First Treatise, par. 10, p. 21 (Mirabeau is a rather odd example, given his famously venal habits!). All other references to *GM* advert to this translation. I note that in par. 11, Nietzsche refers to the "instincts of reaction and *ressentiment*" (p. 23); and in par. 14, tracing how *ressentiment* creates new ideals, he remarks "not being to avenge oneself is called not wanting to avenge oneself, perhaps even forgiveness ('for *they* know not what they do – we alone know what *they* do!'). They also talk of 'love of one's enemies' – and sweat while doing so." So forgiveness is actually the *expression* rather than the forswearing of ressentiment. Nietzsche's argument is usefully explored by M. Scheler in his "Negative Feelings and the Destruction of Values: *Ressentiment*," trans. W. W. Holdheim; in *On Feeling, Knowing, and Valuing*, ed. H. J. Bershady (Chicago: University of Chicago Press, 1992), pp. 116–143. He comments that "thirst for revenge is the most important source of *ressentiment*" (p. 117). I am grateful to Lanier Anderson for discussion of Nietzsche's view of resentment and forgiveness.

exercised through sentiments such as guilt, and in which it is impossible to "say 'yes' to life" (*GM* I, 11, p. 24). On his view, one "forgives" when revenge is impossible; but as this would be insincere forgiveness, one nurses resentment. What Nietzsche does seem to be advocating in this passage is *forgetting* wrongs (this is not dissimilar to the way in which Aristotle's *megalopsuchos* simply overlooks most wrongs or at most responds to the wrong-doer with contempt, or to the way in which Plato's Socrates does not think he can be injured in the relevant sense). That is deeply different from forgiveness even if the effect is to liberate the wronged party from resentment. Simply giving up resentment cannot be a sufficient condition of forgiveness. At the end of the paragraph from which I have quoted, Nietzsche insists that the noble soul will actually admire, indeed love, an enemy truly worthy of the name (cf. *Gay Science* III.169). Forgiveness frequently has as its end reconciliation with one's enemies; Nietzsche praises instead a certain gratitude toward noble enemies with whom – qua enemies – one is *not* reconciled, even if one feels a certain kinship with them. I should think that Nietzsche would say of forgiveness what he says in the *Twilight of the Idols* of pity: "strong ages, *noble* cultures see in pity, in 'loving one's neighbor,' in a lack of self and of self-esteem, something contemptible."[22]

The noble soul seeks autarky, and this is understood as freeing one's self-conception from dependence on what we today might call the "moral community." The perfectionist views I have discussed are embedded in narratives that minimize, if not eliminate, the ethical ties binding the ideal human type to common life as well as the common run of humanity. We have mentioned the seminal Platonic version of this story. Of course the Epicurean version is by contrast deeply anti-transcendentalist, and in some sense is the Nietzschean (the doctrine of the "eternal return" complicates the picture).

Not *every* perfectionist scheme necessarily marginalizes forgiveness as a virtue; and non-perfectionist schemes may also have little place for forgiveness (such seems to be the case in Kant), or simply say little about it (as in Hume and Smith).[23] Yet the influential perfectionist views I have

---

[22] *Twilight of the Idols*, trans. R. Polt (Indianapolis: Hackett, 1997), p. 73.
[23] One reason why Hume and Smith do not count forgiveness as a virtue, indeed scarcely mention the word, may have to do with its religious associations. Ken Winkler suggests to me that Hume may also have connected it with humility (of which he was highly critical). It may be that Hume's optimism about moral and political progress offered comes to a narrative that is insufficiently "tragic" to afford much of a place to forgiveness. Yet Smith does not share that optimism. On Kant, see ftn. 47 as follows.

discussed do marginalize this virtue because of their assumptions about what perfection would involve (and this is distinct from whether or not perfection is attainable – the theories mentioned above differ on that point).[24] I take that to be one constructive upshot of this discussion, as is the recognition that notions such as sympathy, understanding another, common humanity, and fallibility, have long been clustered together. They ought also to be distinguished from one another; excuse, for example, from forgiveness.

If forgiveness is a virtue in a sense of the term "virtue" inspired by Aristotle (in spite of his unwillingness to count it as a virtue), then it will involve several other characteristics: the shaping (habituating) of a passion or emotion or disposition (moral education, in short); being concerned with both feelings and actions; requiring a central role for practical reason or judgment; and assuming a conception of the good to which the agent aims in molding his or her character. It will also be the case that while the virtue lies on a spectrum, it itself occupies a narrow range on it. In spite of common parlance, one cannot be "too forgiving" (for one is then not forgiving but doing something else). To exercise the virtue is by definition to feel and to act just as one should given the particulars of the situation. While one may specify general conditions under which "as one should" obtain, assessment of the particulars is indispensable to the exercise of the virtue. I believe that all of these claims are true of forgiveness. More precisely, the admirable trait of being disposed to forgiveness (in the right way, on the right occasion, and such, as determined by practical reason) – the quality predicated of a forgiving person's character – is "forgivingness," on analogy, say, with "courageousness."[25] Forgiveness is the moral state of affairs that follows upon the expression of the settled character trait in question, and is either completed or under way (forgiveness can carry a "present participle" sense). Forgiveness is what forgivingness expresses, it is what a forgiving person's virtue of forgivingness gives rise

---

[24] For a helpful commentary on perfectionist views and the virtues, see C. Swanton's *Virtue Ethics: a Pluralistic View* (Oxford: Oxford University Press, 2003), pp. 206–211. As an indication of the complexity of the relation between forgiveness and the background issue of perfectionism (or the lack of it), consider that Christ not only declares that "if you forgive men their trespasses, your heavenly Father will also forgive you" (Matthew 6.14), but also in the Sermon on the Mount, and almost in the same breath: "therefore you shall be perfect (*teleioi*), just as your Father in heaven is perfect (*teleios*)" (5.48). *The New King James Bible* (New York: T. Nelson Publishers, 1979).

[25] One of the few commentators to revive the term (taken as denoting the virtuous character trait) is R. C. Roberts, "Forgivingness," *American Philosophical Quarterly* 32 (1995): 289–306.

to (under the specified conditions, and so on). Following standard practice, however, I will be speaking of the virtue of forgiveness, just as one normally would when, say, defining the virtue of courage.

How can forgiveness be seen, in Aristotelian fashion, as a "mean" between excess and defect? An excess of forgiveness would amount to excusing injury too readily; the name for this vice is perhaps "servility," and the dispositional state to which it corresponds would be (as Aristotle indicated) a defect of anger (of resentment and indignation, we might say). A defect of forgiveness would amount to withholding forgiveness when it is due; we may name this vice "hard-heartedness," and its dispositional state would be an excess of anger or resentment. The forgiving person, then, will experience anger in the right way, at the right time, and toward the right object. Good judgment is essential to that effort. Forgivingness is certainly difficult to acquire, and results from proper habituation, practice and moral example. It can also be helped along, or badly undermined, by luck.

At least in the paradigmatic interpersonal scene of forgiveness, there are two parties involved, and I have just sketched the sense in which one of them – the injured party – expresses forgivingness. But what of the person requesting forgiveness? Is there a correlative virtue involved? My argument will imply an affirmative answer for to request forgiveness properly requires judgment and expresses praiseworthy traits of character. For example, the offender should communicate contrition in the right way, at the right time, to the right person. A person who incessantly and compulsively expressed contrition, at times with cause and at times not, would very probably not be a credible candidate for forgiveness. She would exhibit the excess of the requisite virtue. And one who regularly failed to show appropriate contrition would express a defect of the requisite virtue.

If forgiveness is the expression of the virtue of forgivingness owned by the injured person, and "servility" and "hardheartedness" its excess and defect respectively, what is the correlative virtue expressed by the offender?

We do not have a name for this virtue. Some might propose humility; but in addition to its religious connotations – inappropriate to my present investigation – it fails to capture the elements of forthrightness, of taking responsibility for self honesty, good judgment, and the willingness to change one's ways. If a single term is to be applied here, I would suggest integrity, as it can be understood to encompass the nexus of qualities just mentioned. Its defect also has no one name, but would encompass the privations of these qualities, and apply to a person who refused to face up to her wrong-doing and to take the appropriate if difficult steps I shall outline. Perhaps the defect might be termed "evasiveness." The challenge is similar in the case of the excess of the virtue; what is wanted here is a counterpart to servility – a term for the excessive propensity to apologize. That propensity betokens an ongoing fear of finding oneself out of step – even through, say, unintentional or trivial giving of offense – and a correlatively inaccurate sense of one's responsibility for injuries, or even the true character and extent of injury.

On my as well as Aristotle's account, denominating a characteristic disposition "a virtue" appeals as well to an ideal of a human life as a whole – to a "picture" of what a good life would be. What are the ideals that such a life would seek to embody? When discussing the question as to why forgiveness is desirable, and the relationship between narratives and forgiveness (II.viii, ix), I will sketch an answer. As should be clear from the discussion so far, a picture of the world as we have it, including ourselves as embodied, affective, and vulnerable creatures, plays into the judgment as to what will count as a virtue. Virtues express praiseworthy or excellent ways of being responsive to the world, given the sorts of creatures we are. Assessing what they are also requires, then, a view about the obstacles to achieving excellence.

[ii] BISHOP BUTLER'S SEMINAL ANALYSIS

Revenge is a kind of wild justice, which the more man's nature runs to, the more ought law to weed it out; for as for the first wrong, it doth but offend the law, but the revenge of that wrong putteth the law out of office. Certainly, in taking revenge, a man is but even with his enemy; but in passing over it, he is superior; for it is a prince's part to pardon.... This is certain, that a man that studieth revenge keeps his own wounds green, which otherwise would heal and do well.[26]

Resentment and forgiveness are routinely linked in modern discussions of our topic, and this is due in no small measure to the seminal contribution of Joseph Butler. In two consecutive sermons he sets out a justly praised analysis, and it is well worth careful examination both because of its merits and its illuminating limitations.[27] Butler provides a

---

[26] F. Bacon, "On Revenge," in *The Essays*, ed. G. Montgomery (New York: Macmillan Co., 1930), pp. 9–10.

[27] Sermons VIII and IX, in vol. 2 of *The Works of Joseph Butler*, ed. W. E. Gladstone, 2 vols. (Oxford: Clarendon, 1896). All quotations are from this edition; in this section, I have included the pagination directly in my text.

useful path further into the complex terrain of our topic, and I therefore devote the second part of the current chapter to his analysis. The
issues include the reasons for linking resentment and forgiveness; the
nature of the emotion of resentment and its relation to hatred, anger,
indignation, and the desire for revenge; the virtues and vices, as it were,
of resentment; the tendency of resentment to demonize the wrong-doer,
as well as to spin a self-justifying narrative of its pitch and aims; and the
distinction between forgiveness and the administration of justice. As in
the preceding section, my aim here is primarily conceptual; and I make
no claims about Butler's philosophy as a whole.

Butler quotes the same passage from Scripture at the start of both
sermons (Matthew 5.43, 44; "love your enemies . . . "), and in the second
refers back to the first. They are meant to be read together, for an important reason: resentment and forgiveness are on his account intimately tied
to one another. The claims that there is such a tie, and that the tie has
the character he asserts, are not self-evident. Indeed, Butler is regularly
misquoted as defining forgiveness as the "forswearing of resentment."[28]
Butler actually claims that forgiveness is the forswearing of *revenge* (not
that resentment is always left just where it was). Is the misreading of
Butler, regrettable though it may be from an exegetical perspective,
actually the expression of a better understanding of the concept of
forgiveness? What sense are we to make of Butler's view that resentment
is compatible with loving your enemies, in short, with general philan-
thropy? Let us examine his influential analysis in some detail, starting
with the topic of resentment. We shall find that many of his points are
on the mark, that others are not, and that his discussion is incomplete in
crucial and instructive ways.

---

[28] For example, see Murphy in *Forgiveness and Mercy*, ed. J. G. Murphy and J. Hampton
(Cambridge: Cambridge University Press, 1998), p. 15 ("Forgiveness, Bishop Butler
teaches, is the forswearing of resentment"); echoed by Hampton, p. 35. All further
references to Hampton and Murphy advert to their exchanges in this book, and are often
included directly in my text. On the misreading of Butler see also P. E. Digeser, *Political
Forgiveness*, pp. 15–16 ("Bishop Butler, for example, argued that forgiveness required an
injured party to eliminate such resentment"); or again M. R. Holmgren, "Forgiveness
and the Intrinsic value of Persons," *American Philosophical Quarterly* 30 (1993), p. 341.
The definition often seems more or less taken for granted now, even when Butler is
not mentioned; e.g., Strawson's *Freedom and Resentment*, p. 6: "to ask to be forgiven is
in part to acknowledge that the attitude displayed in our actions was such as might
properly be resented and in part to repudiate that attitude for the future (or at least for
the immediate future); and to forgive is to accept the repudiation and to forswear the
resentment."

Each sermon is prefaced by a reflection on the unavoidable fact of human imperfection. While the relevant imperfections are multiple, Butler underlines such traits as fallibility, partiality to self, the resistance of the passions to reason, and of course the tendency to injure others. The question is not why God failed to make us more perfect creatures; but rather, taking human nature and its situation as we find them, what constructive role could so "harsh and turbulent a passion as resentment" (p. 137) possibly play. That it must play *some* such role, Butler takes as given thanks to his theological framework. So one justificatory perspective he offers hinges on the idea of utility; because Creation as a whole is good, the "end" of a passion will lie in its contribution to the good of the whole. This assessment is offered from the standpoint not of the participant but of the observer; however, Butler does not clearly distinguish between the two perspectives in the way that later thinkers such as Adam Smith insisted on doing.

Butler's question can be entertained outside of his theological framework. The controversial argument is that resentment does have a constructive moral role to play, and that resentment in and of itself is "natural" and not intrinsically good or bad (pp. 138–139). He is aware, of course, of the opprobrium normally attached to the sentiment of resentment; indeed the intuition that it harbors something suspect, perhaps mean and belittling (both to its possessor and its object), remains with us. To call someone a "resentful person" is not to compliment. One reason why the passion is suspect is that its ultimate end is the infliction of pain and misery on another person (p. 161). Butler agrees that in a counterfactual state of perfection, resentment would have no place (p. 150); but he also insists that in the world as we have it, it is the "abuse" of the passion only that is the proper object of blame.[29] Let us consider each of Butler's two sermons in turn.

---

[29] In the course of a long excursus on resentment and human imperfection, Adam Smith notes that "resentment is commonly regarded as so odious a passion, that they [most people] will be apt to think it impossible that so laudable a principle, as the sense of the ill desert of vice, should in any respect be founded upon it.... Nature, however, even in the present depraved state of mankind, does not seem to have dealt so unkindly with us, as to have endowed us with any principle which is wholly and in ever respect evil, or which, in no degree and in no direction, can be the proper object of praise and approbation." Smith, *The Theory of Moral Sentiments* (*TMS*), ed. A. L. Macfie and D. D. Raphael (Indianapolis: Liberty Press, 1976), I.ii.3.8 (all further references to *TMS* advert to this edition).

[ii.a] Resentment

What is resentment? Butler distinguishes between two species: the first is "hasty and sudden" anger; the second is "settled anger," which turns out to be "deliberate resentment, malice, and revenge" (as eventually becomes clear, he does not take these terms as synonymous). In the bulk of his analysis, Butler quite rightly uses "resentment" in this second sense only; I should think it clearer to see resentment as a species of anger, than as the obverse.

Sudden anger is normally "instinct" – the sort of response you have when stub your toe against the asphalt step; it is a response to hurt or pain and nothing more. Butler points out that infants and non-human animals feel it (and to anticipate slightly, we might add that non-human animals do not seem to experience "deliberate anger," malice, and the wish for revenge – in short, resentment). The utility of what one could call non-moral sudden anger is that it helps us to defend ourselves, allowing us better "to prevent, and likewise (or perhaps chiefly) to resist and defeat, sudden force, violence, and opposition, considered merely as such, and without regard to the fault or demerit of him who is the author of them." But sudden anger may also be a response to injury, which, as distinct from harm, "suggests to our thoughts" – or may follow from our "representing to our mind" – some "injustice" or other, along with that which is the cause of that injustice (p. 139). Butler is distinguishing, then, between hurt or harm on the one hand, and injury or injustice on the other. Sudden *moral* anger focuses also on the blameworthiness – or to be more precise, the appearance to the victim of blameworthiness – of the cause of one's pain. It "may likewise accidentally serve to prevent, or remedy, such fault and injury" (imagine your immediate reaction upon receiving what looks to be a serious and intentional threat to your child's well being). What unites both types of sudden anger is the swiftness of one's reaction, their relatively brief duration, as well as the support they offer to our self-defense and thus self-preservation.[30]

---

[30] It is interesting that Diderot's *Encyclopédie: ou Dictionnaire raisonné des sciences, des arts et des métiers* (14:186) offers a quite similar definition of resentment (*ressentiment*). I do not know whether this reflects common wisdom about the subject, or shows Butler's influence. For the entry on "Ressentiment," see www.lib.uchicago.edu/efts/ARTFL/projects/encyc/. Also Smith, *TMS* II.ii.I.4: "Resentment seems to have been given us by nature for defence, and for defence only. It is the safeguard of justice and the security of innocence." The distinction between sudden anger and resentment seems ancient; see Homer's *Iliad* I.80–84, where the words are *kholos* and *kotos* respectively. The latter seems bodily (one can "swallow" it down). *Mênis* (the first word of the poem) is

By "deliberate," Butler does not mean that it is entered into "on purpose"; but rather that it is sustained over time, has in view the presumed cause of one's injury, is purposeful (as when one seeks to "even the score"), plots the means of its gratification (in that sense deliberates), and in some way or other is associated with moral judgment. So the temporal projection of self into the future is one important way in which sudden and deliberate anger are distinguished. Settled anger is *never* occasioned by harm alone (p. 144); and it would seem that non-moral sudden anger never leads to desire for *revenge*. Sudden anger defends us by attempting to make the pain stop forthwith; settled anger seeks to defend us by attempting to punish the source of injury and not simply to stop the injurer from inflicting the injury. Butler rightly associates *malice* with resentment; one does not feel malicious when angry unless there is a moral component to the emotion.

While the duration of "sudden" and "settled" anger cannot be fixed a priori, the etymology of "resentment" favors Butler's seemingly awkward distinction between them. For to resent is to feel a sentiment again, and therefore later in time. The English word derives from the French "ressentir," where this point is clearer. The reproduction of anger considerably past the event that occasioned it requires not just memory of that event, but a memory that continues to provoke; and the recurring idea, kept alive by the imagination, of the uncorrected "wrongness" of the event, is a prime candidate for the job.[31]

Indeed, even non-moral anger that continues for a long period of time often takes on an overlay of resentment. Imagine that your body is attacked by an intermittent, painful, and persistent disease that you had no part in bringing upon yourself; the "sudden anger" each stab of pain would prompt may turn into a settled anger at, even hatred of, the illness. I think it likely that this hatred might *feel* like resentment, and call itself by that name, in part because the on-going pain seems so *unfair* ("what did I do to *deserve* this," one asks). The diminishment of one's capacities and prospects – in short, of the duration and quality of

also sustained anger or fury, is normally ascribed to the gods, and in the *Iliad* is used only of Achilles. For discussion of anger terms in Homer and elsewhere, see W. Harris, *Restraining Rage: the Ideology of Anger Control in Classical Antiquity*, ch. 3; and Konstan's *The Emotions of the Ancient Greeks* ch. 2 ("Anger"). (My thanks to Richard Martin for references and discussion.)

[31] Butler's analysis could usefully be deployed to understand ongoing social resentments, given the essential role of memory in settled anger and that such memory can be socially shaped and nurtured.

one's life – caused by the accursed illness, as well as the need to develop strategies of self-defense against an active threat, feel like an injury (possibly even a punishment) and not just on-going harm. Of course, the use of "resentment" in such a case may not be quite proper.[32]

Butler's first illustration of resentment (that is, of longer term, settled, deliberate anger) is actually what Adam Smith would call sympathetic resentment, that is, *indignation*. Reading a powerful fictional account of villainy, the moral sentiments are aroused though we are not touched personally by the matter (this must be implicit in Butler's example), we nonetheless object, on behalf of the injured party, to deliberate or designed wrong-doing against anyone, including this victim. This "fellow-feeling" is one of the "common bonds" – granted, not always a very strong bond – that unites us (p. 141). The more vivid the imagination, the closer the injury to those with whom we identify, the more acute the indignation, and the more eagerly we will wish for the wrong-doer to be punished.[33] It is noteworthy that Butler's first example is literary; the choice implicitly underlines the importance of *narrative*.

I have used the word "hatred" several times; is hatred to be distinguished from resentment? Butler uses the word sparsely, and in a way that suggests that he takes it as synonymous with resentment, as in his

[32] The territory here is complex: consider, by contrast, the settled feeling of anger one might have toward a wrong-doer who is "criminally insane"; as such, the wrong-doer is more like a force of nature than an accountable agent. Or yet another case: a loved one who has acquired Alzheimer's, behaves viciously toward you (his caretaker) on a regular basis, and is in general a heavy burden. You might feel, among other things, on-going anger. Do you feel *resentment*, properly speaking, in either case? Of these sorts of examples, Strawson argues that we would not feel a range of reactive feelings including "resentment, gratitude, forgiveness, anger, or the sort of love which two adults can sometimes be said to feel reciprocally, for each other," for we would likely have taken an "objective" (rather than "participant") attitude toward the person (*Freedom and Resentment*, p. 9). We do, though, sometimes feel anger, even while *also* taking the objective attitude; and possibly also feel guilty about feeling angry. Presumably we feel resentment, in such cases, while not believing that the target of our resentment is really to blame (hence the feeling of guilt, as one is having a feeling one knows is not warranted).

[33] Smith, *TMS* II.i.2.5: "When we see one man oppressed or injured by another, the sympathy which we feel with the distress of the sufferer seems to serve only to animate our fellow-feeling with his resentment against the offender. We are rejoiced to see him attack his adversary in his turn, and are eager and ready to assist him whenever he exerts himself for defence, or even for vengeance within a certain degree." Should the victim be killed, we feel an "illusive sympathy with him," and "that resentment which we imagine he ought to feel, and which he would feel, if in his cold and lifeless body there remained any consciousness of what passes upon earth. His blood, we think, calls aloud for vengeance."

grouping of "hatred, malice, and revenge" (p. 138), or as when he writes: "anger also or hatred may be considered as another [in addition to self-love] false medium of viewing things, which always represents characters and actions much worse than they really are" (p. 162; this in the paragraph admonishing us from treating wrong-doers as though they are "monstrous"). It does indeed seem both that hatred is kin to deliberate rather than sudden anger (I don't *hate* the asphalt on which I stubbed my toe), and that one can hate persons as well as their actions. The objects of hatred are of wider scope than those of resentment, including inanimate things, conditions such as illness, theories or principles, groups of people (all rapists, for example), states of affairs such as poverty, and oneself (in modern English, one would strain in saying "I resent myself," but not "I hate myself"). Retribution does not necessarily follow from hatred, as it so naturally does from resentment. Misanthropes may hate humankind, but without believing they've been injured by them, or wishing to inflict punishment. Even moral hatred is not necessarily provoked by injury to self or to near and dear, as when one hates a racist political outlook (granted, the possible injuriousness of the outlook is part of what makes it hateful). One can hate without resenting (in the sense of the term being explored here). At the same time, "hatred" may be used when malicious envy is meant; this captures one sense of "ressentiment" and some uses of "resentment" (as in, "class resentment").

Jean Hampton argues that "whereas the object of hatred can be and frequently is a person, the object of resentment is an *action*. When resentment is directed at a person, it is in response to what he did, not who or what he is. Hence we say 'I hate you,' and 'I resent what you *did*' but not 'I resent *you*' (unless 'resent' is used to mean 'envy')."[34] If hatred is distinguished from envy, then this does not seem quite right: for if I hate you as a person, it is either because of what you did, what you threaten to do, or what you stand for(as noted, the hateful principles you stand for are in practice injurious). Nonetheless I don't *resent* you on account what you stand for unless the tie-in to action or possible action is tight; this reflects the link between resentment and injurious deeds. But when the tie-in is tight – when you may be credited with the injurious action – then you are the proper object of the action. We do not resent the action; we resent you for doing it, you as its author. So it is misleading to say that "the object of resentment is an *action*."

[34] J. Hampton, "Forgiveness, Resentment, and Hatred," in *Forgiveness and Mercy*, p. 60.

Can one resent without hating? If the cause of the resentment is relatively minor, then surely one may do so; but "settled anger" concerning
a significant injury does seem describable as moral hatred.[35]

Resentment, then, is a moral sentiment in the sense that it is aroused
by the perception of what we (the spectator to the scene, or the victim)
take to be unwarranted injury. It is therefore not just a "raw feel" but
embodies a judgment about the fairness of an action or of an intention
to do that action. Properly speaking, it is provoked by the appearance of
moral, not natural evil. The object of the sentiment is not just the action
but also its author. And it is a reactive as well as retributive passion that
instinctively seeks to exact a due measure of punishment. When felt on
behalf of another, "in a generalized form" as Strawson says, it is typically
referred to as indignation (sympathetic resentment); though we may also
speak of indignation when we ourselves are the victim, and quite rightly
as I argue below (ch. II.ii).[36] The sentiment assumes that the wrong-doer
is responsible for the deed (if it was caused by carelessness, then one
assumes he is responsible for being careless, *ceteris paribus*). The degree
of the resentment ought to be in proportion to the degree of the evil
intended, and the degree to which the deed has the intended effects (we
resent the evil deed more than we do the intention to do the evil deed
(p. 143); unlike Smith, Butler does not address the "moral luck" issues
this brings in its train). It is important to note that the sheer pain that
prompts sudden anger is assumed by settled anger or resentment, even
if it is preserved and revisited in memory – especially easy to do when it
was non-physical pain to start with (such as an insult to one's reputation
and dignity). I accept this broadly Butlerian view of resentment, and its
distinction from anger or hatred as such, in what follows.

[35] By contrast, at *Rhetoric* 2.4, 1382a1–14, Aristotle defines *anger* as about what happens
to oneself, as directed at individuals, as wanting to inflict pain, and in that sense as
retributive; whereas *hatred* (*to misein*) can be directed at a type of person (all rapists, for
example), does not necessarily seek to inflict pain so much as harm, and may result from
harm done to others. While his "anger" resembles what Butler is calling "resentment,"
these distinctions do not map onto ours perfectly. E.g., Aristotle also sees anger as aroused
by an insult and not just injury; in the passage referred to, he also does not distinguish
between moral and non-moral anger, or between short term and deliberate anger.

[36] Strawson, *Freedom and Resentment*, p. 15. As he also puts it, this "sympathetic or vicarious
or impersonal or disinterested" reactive attitude of indignation is felt "towards all those
on whose behalf moral indignation may be felt, i.e., as we now think, towards all men"
(pp. 14–15). This seems part of what makes indignation "impersonal," though the fact
that "one's own interest and dignity are not involved" (p. 14) also plays a role. On p. 14
he concedes that "one can feel indignation on one's own account."

As noted, the natural "end" of this passion is self-defense against actual or possible injury (it may "prevent or remedy" injury, as Butler says on p. 144). Presumably it is effective against possible injury because the person who contemplates doing the injury knows that he will be the object of indignant resentment, and therewith of the desire for retribution. As to *why* injury – and we should here include, with Butler, not just cruelty, but other forms of disrespect – leads us to defend ourselves, Butler does not say; it is taken as a given. A deficiency of an appropriately resentful response is taken as a moral defect in the agent, as we have seen is the case for Aristotle as well.[37]

As to why self-defense against injury (as distinct from harm) leads us to retaliate (and not just stop) the offender, Butler also does not say. He does argue that its effects can be salutary. Were resentment not in principle aggressive in this way, pity and compassion might prevent our punishing injustice and cruelty: for we would feel as much pity toward the offender as we do toward the victim; and compassion with the suffering that punishment would cause the offender would disincline us to administer it (p. 147). Butler takes it that reason alone is not reliable enough to prevent us from doing wrong, or to lead us to punish it (p. 148). Moral evil is cause for reprobation, but in his benevolence, God did not leave us without weapons with which to respond: resentment, a "generous movement of mind" (p. 149) in Butler's startling phrase, is our primary weapon. Butler does not offer the unlikely proposition that such third-personal considerations of utility explain resentment's well established proclivity for retribution.[38] What then does?

Perhaps it feels as though the only way to relieve oneself of the ongoing painfulness of the injury is to shift it to the agent who caused it (hence the pervasiveness of terms such as "getting even" and "payback"). That

---

[37] So too Smith, *TMS* I.ii.3.8. At II.i.5.9, Smith notes that "Upon some occasions we are sensible that this passion [resentment], which is generally too strong, may likewise be too weak. We sometimes complain that a particular person has too little spirit, and has too little sense of the injuries that have been done to him; and we are as ready to despise him for the defect, as to hate him for the excess of this passion."

[38] Its unlikeliness is insisted upon by Smith at *TMS* II.i.2.4; but he perceptively adds that when the wrong-doer is about to meet his just punishment, is no longer a cause of fear, and shows repentance, "generous and humane" spectators begin to feel pity rather than resentment, and are "disposed to pardon and forgive him." Such reflections should be counterbalanced by considerations of general utility (the requirements of upholding the rule of law, and such). See *TMS* II.ii.3.7.

strategy is not necessarily successful – bringing the wrong-doer down to your level of misery does not in fact relieve your misery.[39]

It seems to be part of the primitive idea of retaliation both that the injurer should be made to suffer for the particular injury caused *to me*, and that punishment should not come about adventitiously (say, through the injurer's contracting a suitably horrible disease) but deliberately. The wrong-doer is to suffer and know that he suffers because of the particular wrong he caused this particular person (as Smith notes, *TMS* II.i.I.7). "Ideally" all this is not only to be performed in full view of the victim, but performed by the victim's hands in full view. For the "publicness" of the wrong-doer's deserved suffering seems wished for by revenge; perhaps this has something to do with wanting to ensure that the wrong-doer's "life story" be permanently marked. Were the wrong-doer successfully to pass himself off as an innocent, insult would be added to injury. The unforgiving resentful person imagines that the ideal way to bring about these ends would be to administer the punishment oneself, all the more fully to enjoy the so-called "sweetness of revenge." Such are the fantasies and the fallacies of revenge.

There is a kernel of another thought that is expressed in the retributive impulse, namely that the wrong-doer be made to see and acknowledge that he cannot simply treat others as though they were of no account. Revenge, on this view, is a (misguided) way of communicating moral protest and of demanding accountability. Smith put this well:

the object, on the contrary, which resentment is chiefly intent upon, is not so much to make our enemy feel pain in his turn, as to make him conscious that he feels it upon account of his past conduct, to make him repent of that conduct, and to make him sensible, that the person whom he injured did not deserve to be treated in that manner.

What enrages us is the wrong-doer's

absurd self-love, by which he seems to imagine, that other people may be sacrificed at any time, to his convenience or his humour. (*TMS* II.iii.I.5)

Vengeful resentment may seek to communicate a moral principle that all reasonable people would acknowledge, and whose acknowledgment

---

[39] Cf. Nietzsche's comments on the demand of *ressentiment*, to which revenge (ineffectively) responds, for the "anesthetization" of pain; *GM* III.15. And if the injury takes the specific form of an insult, revenge may relieve one's anger, as Aristotle notes (*Rhetoric* II.2).

is required if one is to form part of the moral community.[40] The wish that the revenge be public would express the implicit universality of the moral claim being made (viz., "nobody may be treated in this manner," "a person is accountable for doing this sort of thing"). Seeing the retaliatory impulse in this way helps, in turn, to understand the conditions ideally required if forgiveness is to be granted. It is one reason for seeing revenge as an "abuse," viz., that it actually obscures rather than establishes the type of implicit moral point just sketched. Even when badly expressed, however, resentment and revenge engage their owner in a morally tinged exchange with the community. This is, once again, one of the reasons that the advocates of "perfectionism" discussed above wrote resentment and revenge out of their narratives of the accomplished, self-sufficient life.

Perhaps there is another impulse implicit in revenge, and articulating it helps shed light on the task confronting forgiveness. Revenge seeks to change the past by punishing the agent who made the relevant aspect of the past painful and injurious – for it conceives of no other way of getting at and changing what has been done. In the eyes of revenge, the alternatives must seem to be either condonation, or passive acceptance and resignation. Both would seem to betray a deep lack of respect for self and for the injured or dead. It is as though revenge believes itself morally bound to make the past come out differently.

Not only is this view of the "either condonation or resignation" alternatives false – as the possibility of forgiveness shows – but its own path is futile. For the past cannot ever be changed, and it is a sort of metaphysical delusion to imagine otherwise. Violence directed at the agent of injury will certainly not undo the effects of the past deed. Forgiveness accepts that the past is unchangeable, but asserts that our responses to it are not (and these include our decisions about the future). It denies that the alternatives to vengeful violence are either condonation or resigned and submissive acceptance. And it claims to express both respect for self and the dead or injured. I am arguing in this book that truth-telling is an essential component of that expression of respect.

To return to Butler: the next step to seeing how he connects resentment with forgiveness is to understand the possible abuses of this form of anger, and he provides us with a list. The most important possibilities are widely remarked upon: settled or ongoing anger can be "imagined,"

---

[40] Stephen Darwall has brought out with force and clarity this aspect of Smith's thought; see his *The Second-Person Standpoint: Morality, Respect, and Accountability*. See also Strawson's "Freedom and Resentment," pp. 14–15.

in the sense that it can be misinformed (for example, about the identity of the true author of the injury), or be out of proportion to the injury done. Importantly, demands for retribution are easily fueled by the passion's drive to gratify itself, a drive "justified" by a certain narrative. Unchecked, resentment consumes everything and everyone, including its possessor.[41] The passion evidently gives some satisfaction to its owner, presumably that of standing so shiningly in (what feels like) the right, and perhaps of being the object of sympathetic resentment. Butler perceptively speaks of the "great mixture of pride" that can accompany settled anger. It is a potentially toxic brew.

The passion of settled anger has, then, a powerful tendency to feed on itself and to justify its own aggrandizement.[42] And this tendency to self-justification brings out another point of some importance to my account: resentment is a story-telling passion. Resentful people create narratives about their injurers, the injury, and their victimization. The classic formal elements of narrative are normally present – a beginning, middle, end, plot structure, conflict and resolution, vividly drawn characters who learn (in this case) through suffering, and a 'moral' to the story. A person in the grip of resentment often demands that the narrative be heard, and yearns that it be published, so to speak (resentment loves company). The content of the narrative will of course depend in large part on the type of injury, and thus the type of resentment, in question. Presumably the sting of a possibly damaging public insult is resented differently than a physical assault; injury that is connected with betrayal has a different texture than one connected with violation by a stranger; and so forth. As we will see, the forgiver too tells a narrative, but one that requires changes in resentment's tale. This is achieved in part by virtue of its incorporation into a larger account in which resentment becomes but a chapter.

---

[41] The phenomenon has long been noted. Recall Achilles' words about the sweetness of anger, quoted at the start of this book.

[42] Not, perhaps, a characteristic unique to resentment, but especially dangerous in its case. Smith remarks that "when we are about to act, the eagerness of passion will seldom allow us to consider what we are doing, with the candour of an indifferent person. . . . every thing appears magnified and misrepresented by self-love. . . . We cannot even for that moment divest ourselves entirely of the heat and keenness with which our peculiar situation inspires us, nor consider what we are about to do with the complete impartiality of an equitable judge. The passions, upon this account, as father Malebranche says, all justify themselves, and seem reasonable and proportioned to their objects, as long as we continue to feel them" (*TMS* III.4.3; Smith cites Malebranche's *De la recherche de la vérité* V.11).

Note that there is no dispute here that the person resented ought to be punished, assuming the injury to be of the relevant sort. The point is that unchecked resentment is not a stable basis for assessing whether or when punishment is due, and cannot by itself assess whether it has attained the appropriate pitch. It comes as no surprise that Butler underlines, as one of the greatest abuses of resentment, the *partiality* of perspective the emotion can engender in its owner. He is committed to the view that one can feel resentment wrongly (in the wrong way, or to the wrong degree, or toward the wrong person), and so to the view that there is a standpoint, other than that of the agent at the moment, from which such an assessment can be made. But he is not claiming – indeed, it is important for his account that it not claim – that resentment is in principle and always distorting of perspective. Rightly focused, it is the legitimate response to injury (Butler even claims that it "is an inward witness on behalf of virtue," that is, of "the reality of virtue"; p. 148). Hence he never recommends extirpating resentment altogether.

For reasons such as these, Butler holds that self-defense against injury that provokes settled anger – revenge, in short – is not to be confused with the "administration of justice" (p. 140). That crucial distinction helps to ground the qualified defense of resentment, and I shall return to it. To his list of abuses of vengeful resentment, I add the "metaphysical delusion" (perhaps this should be called a mistake rather than abuse) mentioned in this section. I realize that the point may bear on the morality of even the judicial administration of punishment. But the rationale for judicial punishment is not exhausted by the (faulty) idea of changing the past.

[ii.b] Forgiveness

Butler's argument leads to the conclusion that it is "only the excess and abuse of this natural feeling [resentment], in cases of personal and private injury" that are forbidden (p. 152). The "abuses" mentioned thus far are moral vices, and are pretty easily recognizable as such. Now, Butler does not suggest that refraining from *abuses* of resentment in and of itself amounts to forgiveness, and certainly does not say that forswearing resentment itself is forgiveness. That virtue enters when he turns to the most dangerous abuse of the passion, viz. *revenge*; it is the most dangerous because it expresses the emotion in actions designed to cause pain and misery, and because its character as a vice easily escapes us. Indeed, ethical systems grounded in notions of honor do precisely that, Butler correctly claims (p. 153). In effect they valorize what Butler wants to think of the ultimate abuse of resentment; for "nothing can with reason be urged in justification of revenge" (p. 157).[43]

Butler does not quite say this clearly enough, but by "revenge" he means retaliation by an individual as he or she judges to be appropriate. And as noted, Butler also means to distinguish revenge from the "administration of justice" (p. 140). What he is counseling, in other words, is that proper resentment at a wrong-doer be expressed in punitive action when and as judged appropriate by independent agents, in accordance with established principle. He does not here spell out what exactly the impartiality of agents and law would involve, though he offers two suggestions discussed below. But he does spell out the distortions that its absence entails, and then goes further in noting that just as resentment feeds on itself, so too revenge (understood in the sense just adumbrated) will "propagate itself" (p. 153). That violence begets violence, leading to an ever worse spiral of retaliation, has of course been endlessly observed, and the desirability of stopping the spiral is often cited as one of the main motivations for prohibiting revenge.

This is the resolution of an apparent paradox in Butler's account, namely that he commends the utility of resentment because it helps "prevent or remedy" injury, and yet prohibits revenge. For if the passion were not followed by retaliation, how would it accomplish that useful goal? The answer seems to be that the passion prompts retaliation, and its natural goal is accomplished when expressed impartially through the administration of justice. As noted, Butler is making a crucial distinction between the sphere of justice, and a sphere of other moral relations. He is opposing himself to an outlook, most prominently one centered on codes of honor, that runs together this distinction between public and private expressions of anger and demands for right. In so doing he is preparing the ground for the now standard view that forgiveness is, so to speak, a "private" matter between the wronged and the wrong-doer, and "about" that as well as the relation of an agent to his sentiments (such as resentment, or guilt). This in turn opens up the possibility that the

---

[43] Individuals acting corporately – as mobs, families, formal associations, or even states – can also take revenge in the sense of expressing punitively their partial, "deaf" resentment; and I see nothing in Butler's analysis that would prevent him from recognizing that fact. But he is here concerned with the paradigm case of an individual's unleashed resentment. There may nonetheless be reason to think that resentment is expressed as revenge all the more easily where the injured party is joined by sympathizers.

wronged person could forgive, while also insisting that the wrong-doer be judicially punished.[44]

What role then does Butler leave for forgiveness? The answer is by now pretty clear, viz., it is first and foremost the forswearing of revenge, and secondly, of the other abuses of resentment. He puts the point by reintroducing the idea that we are to love our enemies: "this supposes the general obligation to benevolence or good-will towards mankind: and this being supposed, that precept is no more than to forgive injuries; that is, to keep clear of those abuses before mentioned." That this does not require forswearing resentment *simpliciter* is explicit:

Resentment is not inconsistent with good-will. . . . We may therefore love our enemy, and yet have resentment against him for his injurious behaviour towards us. But when this resentment entirely destroys our natural benevolence towards him, it is excessive, and becomes malice or revenge. (p. 158)

At first sight this seems impossible: how can one simultaneously love and resent the same person?

Butler alleviates the tension by noting that "it cannot be imagined, that we are required to love them [our enemies] with any peculiar kind of affection" (p. 160). In other words, "love" is being understood here not so much as a feeling but as the recognition that others are not to be treated unjustly (which, by stipulation, revenge has the tendency to do); and still more deeply, as the recognition that even the most heinous human being is still "a sensible creature; that is, capable of happiness or misery." The obligation to recognize him or her as such prevents the resentful victim from taking a step that it is very easy to take, viz., of *demonizing* the wrong-doer; indeed, the demonizing, or dehumanizing, or objectification of one's enemies is a commonplace. In addressing yet again the way in which unchecked resentment distorts perspective, Butler comments on the tendency to see the "whole man [the wrong-doer] as monstrous,

---

[44] In similar spirit, J. D. Mabbott writes: "No one has any right to forgive me except the person I have injured. No judge or jury can do so. But the person I have injured has no right to punish me. Therefore there is no clash between punishment and forgiveness since these two duties do not fall on the same person nor in connection with the same characteristic of my act." "Punishment," *Mind* 48 (1939), p. 158. I take qualified exception to the first premise; and agree with the conclusion, though this question still nags: if the offender somehow escapes just punishment – say, because of a "miscarriage of justice" – is it not more difficult to forgive him? The question was poignantly raised in South Africa, following the work of the Truth and Reconciliation Commission (and thus arguably not because of the miscarriage of justice, but for other reasons). See L. S. Graybill, *Truth and Reconciliation in South Africa* (Boulder: Lynne Rienner Publishers, 2002), p. 49.

without any thing right or human in him"; and he is plainly denying
that there are any "moral monsters." The "whole man" is not "without
any thing right or human in him," so we should refrain from resenting
him without qualification (p. 139). Resentment has, one might say, this
totalizing tendency; and that is surely one of its dangers. To refrain from
totalizing one's negative judgment is referred to in the recent literature
as "re-framing" the wrong-doer, as seeing that he is, in some sense, not
reducible to his injurious behavior – a theme to which I return in below.
Demonizing the wrong-doer is a reductive move: the wrong-doer is nothing but a wrong-doer, and thus "monstrous." Forgiveness is "love" in the
sense that it affirms our commonality, as human beings, with the morally
worst amongst us. Butler infers that nobody is in principle unforgivable.[45]

Butler is not requiring that we either give up feeling resentment altogether, or that we acquire the *feeling* of love toward those who have injured
us. His "forgiveness" does not, though, leave the sentiments altogether
untouched. First, the requirement that we see the wrong-doer as human-
like-us, and not as monstrous, checks the degree of resentment one is
entitled to feel. Second, the injurer also injures himself, presumably by
degrading himself; and is therefore the proper object of compassion.
Butler only provides the barest assertions here, but does suggest that
feeling compassion for the wrong-doer, for this reason, is an ideal. His
example of this "utmost perfection" of forgiveness is Christ on the cross
praying compassionately that his torturers be forgiven on the grounds
that "they know not what they do."[46] Third, Butler is insisting that all
the "abuses" of forgiveness be given up; and this means that resentment
guided by partial or misinformed beliefs be modified (normally, that
would mean moderated). The emotion is to be proportionate to the
offense, and this too has affective consequences.

What is the criterion of proportionality (or, as previously, of impartiality)? Butler seems to suggest two answers to this question here,

---

[45] I discuss the question of "the unforgivable" in II.vii. Butler's conception of "love" as
a disposition rather than affection raises the question as to whether forgiveness is an
emotion or feeling, or has an affective dimension. Does the moderation or forswearing
of resentment produce a specifiable feeling? If so, I do not know what it is. *Not* feeling
resentment doesn't seem to me to be this or that specific emotion.

[46] It is striking that Christ does not himself forgive his torturers. He authorizes (or implores)
God to forgive them on his behalf. This looks like an exercise in third-party forgiveness,
or better, judicial pardon by the supreme Judge. B. Lang notes that Christ implies that
his torturers do not request forgiveness (they do not even know that they do wrong).
Lang, "Forgiveness," *American Philosophical Quarterly* 31 (1994), p. 108. It is a strange
choice of a paradigm for forgiveness, from the perspective of Butler's general line about
forgiveness.

neither sufficiently worked out, and neither clearly related by him to the other. The first is offered from the detached "objective" or theorist's standpoint that considers the pitch of the passion best suited to the given passion's doing its job in the whole – in this case, contributing to self-defense, deterrence, and punishment. Resentment "ought never to be made use of, but only in order to produce some greater good," viz., the "remedy or prevention of evil" (p. 155). Now, the achievement of *that* goal falls first and foremost on restraining designs for *revenge*; and I suggest that it is an important reason why Butler stresses the importance of forswearing, through forgiveness, revenge rather than resentment altogether. The natural end of resentment is not just to feel a certain anger, but "to *do* mischief, to be the author of misery...this is what it directly tends towards, as its proper design" (p. 157, emphasis added).

The second answer is mentioned only once by Butler; it was later to become, in a much more developed form, the core of Adam Smith's reply to the question I posed at the start of the preceding paragraph. Butler writes that the person injured "ought to be affected towards the injurious person in the same way any good men, uninterested in the case, would be; if they had the same just sense, which we have supposed the injured person to have, of the fault" (pp. 160–161). Note that "uninterested" does not mean without interest; the spectator (to use Smith's term) is uninterested – or better, disinterested – in the sense of not herself being the victim of the wrongdoing. As a "good" person, she will bring to bear her "fellow feeling" (p. 141), the right dispositions, understanding, imagination (recall my discussion of Butler's example of our reading the "feigned story" of wrong-doing, and feeling sympathetic resentment). In short, he brings *perspective* to bear, if "placed at a due distance" (p. 162) from the scene. Unlike the perspective of the detached theorist, this second perspective – that of the disinterested spectator – is fundamentally social. Butler assumes but does not here explain why the two perspectives – the theorist's, and that of the sympathetic bystander – should endorse the same judgment, but assumes that they do.[47]

---

[47] The first of Butler's answers, unlike the second, is consequentialist in form. It does seem that forgiveness fits rather easily into a consequentialist moral framework, as is noted by B. Lang, "Forgiveness," p. 110. He there adds that it does not fit as easily into a deontological framework, citing inter alia Kant's view of moral agency: "the person who, acting as a rational agent, at one time harmed someone else, is identical to the person who now (let us say) seeks forgiveness – or who, now or later, might commit the same violation again.... Consistent with this, there is for Kant no third-level duty to forgive that supervenes on the first-level obligation to do what one ought to do and the second-level obligation to punish violations of the first-level duty." Cf. J. R. Silber's comments in his "The Ethical Significance of Kant's *Religion*," in *Religion within the Limits of Pure*

Butler has in effect defined forgiveness as (i) the forswearing of revenge, as well as (ii) the moderation of resentment as judged appropriate by a sympathetic "good man" and the informed objective observer. Resentment has been distinguished from anger or hatred generally. He has commended a forgiving resentment, if I may use so paradoxical a phrase, on the grounds that it defends us against injury, recognizes the humanity of the injurer, and for one further reason with which he concludes: viz., that the injured too has caused injury. Of the "man of antiquity" who said "that as he never was indulgent to any one fault in himself, he could not excuse those of others," Butler is harshly critical (p. 164). Because we are ourselves in need of forgiveness, consistency demands that we be forgiving of others (p. 167).

By way of concluding my analysis of Butler's two sermons, let me revisit the question as to why he sees forgiveness as the forswearing of revenge rather than of resentment simply. I offered two reasons as to why he takes this line. The first is a defense of *moderated* resentment on the grounds that it is an appropriate response to injury, helps us to identify the injury for what it is, and indeed is an "inward witness on behalf of virtue." Secondly, Butler is concerned with the social benefits of properly focused resentment, and the disastrous effects of resentment unleashed. By contrast, another commentator has argued that Butler takes the position he does because his theory of the emotions is non-cognitivist. It would make no sense for Butler to commend something which it is not in an agent's

---

Reason Alone, trans. T. M. Greene and H. H. Hudson (New York: Harper and Row, 1960), p. cxxxii: "Kant could see clearly the incompatibility of forgiveness and absolute freedom"; and "we cannot ignore the problem of forgiveness nor can we accept Kant's futile resolution of it" (p. cxxxiv). Note however that the context of Kant's discussion in *Religion* is that of *divine* forgiveness. While the issues are too complex to explore in this chapter, it is not clear to me that forgiveness largely drops out of Kant's moral philosophy because of his view of our "absolute freedom"; indeed if we were not free, excuse would replace it. I note that Kant mentions "Vergeben" (forgive) just once in *Religion*, in a religious context, though one could argue that the idea is at play in the discussion of "reconciliation" or "atonement" (*Versöhnung*). For the reference, see *Religion within the Boundaries of Mere Reason*, ed. and trans. A. Wood and G. di Giovanni (Cambridge: Cambridge University Press, 2004), p. 88. Elsewhere, Kant does claim, almost in passing, that it is a "duty of virtue" to refrain from revenge and to be forgiving, and discusses an imperfect duty to gratitude as well; it is difficult to see in principle why on his account forgiveness ought not merit a similar place. See *The Metaphysics of Morals*, trans. M. Gregor (Cambridge: Cambridge University Press, 1991), pp. 253 and 248–249. It certainly seems that Kant downplays, perhaps is ambivalent about, non-divine forgiveness as a virtue. For a very helpful discussion of the matter, see D. Sussman's "Kantian Forgiveness," *Kant-Studien* 96 (2005): 85–107. I am grateful to Eckart Forster and Allen Wood for discussion of Kant's views of the matter.

power to do, viz. subdue an emotion by changing his [the agent's] understanding of its appropriateness, proportionality, or what have you.[48] The problem with this interpretation is that while Butler certainly does not claim, with the Stoics, that emotions just are judgments or beliefs, he characterizes resentment in terms that assume that it has a strong cognitive component, as when he remarks that "reason suggests to our thoughts that injury and contempt, which is the occasion of the passion," and that reason "can raise anger" only "by representing to our mind injustice or injury of some kind or other" – a phrase that underlines the capacity of reason to do just that. He speaks of instances of resentment as "the effect of reason." Sudden anger, by contrast, does not require a *moral* thought of any sort; plain hurt and pain will do, for they are "occasioned by mere sensation and feeling" (p. 140).[49]

All of this is compatible with the view that while the emotion of resentment at a person may evaporate quite quickly in light of emended beliefs of a certain sort (typically a factual sort, having to do, for example, with one's mistaken identification of the wrong-doer), cognitive emendations of other sorts (say, to the effect that the wrong suffered was not all *that* bad, that one's response is disproportionate) may take time to get a grip on the emotion, and may require significant effort on the agent's part. And there is that brute sting of pain; it may simply take longer to subside than the relevant emended beliefs warrant. An emotion such as resentment is quasi-cognitive; we do not credit it to pre-linguistic humans, which suggests that it includes beliefs (whose content can be stated propositionally). But it also is an affective, bodily state.[50]

---

[48] I refer to P. Newberry, "Joseph Butler on Forgiveness: A Presupposed Theory of Emotion." *Journal of the History of Ideas* 62 (2001): 233–244.

[49] As A. Speight nicely puts it, for Butler (as for Hegel) forgiveness includes a "revision of judgment." See his "Butler and Hegel on Forgiveness and Agency," *Southern Journal of Philosophy* 43 (2005), p. 299.

[50] The debate over the extent to which the emotions are cognitive is intense and on-going. For an argument against the view that emotions are beliefs (the straight cognitivist standpoint) see P. E. Griffiths, "Towards a 'Machiavellian' Theory of Emotional Appraisal," in *Emotion, Evolution, and Rationality*, ed. D. Evans and P. Cruse (Oxford: Oxford University Press, 2004), pp. 89–105; his *What Emotions Really are: the Problem of Psychological Categories* (Chicago: University of Chicago Press, 1997); and the first two chapters of C. DeLancey's *Passionate Engines: what Emotions Reveal about Mind and Artificial Intelligence* (Oxford: Oxford University Press, 2002). Among the many complex issues at stake is the meaning of "cognition" itself.

2

Forgiveness at Its Best

> We should resent more from a sense of the propriety of resentment, from a
> sense that mankind expect and require it of us, than because we feel in our-
> selves the furies of that disagreeable passion. There is no passion, of which
> the human mind is capable, concerning whose justness we ought to be so
> doubtful, concerning whose indulgence we ought so carefully to consult
> our natural sense of propriety, or so diligently to consider what will be the
> sentiments of the cool and impartial spectator. . . . It must appear, in short,
> from our whole manner, without our labouring affectedly to express it, that
> passion has not extinguished our humanity; and that if we yield to the dic-
> tates of revenge, it is with reluctance, from necessity, and in consequence of
> great and repeated provocations. When resentment is guarded and quali-
> fied in this manner, it may be admitted to be even generous and noble.
>
> Adam Smith, *TMS* II.i.5.9

In this chapter, I build on the considerations offered so far in order to
define forgiveness. Among the topics to be discussed are the relation
of forgiveness and self-respect; the conditions that offender and injured
would ideally meet; the "moral monster" and the "unforgivable"; why
forgiveness is desirable; the role of narrative (the "story" we tell ourselves
and each other about forgiving or being forgiven); and the relation of
forgiveness to reconciliation. The "paradigmatic" sense of forgiveness
frames my discussion in this chapter.

[i] FORGIVENESS, REVENGE, AND RESENTMENT

Is Butler right in understanding forgiveness as requiring the forswearing
of *revenge*? The answer seems to me affirmative. It would be incomprehensible to hold that X has "forgiven" Y when X is intent on taking revenge

on Y. I repeat that this is compatible with X endorsing whatever judicial punishment has been impartially allotted to Y, which is to say that forgiveness is primarily about the moral relations and sentiments between X and Y, rather than about the administration of justice. On this view, which I endorse, there is no inconsistency between a retributive or consequentialist theory of punishment and interpersonal forgiveness. And that is a fortiori so with respect to the relation between the duty to punish (however that duty is understood) and forgiveness. A judge in a court of law has no business basing judgments about justice on considerations of forgiveness (the judge's, or someone else's) – which is not to say that considerations of mercy or pity are inadmissible – and one could forgive one's offender while also insisting that judicially determined punishment be carried out (it is not as though a victim's forgiveness exempts the offender from impartially administered justice).

As I have noted, many now view it as self-evident that forgiveness is in part the forswearing of resentment. This is ultimately true, in my view, but it is not self-evident. Let me go through this complicated issue step by step. The claim being examined is not that forgiveness is the forswearing of anger or hatred, but of that species of anger or moral hatred Butler defines as resentment. One may be angry without feeling resentment (in the sense I have defined it, following Butler), and hence giving up that anger is not forgiveness. I could be angry that I have cancer, for example; or angry that the economy is doing badly; or angry that that the politicians in power have mismanaged the economy. Forswearing anger in such cases is not forgiveness.

Why should our understanding of forgiveness as a virtue mention resentment at all, even granting that resentment is the normal affective response to injury?

Forgiveness is a certain kind of ethical response to injury and the injurer. Following Butler, we have characterized resentment as a species of moral hatred that is "deliberate" rather than sudden, is aroused by the perception of what we take to be unwarranted injury, embodies a judgment about the fairness of an action or of an intention to do that action, is provoked by moral not natural evil, is aimed at the action's author, and is a reactive as well as retributive passion that instinctively seeks to exact a due measure of punishment. It also seeks to protest the wrongness of the (intended) action. We have defended the view that it is appropriate (for us non-Sages) to respond with anger when wrongly injured (I return to this later). The intuitive tie between forgiveness and the moral anger one feels at being unjustly treated is unbreakable.

If one felt *no* resentment in response to someone's injurious action against oneself, it would make no sense to forgive them for their deed. The case is similar in definitions of other virtues of character: for example, courage would mention (or entail a view about) the courageous person's relation to fear. It is possible to be unjustly treated and not feel the corresponding resentment, of course; but one is then either very much above common life (say, because one is a Sage), or insensible for any number of other reasons (say, because one is self-deceived, or emotionally blocked for some psychological or cultural reason). In such cases, one is not actually in a position to forgive – even if one ought to be thus positioned. It is also possible to be unjustly treated and not know that one has been (say, because one is an infant, or "brain washed," or what have you): again, whatever one is doing in overlooking the injury and feeling no anger toward the offender, it is not forgiveness.

Of course it is possible not to take revenge and still feel just as much anger; but in such a case we might speak of pardoning the offender, or simply of refraining from revenge for a prudential or social reason, as the case may be. And as already noted, if X stops resenting Y, it does not follow that X has forgiven Y; amnesia, for example, is not the same thing as forgiveness. So forgiveness cannot *simply* be forswearing resentment, even though it does require at least the moderating of resentment. We recognize a different phenomenon, namely that of letting go of resentment for moral reasons, as well as of revenge, without forgetting the wrong that was done, and even in some cases (re)accepting the offender as a friend. This is what we are calling forgiveness.

Is defining forgiveness in terms of the letting go of resentment (for the right reasons) too narrow? One author argues that "it should also count as forgiveness to abandon contempt for someone or disappointment in him. Taken together, these suggest that to forgive someone for having wronged one is to abandon all negative feelings toward this person, of whatever kind, insofar as such feelings are based on the episode in question."[1] On this view, abandoning resentment is neither a necessary nor sufficient condition of forgiveness.

By way of reply, I argue that the reactive sentiment under discussion is quite specific, and involves the attribution of responsibility to the wrongdoer, as well as the belief that one has been wrongly injured. Disappointment could be one emotion felt in connection with this situation, but it is not, I think, a direct response to it. It would stem, we are imagining, from

---

[1] N. Richards, "Forgiveness," *Ethics* 99 (1988), p. 79.

the recognition that the person is not as trustworthy as we had thought. But we may have had no such thought about the offender. Disdain may also be felt in this connection, but may not be; one can have disdain for persons (individually or in groups), or indeed for theories, even when they do no personal injury. Or take disgust: I may be disgusted with you, though you have caused me no injury whatever. The reactive sentiment directed at the wrong, then, is primarily and properly resentment (defined along Butlerian lines).

Forswearing resentment does not require giving up *every* "negative" feeling associated with the injurious event. One may forgive, but still feel sorrow in regard to, or disappointment with, the offender. Or I may be depressed by what you have done; but overcoming the depression is not necessarily forgiveness (if, say, I do not think you intentionally aimed to injure me). Forgiveness does however mean overcoming negative feelings that embody and perpetuate the key features of resentment, feelings that very often accompany resentment – such as contempt and scorn – *insofar as* they are modulations of the moral hatred in question.[2] Scorn may be (but is not always) the expression of resentment, such that though they are distinct, to forswear the one requires doing so with the other. The phenomenology of the moral sentiments is subtle and variegated; my point is that the moral sentiment(s) given up by forgiveness must embody the features evident in resentment, for the context to which the relevant sentiments respond have the features stipulated (a responsible agent inflicting unwarranted injury, etc.). And this is entirely consistent with my view that forgiveness is a virtue.

Granting then that forgiveness is connected with the letting go of resentment in particular, we next ask whether it requires *forswearing* resentment. Certainly, it would be counter-intuitive to claim that X has forgiven Y if X is seething with resentment against Y. Yet Butler's theory holds that it includes the *moderating* of resentment to an appropriate level as judged by a suitably informed and sympathetic third party. In principle this could endorse a continuing high level of moral anger, though Butler thinks that in practice it will most often bring resentment down to a level much lower than that dictated by unrestrained passion (p. 162).

There is something right and something wrong about this view. Resentment ought certainly be corrected for its "abuses," and this will

---

[2] On these points I am in agreement with P. M. Hughes, "What Is Involved in Forgiving?" *Philosophia* 25 (1997), pp. 37–40. My disagreement with Richards is consonant with that of Hughes.

normally mean moderating it, such that it is proportionate to the injury. Forgiveness would be impossible without *that* much. But *only* that much seems to give us some virtue other than forgiveness; something like the virtue of standing up for oneself, a mix of righteous indignation and pride. Butler seems right to hold that we are entitled to say "X forgives Y" even though X continues to feel resentment that is not stronger than is proportionate to the injury, but the concession holds only if the resentment is felt *for a time only*. Let me explain why.

Keeping in mind our brief discussion of resentment as a quasi-cognitive emotion, I propose that forgiveness requires that resentment for the relevant injury be appropriately moderated *and* that the agent make a further commitment to work toward a frame of mind in which even that resentment is let go. Forswearing the emotion is indeed the ultimate goal. Where the injury is small, the end may quickly be achieved. But where it is not, "I forgive" is not necessarily a report of a warranted affective state (say, that resentment has disappeared, for the right reasons) – not, that is, of a completed *achievement* – but a report of a feeling (say, that resentment has been brought down to the proportionate level, for the right reasons), *and* an expression of an ethical commitment to see one's relation to the wrong-doer in a light that leads resentment out the door, so to speak, *and* a trustworthy report that resentment is in fact moving out the door – all under conditions where the offender has taken the appropriate steps.[3] "Forgiveness" may either refer to that process or to the end-state. I am proposing that the former, "present participle" sense is legitimate (assuming, to repeat, that the offender has taken the appropriate steps), even while granting that qua process forgiveness is incomplete relative to the "perfect tense" sense. This distinction should not be confused with that between what I am calling "paradigmatic" and "non-paradigmatic" kinds of forgiveness, for it obtains also within paradigmatic cases.

The merit of this approach is that it preserves the credibility of much of our talk about forgiveness (for we frequently forgive while still experiencing *some* anger); preserves the intuition that fully achieved forgiveness would let go of resentment altogether; and acknowledges that a sentiment such as resentment does not respond immediately and wholly to cognitive

---

[3] I share this conclusion with J. G. Haber, *Forgiveness* (Lanham: Rowman and Littlefield, 1991), p. 7; and H. J. N. Horsburgh, "Forgiveness," *Canadian Journal of Philosophy* 4 (1974): p. 273. However, our three analyses of forgiveness differ in important ways, and therewith our arguments for this conclusion. My third proviso in the sentence to which this note is appended is meant to respond to the possibility that the resentment fails to "move out the door": were that the case, we should say that the commitment ultimately failed, and with it, forgiveness.

emendations or to one's will. Still further, this approach recognizes that forgiveness may be a difficult achievement for a host of reasons having to do both with the wronged and the wrong-doer, while encouraging us to undertake the project with the assurance that it is not an all-or-nothing affair. Forgiveness will require other virtues, such as self-command, understanding, and trust, exercised over time.

A defender of Butler might reply: if resentment *is* moderated to the appropriate level, why aim to forswear it *altogether*? It would seem by definition that the appropriately pitched sentiment is warranted, such that abandoning it altogether – as achieved forgiveness would appear to require – is a vice not a virtue. Aristotle tells us that to fail to be angry when the occasion rightly demands it is to be "slavish," that is, to manifest the view that one does not think oneself worth defending.[4] Hence, the Butlerian temptation to hold that forgiveness is the forswearing of revenge and the moderating of resentment to the appropriate level.

By way of response, I say that we recognize professions of forgiveness when some resentment lingers, *only so long as* there is commitment to its continued abatement. It would be strange to credit complete forgiveness when resentment continues and its continuation is judged warranted; something essential to the process would not have been completed. Indeed, if moderated resentment *is* still warranted all things considered, then forgiveness is impossible or premature. Forgiveness does not attempt to get rid of warranted resentment. Rather, it follows from the recognition that the resentment is no longer warranted. And what would provide the warrant can be nothing other than the right reasons. These specify the conditions the offending party should meet to qualify for forgiveness. What are those conditions?

In order to answer this question, we need to dwell a bit longer on one warrant for continued anger, namely that to let go of it betrays a lack of self-respect.

[ii] RESENTMENT AND SELF-RESPECT

Retribution is an admission of pain. A mind bowed by wrong done to it is not a great mind. Whoever harmed you was either stronger or weaker than you. If he was weaker, spare him; if he was stronger, spare yourself.

Seneca, *De Ira* 3.5.8

---

4 Not everyone agrees with Aristotle's point. Seneca argues in *De Ira* that are better off being cured of anger altogether. As he puts it at the conclusion of Book I (I.21), "there is nothing about anger, not even in the apparent extravagance of its disdain for gods and men, that is great or noble."

The provocative Aristotelian label I just recalled ("slavish") raises a question pertinent to the analysis of forgiveness: is resentment, even when it is warranted by the injury that provokes it, an implicit confession that one has doubts as to whether one is worthy of respect?

In the first chapter of this book I suggested that several classical, and one modern, perfectionist theories did not see forgiveness as a virtue in part because they held that the perfected person would not feel resentment (either on account of invulnerability to injury, or of contempt for anyone capable of inflicting injury). I suggested that forgiveness is a virtue more at home in an ethical scheme that emphasizes our irremediable imperfection. It would seem to follow that resentment is a sign of our vulnerability to others, of our less than perfect natures. And this might seem to come to admitting that when we feel resentment, it is because we acknowledge that there may be some truth – at least a grain of truth – implied by the injury against which we are defending ourselves. By contrast, imagine that the injury consists in a heinous but false accusation. If one were entirely convinced that the accusation is false, why would one resent its author, rather than laugh it off and judge its author a contemptible fool not worthy of precious time and energy?

In light of such questions it is not surprising that Hampton defines resentment as "an emotion whose object is the defiant reaffirmation of one's rank and value in the face of treatment calling them into question in one's own mind" (pp. 59–60). For Hampton, resentment is a response not to the sense of being demeaned or dishonored or insulted (treated as being less in value when one is certain of one's own value; her example is that of a prince's reaction to being treated as a pauper, p. 45), but of being lowered in value, or being diminished. The injurious treatment is received as revealing "a rank that is lower than she thought. So what is lowered is her self-esteem." (p. 50). The resenting person fears that the offender is right in treating her as of little account, wishes that the belief in her low value is false, and accordingly defies or protests it (p. 57). As Hampton puts the central point, "resentment is . . . an emotion which betrays weakness" (p. 148). Someone who "recovers a high degree of belief in her own rank and value" will "thereby overcome resentment" (p. 79). Hence the importance in her view of "malicious hatred," which may follow upon resentment and which seeks to lower the injurer to one's own diminished level – a strategy she rightly sees as self-defeating (pp. 65, 72). This thesis is strikingly similar to Nietzsche's characterization of *ressentiment*.

While resentment *may* betray weakness, I see no reason to believe that it must do so, or indeed normally does so. A failure to manifest proper resentment may manifest low self-esteem (Aristotle's "slavishness"); but manifesting proper resentment need not do so. But if this so, then why *do* we feel resentment when injured by means of insults and such?

I concede that in resentment (which to repeat I am taking to be "settled anger" and distinct from envy) there is indeed a self-defense mechanism at work, just as Butler assumed. In the case of some types of injury, one's social standing may be harmed by allegations about whose falsity their victim entertains no doubt. The potential for that secondary harm is a matter of grave concern to most of us, given that we non-Sages do care about how we are regarded by others.

More importantly, to pick up a point made in the preceding chapter, there is an implicitly impersonal aspect to resentment: *it is wrong* to treat someone like this – the protest that is part of resentment is directed at the sheer "wrongness" or unfairness of the injury. This reactive feeling testifies to a moral standpoint, and also seeks to deny the offender his "absurd self-love, by which he seems to imagine, that other people may be sacrificed at any time, to his convenience or his humour," to quote Smith once again (*TMS* II.iii.I.5). You *must not do* this sort of thing, for it is *not to be done*, pronounces our resentment. In other words, resentment contains a powerful element of indignation.[5] As already suggested, herein lies a reason for the wish that the protest be public: the principles being stood up for are shared, and so too must be the indignation at their violation.

And because you also *do* respect and esteem yourself, your indignant resentment is personal as well; for you stand not just on the ground that "it is not to be done," but that it is not to be done *to you* (and of course this assumes that you have the standing to demand not to be treated thus). So

---

[5] Hampton seeks to distinguish the two, seeing indignation as an impersonal form of anger that does not reveal any doubts about its owner's self-esteem (p. 56). She remarks that the "indignant person experiences neither the fear nor the defiance which is characteristic of resentment" (p. 59). I am disagreeing with her characterization of resentment, and also disagree with her view that indignation does not express defiance. But I agree that indignation (as I am calling it, indignant resentment) does not express the fear that the injury may be warranted by one's moral status (the fear that the victim is, so to speak, properly to be injured). I note that Murphy shares Hampton's tying together resentment and "weakness," and also associates Nietzsche with that view (p. 93). Scheler too accepts the Nietzschean view that *ressentiment* expresses weakness ("Negative Feelings," p. 119), a view with which I do not disagree, because I distinguish between resentment and *ressentiment*. By contrast, Murphy and Hampton are running together resentment and Nietzschean *ressentiment*.

understood, resentment does not seek to diminish, insult, or devalue the
wrong-doer (though of course the wrong-doer may experience it as such,
because her *false* view of self is being rejected), so long as the "abuses"
of resentment so ably set out by Butler are avoided. And it does not
reflect a sneaking suspicion that one is worth the diminishment, insult,
or devaluation communicated by the wrong-doer's behavior.

Resentment embodies the demand that the wrong-doer show the
proper respect, and be accountable for not having done so. Implicitly,
then, it not only expresses the view that the wrong-doer is an accountable
being, but even shows a certain respect toward the wrong-doer.[6] Forgiveness does so as well, as I will shortly argue; it expresses that respect, and
recognition of accountability, by way of a remarkable transformation on
the part of injured and injurer alike.

Resentment does not necessarily express a lack of self-respect, then,
and the reasons for moderating and forswearing resentment do not hinge
on an effort to regain self-respect. This brings us back to the question
posed at the end of the preceding section: what are the conditions defining when resentment is not warranted, and so too when one no longer
warrants being resented? Given the argument thus far, this comes to asking for the conditions necessary for forgiveness.

Whatever the answer to the question before us, forgiveness must not
collapse into either condonation or excuse. Broadly speaking, to condone
is to collaborate in the lack of censure of an action, and perhaps to enable
further wrong-doing by the offender. One may condone in the sense
of accepting while not disapproving (by not holding the wrong-doing
against its author), or in the sense of tolerating while disapproving (a sort
of "look the other way" or "putting up with it" strategy).[7] If forgiveness

---

[6] This would fall under the heading of what S. Darwall calls "recognition respect." See his
"Two Kinds of Respect," *Ethics* 88 (1977): 36–49. This sort of respect "is said to be owed
to all persons. To say that persons as such are entitled to respect is to say that they are
entitled to have other persons take seriously and weigh appropriately the fact that they are
persons in deliberating what to do.... The crucial point is that to conceive of all persons
as entitled to respect is to have some conception of what sort of consideration the fact of
being a person requires" (p. 38); considered as a moral attitude, "to respect something is
thus to regard it as requiring restrictions on the moral acceptability of actions connected
with it" (p. 40); "we are judging that the fact that he or she is a person places moral
constraints on our behavior" (p. 46).

[7] I owe this distinction, and the language of "complicity," to P. Hughes, "Moral Anger,
Forgiving, and Condoning," *Journal of Social Philosophy* 26 (1995), pp. 111–115. He characterizes these two views of condonation as "approving permissiveness" and "disapproving
permissiveness" respectively. He insightfully comments: "Condoners 'treat' wrong-doers
as if they have done nothing wrong, and this is surely the main reason condoning is
thought to be morally objectionable" (p. 114).

were condonation in either sense, it would certainly not be a virtue, and thus would no longer count as true forgiveness. The first amounts to complicity in or collusion with the wrong-doing, perhaps covered up by some form of rationalization. And of course, if its attempts exempts the wrong-doer from responsibility for the wrong action, it amounts to excuse. The second is compatible with continued resentment directed at the offender. But the aim of forgiveness is something quite different: to understand, to relinquish revenge and resentment, all the while holding the offender responsible. It is not mercy, in the sense of the suspension of warranted punishment – for that would be the province of justice, which responds to a quite different set of considerations.

We have established that forgiveness comes with certain conditions or norms, else it would collapse into forgetting, or excusing, or condonation, or rationalization, as the case may be. When satisfied, these conditions qualify the offender for forgiveness and entitle the victim to forgive. They also provide reasons specifying why it would be appropriate for the victim to forgive (and, by implication, criteria for understanding when it would be inappropriate to forgive). I attempt to specify these conditions in sections [iii] and [iv]. In section [v] I revisit several questions, including that of the relevance of conditions for forgiveness: why may not the victim forgive freely, bestow it as a gift? Why is forgiveness not unconditional in that way?

[iii] TO BE FORGIVEN: CHANGING YOUR WAYS, CONTRITION, AND REGRET

The transformations that the offender and victim undergo are mutually dependent, in our paradigm case of dyadic forgiveness, and they are asymmetrical. Both of these features lend forgiveness highly unusual, if not unique, characteristics as a virtue.

I will discuss the injurer's transformation first: why is it necessary, if there is to be forgiveness, and in what does it consist? Butler gives us little guidance here. I will continue to assume that the offender really has done wrong, is responsible for the wrong done, that the wronged person's resentment is warranted, and that the offender (not the injurious act) is the proper object of both resentment and forgiveness.

In the paradigmatic interpersonal scene that provides our touchstone, the offender has injured a specific individual; the offender asks the victim for forgiveness; which if granted, is bestowed on the offender. The victim's resentment is normally provoked by a person's action, but is properly focused on the person for doing the deed; we forgive the agent, not the deed (even though we forgive the agent for doing the deed). These seemingly banal characteristics of the scene have profound consequences for the norms or criteria that define the asking for and receiving of forgiveness. They specify the irremediably *social* character of the process and, as a consequence, the moral interdependence of the two parties in question. But "social" does not mean that society can itself do the moral work, at least not in the way the paradigmatic scene calls for (this changes in non-paradigmatic contexts). The two individuals are the fundamental moral units here; unless that is assumed, forgiveness collapses into something quite different – say, a socially mandated process for peace making. We are assuming that the offender bears responsibility for the injury, that the injury really does matter ethically because it is a wrong to the victim (and not simply because of its consequences for society), and therefore that in the paradigmatic case the victim alone owns the moral right to forgiveness.

If we ask why the offender who has satisfied all of the conditions for being forgiven must wait for the victim to forgive, and not simply claim forgiveness by virtue of having satisfied those conditions, the answer ultimately lies in the two central points just made. First, the original context that gives rise to the issue is interpersonal or social, and that carries forward to the moral action of forgiveness whose purpose is to address that context. The dyadic character of the process permeates it from start to finish.

And second, the moral action arises from individuals. For example, it is not completed unless the injured party's sentiments have changed. That is a project for the injured party, not the offender; so the latter is not in a position to claim to be forgiven simply because he has, according to his own lights, satisfied the relevant conditions. A claim to the contrary adds insult to injury, usurping the victim's prerogative to pronounce forgiveness, and manifesting further disrespect for the victim because it communicates that the victim's assessment and sentiments are irrelevant. And there is also the complicated problem of assessing whether the magnitude of the injury done is forgivable, given its impact on the injured person; in the first instance, that is to be assessed by the person who has suffered the injury (I return to this in discussing the question of "the unforgivable."). Indeed, the relevance of the perspective of the injured party is built into the conditions the offender must satisfy, as we shall see. Whether or not the offender has satisfied several of the conditions must in the first instance be for the injured party to assess (for example, the condition that the offender understand the injury he or she has done, and communicate that regret to the victim). In section [v] of this chapter I will consider a mirror image of this issue, viz. whether the victim may forgive the offender whether or not the latter has taken any of the required steps.

Even if it were somehow determined with complete accuracy – say, by an impartial but sympathetically attuned moral community whose judgment is perfect – that the offender is forgivable, thanks to having satisfied all of the relevant conditions and given the nature of the injury, the decision to that effect strikes us as second best relative to the same decision as made by the injured party. Why? Because one of the implicit ends of forgiveness would not have been accomplished, namely restoration of mutual respect and recognition between the two parties – the minimal state of civility that existed before the injury was done. I do not assume that the two parties knew each other personally prior to the injury; but that as co-members of the moral commonwealth, they were bound by moral regard for each other.

One of the striking consequences of this interdependence is that each party holds the other in its power, in this sense: the offender depends on the victim in order to be forgiven, and the victim depends on the offender in order to forgive. This interdependence is part of the logic of forgiveness, and may well render it unique among the virtues (and in Chapter 1, I have characterized it as a virtue). By contrast, I can be just or courageous whether or not those abusing or threatening meet any conditions other than abusing or threatening me. The interdependence of offender and victim in the scene of forgiveness again illustrates that virtue's rootedness in the human world that is, from the standpoint of classical perfectionist theory, deeply imperfect in just this way: interdependent, social, vulnerable.

The agent requires reasons in order to commit to giving up resentment, or at least, to giving up the judgment that the wrong-doer warrants continued resentment. What are those reasons?

The first of these reasons consists in the wrong-doer's demonstration that she no longer wishes to stand by herself as the author of those wrongs. That is, she must acknowledge, first, that she was the responsible agent for the specific deeds in question. A failure to take responsibility is a denial or avoidance of a fundamental and relevant truth of the matter not only adds insult to injury so far as the victim is concerned, but undermines the possibility of trusting that the offender will not turn around and repeat the injury. To forgive would then collapse into condonation.

Second, she must repudiate her deeds (by acknowledging their wrongness) and thus disavow the idea that she would author those deeds again.

That repudiation (assuming it is sincere) is a step toward showing that one is not simply the "same person" who did the wrong, for the earlier person authored and in some sense espoused rather than disavowed those deeds. The conjunction of the two seems impossible at first blush: one takes responsibility for having done X, and one repudiates the self that did X.[8] While I will not venture here into the extremely difficult problems of personal identity, I note that the core of the repudiation in question actually depends on a recognizable continuity of self, else the moral work that the wrong-doer must perform in order to earn forgiveness cannot be undertaken (she would simply say the equivalent of: "it wasn't 'me' who did the wrong, I had a schizophrenic episode," which is to offer grounds for excuse).

Third, the wrong-doer must experience and express *regret* at having caused that particular injury to that particular person; in our paradigm case, this expression will be addressed to the wronged party. The regret must be specific in this way, and not simply acknowledge the wrongness of the act. This address constitutes an indispensable acknowledgment that the wrong-doer now recognizes the respect due to the injured. Notice that the wrong-doer must not just *feel* regret and contrition; but must communicate it to the person she injured. Forgiveness is in part a communicative act, and in that sense rhetorical (it is an expression that is meant to persuade, though not merely to convince or change the victim's sentiments and judgment). I am of course supposing that forgiveness is sought from, and therefore addressed to the injured party.

These three conditions entail that *memory* is essential to forgiveness (I have been assuming that forgiveness for past acts, not proleptic forgiving for possible future acts, is at issue – I suspect the latter notion is not coherent). The importance of memory will be crucial at the political level as well. At both levels, the pertinent and accurate remembering is inseparable from allegiance to the truth of the matter.

Fourth, the offender must commit to becoming the sort of person who does not inflict injury, and that commitment must be shown through deeds as well as words. Then her repudiation of her "past self" would become credible, and it is her task to make it so, for the "burden of proof" is hers and hers alone to shift. So the "action" of forgiveness is not just rhetorical (in the sense just mentioned), and not just a matter of

---

[8] As is noted by J. Beatty: "in seeking the forgiveness of the other, the offender is asserting both that he is and is not the man who committed the offense." "Forgiveness," *American Philosophical Quarterly* 7 (1970), p. 251.

changing sentiments. These four steps constitute the *contrition* requisite to a convincing appeal for forgiveness.[9]

Forgiveness so understood is not condonation, because it requires that the offender not only take responsibility for her past wrong-doing but for emendation. The sort of case in which the abused spouse "forgives" her abuser, in the sense of lets him off the moral hook and implicitly encourages further objectionable behavior, is blocked by this condition.

Fifth, the offender must show that she understands, from the injured person's perspective, the damage done by the injury. This entails listening to her victim's account, and to grasping it with compassion. The offender is thus required to exercise "sympathy" in the sense of putting herself in the position of the person she injured, and understanding what being in that situation meant for the injured person.

The offender's regretful address would offer some sort of *narrative* accounting for how she came to do wrong, how that wrong-doing does not express the totality of her person, and how she is becoming worthy of approbation. She needs to make herself intelligible by offering up an account that is neither fiction nor excuse making, and that puts the wrong-doing as well as the self that did the wrong in a context. The injured party deserves answers to questions such as "who is this person, such that she could have injured me thus? Such that she warrants forgiveness?" This requirement for account giving is a sixth condition.[10]

Taken together, these conditions ensure that in forgiving the offender, we have accurately targeted that for which the offender is being forgiven, and that we are right to forgive the offender for those deeds. Were the

---

[9] The expression of contrition is not merely a speech act, then. A "merely verbal" fulfill-ment of the requirements I am setting out would not suffice; hence the emphasis on deeds as well as words. Are words required at all? It is not inconceivable that a person could take steps that would be unambiguously understood by the victim as signifying contrition in the way I have defined it (though this takes a stretch of the imagination to conceive!). But in the main, explicit and verbal address will be expected and necessary.

[10] A compelling literary description of this sixth demand will be found in Ian McEwan's novel *Atonement* (New York: Random House, 2001), p. 326. Robbie demands just such an account from Briony, specifically a letter addressed to him explaining "in much greater detail" why she gave false testimony that sent him to prison. Briony turns out to be the author of the novel itself; *Atonement* is her atonement – but not to Robbie directly, who by the (fictional) time of its completion is dead. As she notes at the very end, she is not forgiven, and her musings about different endings she might have given her narrative, as well as her unconvincing analogy between author and God, evince traces of that disregard for truth and confusion about her agency that were responsible for her original wrong-doing. Her atonement is therefore incomplete, for reasons that chime with the argument I am making.

offender to represent the deeds accurately, but not recognize them as
hers, we would not be in a position to forgive her; for the agent is the
primary object or target of forgiveness. We are not forgiving the agent
for not knowing that she did what she acknowledges was done, or in spite
of the fact that she does not know, or worse, in spite of the fact that she
refuses to acknowledge her responsibility for the mutually acknowledged
deeds. Such cases might (or might not) call for excuse, but they are not
cases of forgiveness.

Why should the offender take any of the six steps? Why should she
seek forgiveness? The wish to alleviate the burden of guilt is surely the
most common and pressing *motive* for requesting forgiveness.[11] Guilt is
readily understood as the moral feeling produced by conscience, itself
the internalized voice of moral authority. It is striking not only how compelling "the voice of conscience" can be, but how powerfully it testifies
to our nature as social and interdependent beings. As the result of an
internalized voice of moral authority, it assumes the existence of moral
community. And the thought that guilt is *alleviated* through forgiveness
makes sense if the offender sees herself through the eyes of a moral
community (this may be a notional community), wishes to rejoin that
community, and understands that the injured party has the *standing* to
release her from moral isolation. In the paradigmatic scene under discussion, the moral community defers to the victim to grant (or withhold)
forgiveness.

Smithean sympathy theory offers an intriguing explanation of the psychological mechanisms by which the sense of guilt arises and by which it
can be lifted. A core idea is that self-understanding is socially mediated,
and that acceptance in the community is desired (see *TMS* III.1.1–6). The
offender cannot help but consider the view in which she is held by others,
even when the others articulate no such view of his guilt (perhaps they
do not know of his heinous deed); in which case she views herself as they
would view her, were they in the know (*TMS* III.2.9). For the perfectionist
views sketched in Chapter 1 of this book, by contrast, the virtuous person

---

[11] Might the offender also seek forgiveness in order to alleviate the burden of *shame*? I am
not certain as to the answer to this complicated question, but my guess is that shame
would seek pardon rather than forgiveness. In any case, both the wish to alleviate the
burden of shame, and the burden of guilt, would demonstrate a wish to be readmitted
to the moral community. For a fascinating and instructive discussion of the distinction
between shame and guilt, see B. Williams' *Shame and Necessity* (Berkeley: University of
California Press, 1993), pp. 77–102. For a brief comment on their bearing on forgiveness,
see pp. 90–91.

has to a very large extent – if not completely – freed her self-conception from dependence on the moral community (I have already noted the instability of Aristotle's "magnanimous man" in this connection.). The perfectly virtuous person seems, correspondingly, to have no place for guilt or its alleviation through forgiveness.[12]

An agent who satisfies any of the just specified conditions, let alone all of them, cannot be characterized as a "moral monster" even if the injuries he or she perpetrated are monstrous. I return to the idea of moral monsters, sympathy, and shared humanity in [vi] later.

[iv] FORGIVING: A CHANGE OF HEART, AND SEEING THE OFFENDER AND ONESELF IN A NEW LIGHT

Suppose that the wrong-doer has taken all of the steps just sketched in [iii]; what transformation must the injured party undergo in order to forgive? It is clear that there are conditions the forgiver too must meet, if forgiveness is to take place. Imagine an offender who has taken all the required steps from her side, requests forgiveness, and is greeted by her victim with "sure, whatever, you're hereby forgiven, have a nice day . . . thanks to *Lethe* (a powerful new medication developed by Eternal Sunshine Inc.) I can scarcely remember what you did to me anyhow." The offender would have been dismissed rather than forgiven.

The commitment to forgive is conceptually incompatible with behavior that signals a failure to forgive. I have in mind someone who claims to have forgiven – excepting perhaps the letting go of lingering resentment – but then keeps reminding the offender of her misdeeds. This is a form

---

[12] What will count as "injury," and to what extent is it culturally defined? In private correspondence (referred to here with permission), Amelie Rorty raises the possibility that injury may be erroneously conceived by *both* parties to forgiveness (picture, say, a false view of honor held in a medieval society dominated by warriors, or the "code of honor" to which Butler alluded), and yet that forgiveness may be genuinely requested and granted. In such a case, forgiveness is founded on beliefs that the parties to it truly hold, but which are normatively false. Strictly speaking, the theory I am advancing rules out such a case; and certainly rules out a case in which the genuinely held beliefs of both parties are factually false (say, based on a factual mistake about who did what to whom). Whatever the correct characterization of the forswearing of anger in such case, "forgiveness" is not it. If the parties to the exchange are mistaken normatively or factually, then what is needed is to understand that morally culpable wrong was not committed or suffered. I cannot forgive you for a wrong you did not commit, even if you too believe (erroneously) that you caused the injury (indeed, it would be an insult to forgive you in such a case!). Similarly, my view rules out cases in which both parties suffer from self-deception and then jointly subscribe to normatively or factually false views about injury and forgiveness.

of manipulation, even humiliation. Forgiveness would then have meta-morphosed into an instrument of revenge; yet forgiveness is, in part, the forswearing of revenge. The same is a fortiori true of the incompatibility between such behavior and accomplished forgiveness. Forgiveness is not war by other means. Perhaps the metaphor of "debt" is appropriate in this one way: forgiving the offender is like forgiving a debt in that once it is accomplished, the matter is closed and the offender released. Even when these three steps – the forswearing of revenge, the moderation of resentment, and the commitment to let resentment go altogether – are taken for moral reasons (because it's the right or virtuous thing to do), something else is also required, as Hampton rightly maintains: viz., a change in the injured person's belief that the wrong-doer is simply a "bad person" with whom one ought not consort (Hampton, p. 36). Without that, we should hardly be willing to credit her with forgiveness.

The six conditions sketched in the preceding section are not meant as a therapeutic program. The question is not about what we can do psycho-logically. Rather, these are conditions of a moral nature that may warrant a change of belief about "the bad person's" character, and therefore war-rant that the injured party should emend her view that the wrong-doer is reducible to the agent who did those wrongs. As already noted, this is commonly referred to in the literature as a process of "reframing," and this is a fourth condition the injured party meets. This does not come to dividing off the deed from the doer; Augustine's much quoted (or rather, slightly misquoted) "hate the sin, love the sinner" is mistaken.[13] Let us take a closer look at that point before spelling out the other conditions that the forgiver meets.

Augustine's dictum invites the thought (not one Augustine would have welcomed) that the sinner is always to be *excused* or pardoned – else why *not* hate the sinner for what she did? Such a position risks collapsing forgiveness into condonation. A reply to this worry might run as follows: if it were the case that the target of forgiveness is the past *act* and not the agent, then in theory the agent need not meet *any* conditions in order to warrant forgiving, in particular not have a change of heart or commit to a change of ways.

---

[13] St. Augustine, letter 211, par. 11: "cum dilectione hominum et odio vitiorum" (he is recommending "due love for the persons and hatred of the sin"). Arguably, we should translate "vices" not "sin." In Augustine's *Opera Omnia*, ed. J.-P. Migne, 16 vols., vol. 2 (Paris, 1865). My thanks to John Freccero for his help in tracking down this reference. Cf. Seneca, *De Ira* II.28: "Many of mankind, indeed, are angry not with the sin, but the sinner."

The first response is that the act is the work of the agent. If the act is the object of forgiveness quite independently of the actor, a deep conceptual confusion would prevail. Events in the world devoid of intention are not properly the object of resentment or the forswearing thereof, as argued in section [i] of this chapter and in the discussion of Butler. Forgiving an act without reference to the actor would treat the act as independently motivated; both the phenomenology and the metaphysics of the matter render that idea deeply suspect.

Consider a more sophisticated version of what one might call the Augustinian strategy: resentment of the past act is a form of protest against a threatening *claim* made in or by the act.[14] That is, "resentment protests a past action that persists as a present threat" by embodying the claim that you may be treated in this way (p. 546). On this view it is still the case that the agent is not the target of resentment. For forgiveness, an apology by the actor could suffice, but even that is not necessary; the support of the community or its punishment of the offender might suffice to bring about the victim's reframing *of the act,* such that resentment abates, the significance of the past act for the agent changes, and protest is no longer necessary (p. 553). This is not supposed to collapse forgiveness into condonation because it retains protest against the claim made by the act. And this approach aspires to help avoid difficulties inherent in the kind of account I give, namely those of (a) rendering the victim dependent on the offender's changing her relation to her past act (by disavowing that act, for example), and (b) raising the bar for forgiveness unreasonably high (by making it dependent on conditions so difficult to meet). I reply to (a) and (b) in sections [v] and [ix] respectively of this chapter.

I have myself argued in Chapter 1 that resentment responds in part to a claim implicit in the act, and that a primary goal of the retributive impulse is to make the *agent* understand and if possible "take back" or recant the claim that you may thus be treated. But there is a significant difference between characterizing the protest in this way, and as being directed to the claim in a way that makes it (or the agent for doing it) rather than the agent the primary target or forgiveness. The latter would be more like protesting a potentially damaging falsehood conveyed by an anonymous message, in which case one would be angry, but forgiveness

---

[14] See P. Hieronymi, "Articulating an Uncompromising Forgiveness," *Philosophy and Phenomenological Research* 62 (2001), p. 530. I am much indebted to Hieronymi for correspondence and discussion about these issues. My paginal references to her article are included directly in the text.

would not be at issue (forgive whom?). If some aspect of an *action* is the target of resentment and protest, then the thought of the action is inseparable from that of the actor whose action it is; and that is in keeping with the phenomenology of the subject, as already remarked.

So it must be the case that we resent the actor for doing the act, and have no reason for forswearing that resentment absent conditions being met by the actor (this once again in what I am calling the "paradigmatic" scene; in non-paradigmatic cases, *some* conditions have to be met somehow, however imperfectly – or so I shall argue). If a change of attitude of the person who made the claim changes whether or not the claim is still a "threat," then it is not just the claim that one resents but the person making it.[15] And the addressing of a genuine apology already brings into play several further conditions: the taking of responsibility, recognition that the act was wrong, a change of heart sufficient to disavow the action and to say so to the victim (p. 554), and implicitly the commitment not to repeat the offense (on pain of inconsistency). So the actor's relation to the past act is indeed in play – how else could the actor's apology possibly count as one way to warrant forgiveness?

Suppose contrary to fact that the actor need do nothing in relation to the act or her victim, and that instead the community renders the claim made in the past act not threatening, presumably by punishing the actor or protecting the victim; have I then forgiven, or have I warrant to forgive the act (or, because even the locution makes little sense, let us say forgiven the actor for the act)? It seems to me that the answer is negative because it incorrectly locates the work of forgiveness. Punishing the offender is a matter responsive, as I have said, to considerations of justice, law, and procedure. The victim's forgiveness is not hostage to the community's discharging the obligations of justice. The actor might or might not forgive the offender even if the latter has been duly punished (consider the case in which the offender is unregenerate and ever more vicious because of punishment).

---

[15] Hieronymi writes: "Once the offender *himself* renounces the deed, it may no longer stand as a threat to either the public understanding of right and wrong, to his worth, or to one's own. It has been cut off from the sources of its continued meaning." "Articulating an Uncompromising Forgiveness," p. 548. This seems to me to concede the point I am making, for it is incompatible with the idea that the claim and not the agent making the claim is the target of resentment and forgiveness. Hieronymi's next statement makes this even clearer: "The author has retracted his statement, and anger loses its point. Continued resentment would now constitute mere vindictiveness, betraying a smallness of character or lack of self-esteem, rather than showing an admirable appreciation and defense of genuine goods."

I return to the notion of "seeing the offender in a new light," having further defended my claim that doing so is a necessary condition of forgiveness. Re-framing does not come to the view that the wrong-doer is not to be considered as being the wrong-doer, to "washing away" the fact of her having done wrong (that would be more like amnesia, or excusing, or condonation (of the sort that claims no wrong was really done)). So it must involve something like distinguishing that "part" of the self responsible for the injury from the "whole person." Now, the wrong-doer will very probably be seen "in a new light" not solely or even primarily on the basis of the "whole person" as already evidenced, in part through the offender's narrative, but also on the basis of her projects for reform of self. "Reframing" and forgiving are in this sense forward looking (whereas excusing is typically backward-looking, and assumes that the act does not "really" reflect the agent). The "whole person" is being understood in a temporal framework. The forgiver must therefore be willing to revise her judgments, as well as change her sentiments, in part on the basis of *trust* in the future. This trust will rest on the forgiver's ability to enter sympathetically into the situation and self of the offender, not so as to excuse, but so as to imagine a credible *narrative* in which the offender takes the required steps. The effort will of course build on the narrative that, stipulatively, the offender has already offered. The victim will (in this ideal situation) grasp events from the point of view of the offender, and have reason for trusting that the offender's promise of change is "real." I underline that this process of "reframing" is a necessary, not a sufficient condition, for candidacy for forgiveness; it is possible that grasping the offender's motives and perspective might actually increase the victim's resentment.[16]

We have seen that resentment can provide a certain satisfaction to its owner; it may contain an element of pride, and for such reasons may be difficult to get into perspective. Both because at the cognitive level the story of the wrong-doer and of the wronged may be complicated, and because an emotion such as resentment does not *simply* respond to revision of the relevant beliefs, significant intellectual and affective effort may be required of the forgiver. The *commitment* to forgive may be possible if the wrong-doer meets the six conditions specified in section [iii] of this

---

[16] As is rightly pointed out by Hieronymi, "Articulating an Uncompromising Forgiveness," p. 541, in objection to D. Novitz's account. Hieronymi adds there that if one's justified resentment were eliminated simply by empathetically understanding another's point of view, then one would evince a problematic lack of self-esteem.

chapter, if the offense is not so severe as to be humanly impossible to forgive, and if the injured person has engaged in the process outlined here. As part of that process, the forgiving person comes to see herself in a new light as well. And this should count as a fifth condition the victim meets. I will suggest that it involves dropping any presumption of decisive moral superiority, and recognizing instead the shared humanity of both parties. It also involves dropping any *defining* identification of self as the person injured in this way by that person – a thought to which I return when discussing the role of narrative.

Lastly, I propose a sixth condition that the victim meets, if the full expression of forgiveness is to come about. The victim addresses the offender and declares that forgiveness is granted (even if in my "present participle" sense). Why should this be counted as a condition that it would be admirable for the victim to meet? The answer is multi-faceted. The offense by its very nature disavowed the respect due to the victim, and the offender has explicitly expressed contrition for having done so. The offender explicitly puts a request to the victim. The appropriateness of responding in kind, through a communicative act that is and is taken to be an expression of forgiveness – an answer to the request – is perhaps underlined by this thought: what rationale could one offer for the refusal to say to the offender that one forgives when one has forgiven? I can think of none, given the stipulated conditions of the scene, and there are good reasons *for* the explicit statement. The lack of symmetry in address would presumably be understood by the offender as the withholding of forgiveness – how else is she to know that she is forgiven, absent a statement of forgiveness, or to interpret a refusal explicitly to grant the request? To withhold it would at a minimum mean that the bilateral or interpersonal dimension that is intrinsic to forgiveness is not fully recognized, and the given social relation is not restored to its previous status. Further, the victim who claims to forgive but cannot bring herself to say it to the offender has reason to doubt her own claim; obversely, if she does say it to the offender, her claim acquires further confirmation in her own eyes. The explicit statement of forgiveness would presumably help both parties accomplish the ethical goals involved – such as overcoming guilt and lingering resentment, and growth in direction of a future that does not simply reiterate the evils of the past.

I have specified the necessary conditions if the offender is to qualify for forgiveness, as well as those under which the victim may forgive. Taken together they still do not give us the sufficient conditions for the moral state of affairs referred to by "forgiveness," for there is another element to consider: whether the nature of the injury is unforgivable. If so, then the perfect satisfaction of all the conditions described thus far could not permit forgiveness. Another necessary condition for forgiveness is that the injury be in principle forgivable. I discuss that complicated issue in section [viii] of this chapter.

The conditions for bestowing or qualifying for forgiveness are relatively general in nature, and fulfilling them in any specific context is not a mechanical process. To determine how to meet them, or whether or not they have been met, requires the exercise of something like good judgment or practical wisdom that is well attuned to the particulars. Was that *really* contrition? enough thereof? expressed in the right way at the right time? The circumstances are often complex, the gradations and nuances many, and the temptations to misconceive ample. And this is one of the ways in which forgiveness is a virtue; as Aristotle argued, virtue requires practical wisdom and good discernment.

[v] THE CONDITIONS OF FORGIVENESS: OBJECTIONS AND REPLIES

> The forgiveness! I know it
> will be freely offered
> or it won't, and that is all –
> and no one may bestow it
> on himself.
> If it is to come
> it will come of itself like a separate
> being,
> a mystery, working
> unseen as a wind causes still
> leaves or water to move once again.
> And hide me in the shadow of Your wings.
> Let the heart be moved again.
>   Franz Wright[17]

The theory of forgiveness set out thus far is open to a number of objections. Have too few or too many conditions been specified? Why can we not conceive of forgiveness as the dismissal of a debt, or as a "gift"? And what about the role of appeals to common humanity, anciently thought to

---

[17] F. Wright, "East Boston, 1996," in *God's Silence* (New York: Random House, 2006), p. 9.

figure into forgiveness? In this and the next section, I consider objections along these lines, and offer replies.

[v.a] Atonement and the Payment or Dismissal of a Debt

It might seem natural to propose atonement as another condition of forgiveness that must be met by the offender. However, unless the notion simply means the same as "repentance" or "contrition," the notion is out of place in the secular framework I have stipulated.[18] It might however be thought that a secular analogue to atonement does have a place in qualifying for forgiveness, namely with respect to the offender "making it up" to the injured by means of compensation for the injury done. May meeting the conditions for forgiveness be understood as a sort of repaying of a debt?

An affirmative answer might be suggested by the language of debts and repayment long associated with the topic. As mentioned already, the New Testament word for forgiveness carries the connotation of the dismissal of a debt. It is not impossible that historically the idea of forgiveness arose out of debtor-indebted relations, along with notions such as "guilt" (witness the senses of the German word "Schuld," for example). And we use the vocabulary in related contexts, as in speaking of a "debt of gratitude."

A contemporary philosopher argues that

> For perfect removal of guilt, then, the wrong-doer must make atonement for his wrong act, and the victim must forgive him. Atonement involves four components – repentance, apology, reparation, and what, for want of a better word, I shall call penance (though not all of these are always required). They are all contributions to removing as much of the consequences of the past act as logically can be removed by the wrong-doer.

The first premise from which this conclusion is drawn is apparently that "guilt is analogous to a debt." But in that event, the guilty party need not necessarily offer reparation at all; as Swinburne here notes, the victim could simply dismiss the debt unilaterally. Hence, the point that the consequences of the past act are to be removed as far as possible, and

---

[18] Here I am in agreement with A. Kolnai, "Forgiveness," *Proceedings of the Aristotelian Society* N.S. 74 (1973/74), p. 95. In its etymological sense "atonement" means at-one-ment, the (re)gaining of an original unity or harmony. But one may forgive without reconciling in this strong, unity-making sense (as is argued in the concluding section of this chapter). Similarly out of place in a secular context is the notion of penance.

that includes the harm as distinguished from the "purposive attitude of the wrong-doer."[19] Let us examine these premises in turn.

The most compelling reason for disentangling the notions of forgiveness and of dismissing a debt lies in the deep and crucial disanalogies between the two. When X wrongs Y, she does not borrow and is not loaned something. She forcibly *takes* something from Y without her consent. By contrast, the taking on of a debt is consented to by the lender, who is (as she thinks) benefited thereby. Further, as Swinburne himself notes, indebtedness can in principle be dismissed unilaterally by the person to whom the debt is owed (I return below to the question of "unconditional" forgiveness). And if to injure were to incur a debt, the "guilty" party could unilaterally wipe the slate clean by repaying the debt. No commitment to change, to truth telling, or even to taking responsibility would be required. Debt repaid, the attitude and sentiments of the "lender" – in this analogy, the victim – are irrelevant to the completion of the moral exchange. But none of this is true of forgiveness.

I do not doubt that many societies have developed rituals for wiping the slate clean that are analogous to repaying a debt.[20] But in spite of the family resemblance, these conflict-resolution procedures are importantly different from forgiveness. The resentment, perhaps hatred, of the parties may well remain intact, even if revenge has been forsworn thanks to payment of a socially sanctioned fine in the approved manner. There need be no change of heart, no "reframing" of either party, no commitment to change. In effect these procedures are ways of administering justice and perhaps of securing civic peace. The juridical and political spheres are indeed those within which compensation and reparation should be determined. To construe forgiveness as the dismissal of a debt confuses the claims of morality with the claims of justice and politics, to the detriment of both (I develop this argument further in Chapter 4). And this undermines the force of what I am taking to be Swinburne's second premise, namely that the offender is to undo the consequences of the wrong action as far as is "logically" possible, if forgiveness is to take place. The logic of *forgiveness* does not require compensation and

---

[19] All three quotations are from R. Swinburne, *Responsibility and Atonement* (Oxford: Clarendon Press, 1989), p. 81. On p. 82 he adds "I remain guilty for hurting you if I do not do what I can to remove the harm I have done you." On pp. 84–85 he makes clear that forgiveness is the appropriate response to reparation, apology, and penance.

[20] For examples, see N. Tavuchis, *Mea Culpa: a Sociology of Apology and Reconciliation* (Stanford: Stanford University Press, 1991). I return to the issue of "forgiveness rituals" in Chapter 4.

reparation; but this is perfectly compatible with the view that *justice* requires them.

It is also compatible with the view that it may be appropriate for the offender to offer reparation from a different motive than that analogous to repaying a debt, namely to signal that her professions of contrition are credible. The wronged party must be convinced that the offender means those professions, and one way to show that is to make serious efforts of this kind. In this case, compensation is offered for its symbolic or expressive value, and neither satisfies the claims of justice nor obviates the role that other conditions must play.

The idea of indebtedness carries with it a thought that is detachable from it and is relevant to forgiveness, namely that of a certain kind of *dependence*. The offender is dependently tied to the wronged person in that she does "owe" it to her to take the steps I have specified. In appealing for forgiveness, the person who did wrong expresses her dependence on the injured party; she places herself in the hands of the victim both in asking for something – forgiveness – and in that the steps she has taken do not "count" as being forgiven unless the victim accepts them as such (at least in our paradigm sense). Even here, though, the disanalogy with debt dismissal comes through. For if the debtor pays the debt – the envelope slipped under the door at night containing the required sum – then it is counted as paid even if the lender returns it, throws it away, or what have you. Perhaps this is why Swinburne switches from the language of debts to that of gifts, though strangely, he refers to the offender as the giver, and acknowledges that a gift not received does not count as given.[21]

Granting that qualifying for forgiveness does not require the additional steps of atonement or debt repayment, why may forgiveness not be thought of as "free," as a "gift"?

[v.b] Forgiveness as a Gift and Unconditional Forgiveness

In spite of my objections to understanding forgiveness on the model of debt repayment or dismissal, my talk about "conditions" for forgiveness may make it sound as though forgiveness is an economic transaction, and is therefore inferior to something like "absolute" forgiveness (just as, say, love that is contingent upon the beloved satisfying various conditions

---

[21] "In making apology, reparation, and penance, I am giving you something. All gifts have to be accepted (explicitly or implicitly) or else they remain with the giver." *Responsibility and Atonement*, p. 84.

would seem inferior to unconditional love). With something like this in mind, forgiveness is sometimes referred to as a "gift," as we have just seen; but a gift that comes with quid pro quo strings attached is no gift. The worry motivating the gift language here may be that if forgiveness comes with conditions, especially when it comes to great evils such as "crimes against humanity," it will be politicized and reduced to something like negotiated pardon.[22]

This strikes me as a confusion. It is true that forgiveness can be trivialized, politicized, and otherwise misunderstood – but that is just to say that we need to get clear on the conditions whose achievement it assumes. To infer from the possibility of its abuse to the conclusion that true forgiveness is "unconditional," or from its coming with conditions to the conclusion that forgiveness is an economic transaction, is in each case a non sequitur.

Furthermore, the vocabulary of "gift giving" does not accomplish the intended purpose. For while it is true that a gift given in expectation of a quid pro quo is suspect, gifts are normally accompanied by the expectation of reciprocity.[23] We find it perfectly intelligible to think that a gift be may be wrongly given in any number of ways – for example, to the wrong person, or at the wrong time, or of an inappropriate amount, or in a way that is self-serving or signals a corruption of judgment (here is with the *quid pro quo* becomes suspect). The same may be said about receiving a gift. So gift exchange is subject to norms, just as is forgiveness.

Perhaps the ground level assumption is the belief that forgiveness has to be elective, in the sense of not being a response that is morally appropriate (not, therefore, something owed to the offender), if it is to have full moral worth. It must be undeserved and unjustified. I see no reason to endorse that assumption, and reasons not to. To forgive someone undeserving of the honor, under the banner of a "gift," may condone the

---

[22] Derrida argues that the "absolutely heterogeneous" elements of the unconditional and the conditional are "irreducible to one another" (even though also "indissociable"), else we are lead to confusions such as the reduction of forgiveness to amnesty, amnesia, acquittal, and to "some political therapy of reconciliation, in short to some historical ecology." *Cosmopolitanism and Forgiveness*, trans. M. Dooley and R. Kearney (London and NY: Routledge, 1997), pp. 44–45. His examples of *le pardon* in modern French history (p. 40–41) are examples of amnesty and perhaps amnesia, not forgiveness. Given the confusion, it is not surprising that Derrida declares forgiveness "mad" and "unintelligible" in principle, since aimed at the unforgivable (p. 49).

[23] For an interesting commentary on this point, see P. Bourdieu's "Marginalia – Some Additional Notes on the Gift," in *The Logic of the Gift: Toward an Ethic of Generosity*, ed. A. D. Schrift (New York: Routledge, 1997), pp. 231–241.

wrong-doer, and even provide encouragement to more offenses. And it also risks undermining the agent's sense to her entitlement to warranted resentment.

Another argument to the effect that forgiveness is unconditional should be responded to. An argument advanced by Garrard and McNaughton in favor of "unconditional forgiveness" has both negative and positive sides. On the negative side, they seek to show that standard objections to the effect that forgiving when the offender has not met the requisite conditions amounts to condonation and evinces a lack of self-respect are unpersuasive. On the positive side, they argue that the recognition of shared frailty and human solidarity endorse unconditional forgiveness.[24]

Let us look briefly at each branch of their arguments, starting with the negative. They write: "On our view, to forgive involves not requiring either apology or penance. To insist on an apology is to insist that the wrong-doer humble himself before one, and this implies that there is still some residual resentment" (p. 47). Now it is certainly true that there is residual resentment; and the point is precisely that the victim rightly requires a reason that is not merely self-regarding (not just about one's own mental health, for example) in order to *forgive* the offender and thus give up the resentment. Garrard and McNaughton paint apology in quite unacceptable terms; for it is not the case that it requires either that the offender humbles herself in a way that is demeaning, or that the victim engages in "relishing" (p. 47) the offender's subservience. So that objection to requiring apology if forgiveness is to be granted does not succeed. They agree that to forgive is not to condone; and it is a central tenet of their argument that unconditional forgiveness does not condone in the sense that the forgiver does not "overlook a wrong that should not be overlooked," or "excuse what is not excusable" (p. 49). But what their argument fails to register is that as a communicative or bilateral act, "forgiveness" that requires *nothing* of the offender (putting aside submission to judicially mandated punishment) does communicate to her, as well as everyone else, that she is not being held accountable. The victim may subjectively feel that she is not overlooking the wrong done; but if the forgiveness is unconditional, the intrinsically interpersonal character of (paradigmatic) forgiveness is lost. And experience teaches, we

---

[24] E. Garrard and D. McNaughton, "In Defence of Unconditional Forgiveness," *Proceedings of the Aristotelian Society* 104 (2003): 39–60. My paginal references to this article are included directly in my text.

might add, that the offender is very likely to draw the conclusion that her wrong-doing has been condoned.

Garrard and McNaughton also want to argue that unconditional forgiving is compatible with fighting against the wrong, "and thus with maintaining self-respect" (p. 51). Their premises for this conclusion are a bit mystifying. They agree that forgiveness is the forswearing of resentment, and do not wish to collapse forgiveness into condoning. So they must be imagining a case in which the offender voluntarily continues to wrong you, you fight back, and at the same time you forgive her and thus forswear resentment. I find that psychologically implausible and morally baffling; *why* forswear resentment under such conditions? And what of the argument that to do so is to evince servility, a lack of self-respect? They answer that if the injured person fights back, then her self-respect is intact. Supposing for a moment that it is psychologically possible to do what they are claiming, the key "self-respect" objection is not answered. It is not just a matter of fighting back, but of experiencing the appropriate sentiment (anger or resentment) that expresses one's regard for self as one-not-to-be-treated-in-this-manner. To give up *that* sentiment is perhaps (on the best construal) to stand up for oneself "on principle"; but that is not for *you* to stand up for *yourself,* so much as for you to sacrifice yourself for a general principle.

As to why one would forswear appropriate resentment without the offender meeting conditions – to turn to the "positive" part of their argument – the reasons offered are "respect for persons, and human solidarity" (p. 52). They themselves provide a compelling set of reasons for dismissing the "respect for persons" view (including Govier's modulation that because wrong-doers have the capacity for change, we owe it to them as a matter of respect not to judge them to be unforgivable; p. 53). Similarly, they offer trenchant and related criticisms of the second ground for unconditional forgiveness, but nonetheless conclude that "the appeal to common humanity as a ground for forgiveness is not an appeal to *respect.* Rather it is an appeal to human *solidarity,* the concern for the well-being of those who one feels are in the same condition as oneself" (p. 55). The thought seems to be that had we been in similar circumstances, we might have done the same or similar wrong (p. 55). The recognition of "our common moral frailty" and of moral luck "isn't the comfort of excuse but of companionship" (p. 57). Somehow this is supposed to provide, on their account, an argument for unconditional forgiveness – but how exactly? The connecting steps simply are not spelled out, let alone in a way that persuades that the acknowledgement of "human solidarity" is *sufficient* for forgiveness. Am I to forgive the wrong you have done me because by doing so I "comfort" you with the acknowledgment of the universality of sin? But why should I comfort you in any way? Were I to want to comfort you by asserting that I too am frail, why would that come to forgiving you for this wrong? Why does not forgiving on this basis come to condoning or excusing?

Note, finally, that the argument would entail that one should ongo-ingly forgive wrongs, that is, forswear resentment altogether (since the sufficient reason for doing so is permanent (p. 52)). The ideal is not the forswearing of resentment, but its abandonment altogether. But then we are either back to the perfectionist ideal examined in Chapter 1, or we are dressing up servility as a virtue. I agree that forgiveness "involves a kind of humility, a readiness to see the forgiven one as not so markedly inferior to oneself" (p. 58), and argue in this chapter that some such view is important to defeating false assumptions about the offender as a "moral monster" as well as to countering an unwarranted resistance to forgiveness. But to claim that the acknowledgment of our humanity is a sufficient reason for forgiveness has not been shown. The "common frailty" thesis might just as well lead to the view that it is all the more important – just because we are so frail – to hold ourselves and each other accountable by *not* forgiving unless there is warrant for doing so.

I have been discussing the "unconditional forgiveness" proposal with the paradigmatic scene of forgiveness in mind, and arguing that it is not persuasive. But what about non-paradigmatic forgiveness? Something like unconditional forgiveness might arise in that context; say, one in which the victim is deceased. But as I shall argue, even here the offender would have to be make herself worthy of forgiveness, and imagine not from her own perspective but from that of the moral spectator that all things con-sidered the victim would forgive her were she able. A similar line of rea-soning pertains if the victim is alive and the offender deceased. The ideal conditions cannot, under such conditions, all be met, or met perfectly; but it does not follow that forgiveness becomes unconditional.[25]

---

[25] C. Bennett argues for unconditional forgiveness on other grounds: "overcoming the morally inappropriate reaction of resentment and putting the wrong behind you in this way is *personal forgiveness*," and it is unconditional. "Personal and Redemptive Forgive-ness," *European Journal of Philosophy* 11 (2003), p. 139. He is referring to what I have called, following Nietzsche, *ressentiment*; for it is a matter of giving up anger one feels because of one's "insecurity" (p. 140). But that is not forgiveness; it is correcting an unwarranted sentiment. Myriad instances of disproportionate and interpersonally hos-tile sentiments present themselves in common life, and they may have real effects on

Advocates of unconditional forgiveness have other obstacles in their way: if the victim may bestow forgiveness unilaterally, without regard to whether or not the offender has fulfilled the relevant conditions, then why cannot an informed and sympathetic third party do so as well? Indeed, why cannot the offender self-forgive for injury done to another, especially when he *has* (though not because he has) met all of the relevant conditions for qualifying for forgiveness? It may be replied that the injured party alone can forgive; but that still leaves us with the first question. May the injured party rightly forgive (or withhold forgiveness) with no conditions attached? What if he is insane, or suffering from mental blocks that have nothing to do with the relevant events, or seriously unbalanced: is whatever he decides with respect to forgiveness acceptable? I have argued throughout for a negative answer to these last two questions.

We may still be missing a compelling thought buried in the view that forgiveness is a gift. Perhaps the point is not so much that forgiveness is like the free dismissal of a debt, but that it is supererogatory in the sense that it is not something that can be morally demanded, but is good to do.[26] And yet I have repeatedly said that under certain conditions it would be blameworthy not to forgive, which implies that it may indeed be morally demanded, and that forgivingness is a praiseworthy virtue. I have certainly implied, as well, that it would be blameworthy not to seek forgiveness (by taking the appropriate steps). The expression of forgivingness is not elective in the sense that one can *arbitrarily* decide, without blame, to withhold it. The same could be said of gratitude. Under the appropriate conditions, the victim has reasons for committing to forgive (or not); to forgive (or not) would be what a good or virtuous person would do.

I now want to add that offender has no right to forgiveness. The offender ought not *demand* or *insist* that the victim commit to forgiveness, and certainly ought not seek to compel forgiveness. In this sense, forgiveness *is* elective. Why?

our moral relations to others. If the correcting of those sentiments were "forgiveness," the term would lose all meaning, Bennett's asseveration to the contrary notwithstanding (p. 141). That correcting the sentiment of *ressentiment* and agreeing to cooperate again with the offender may produce contrition (p. 141) does not show that forgiveness has taken place; it is merely a happy outcome of another process that prepares the ground for forgiveness.

[26] Consider D. Heyd, *Supererogation: its Status in Ethical Theory* (Cambridge: Cambridge University Press, 1982), p. 162: "Forgiveness is 'touching' ... because of its free, optional character, that is its being more than could be morally expected or claimed. ... For it is exactly the giving up of something which one has the full right to harbour (hostility feelings), which makes the restoration of friendship and mutual respect meaningful."

Were the offender to demand forgiveness, in the case of serious wrongs, she would once again manifest a distinct lack of respect for the victim, attempting to bend the victim to her will once again. As a matter of respect, she owes it to the victim not only to take the steps I have described, but to underline, by *not* insisting or demanding, that she had indeed changed her view of the victim, has understood that the victim is not to be coerced and indeed may have a hard road to travel in giving up resentment or even committing to do so.[27]

Forgiveness cannot be compelled because its moral value lies in part in a change of heart on the victim's part, the letting go of resentment, and seeing the offender in a new light. These commitments cannot be meaningfully compelled by a third party, for the sincerity and whole heartedness with which they are adopted by the agent are essential to their moral value. An analogous argument would hold with respect to the offender requesting forgiveness. Without that honesty, the exchange is at best morally empty, at worst disrespectful of the other party. And because the sentiments are not wholly at the command of the will, the forswearing of resentment cannot be obligatory let alone subject to coercion.[28] We blame a person who fails to show proper gratitude, though we do not dream of compelling her to do so; why should forgiveness not be thought of as analogous?

A possible motivation for the view that forgiveness must be unconditional may lie in the worry that if it is not, considerations of forgiveness will be subsumed under those of justice. I would agree that such a result is to be avoided, and believe that my argument does avoid it. The offender does not have a right to forgiveness; and there are no rules for forgiveness comparable to those used by a court of law to decide conflicts. It is not unjust for a victim to fail to forgive the offender, though it may be blamable.

I have argued that we should not understand forgiveness on the model of the forgiveness of a debt, but that the alternative is not to see it as a "gift," if that is taken to mean "elective" in a sense that is not responsible to any moral reasons. The "either the obligatory forgiving of a debt or the unforced gift of forgiveness" dilemma leads to unacceptable conclusions. It is a false dilemma that, at least in the case of one author, seems motivated

---

[27] This line of reasoning was suggested to me by Ken Taylor. He puts it well: by inviting rather than demanding forgiveness, the offender shows respect and sympathy for his victim, and also that he has indeed repudiated his wrong-doing. See his "blog" at http://theblog.philosophytalk.org/2005/05/why_forgiveness.html.

[28] Richards argues along similar lines. "Forgiveness," p. 96.

by the mistaken views that if a wrong-doer deserves to be forgiven, then there is nothing to forgive, and/or that forgiveness is properly a response to a wrong-doer who has *not* taken any steps to deserve forgiveness.[29]

On my account, then, forgiveness cannot be "unconditional" either in the sense that it lacks conditions that define what would count as forgiveness, or that there are no constraints on when it is the right thing to do in the sense that it is what a virtuous person would do. I have also argued that forgiveness may not be demanded or compelled: nobody has an (enforceable) "right" to forgiveness. Forgiveness is certainly elective in the sense that it is voluntary. It now remains to explain further why conditional forgiveness – predicated upon the conditions I have specified having been met – should be given. This comes to explaining why conditional forgiveness is praiseworthy.

[v.c] Praiseworthy Conditional Forgiveness

What is the argument in favor of the view that forgiving – under the right conditions as specified above, and when the wrong is not in principle unforgivable – is something one should do? The answer would seem obvious: forgive, because forgivingness is a virtue, and the relevant conditions for its expression have been met. The matter should however be examined more closely.

Under the conditions stipulated, forgiveness is commendable because it is what the offender is due. A range of other reasons also commend forgiving. Forgiveness recognizes that resentment for injuries should be proportionate; that a wrong-doer who has taken all the necessary steps to rejoin the moral community would be disrespected in turn if forgiveness were withheld; that sustaining the moral community is a good to be

---

[29] I refer to C. Calhoun, "Changing One's Heart," *Ethics* 103 (1992), pp. 80–81. Calhoun distinguishes between "minimal forgiving" – forgiveness that is warranted by the wrong-doer's remedial actions and statements, and which is therefore due – and "aspirational forgiveness" which is "a gift, not the paying of a debt or the remission of a debt whose collection would prove too costly" (p. 81). She is forced to the strange view that "the forgiveness we aspire to get (and give) is forgiveness for culpable, unrepentant, unpunished, and unrestituted wrongdoing. . . . When I ask aspiringly for forgiveness, I ask you to forgive me for something that renders me undeserving and entitles you to hard feelings toward me" (p. 80; to whom do this "I" and "we" refer?). This is what makes aspirational forgiveness "elective," and "conceptually connected with supererogatory acts of generosity and charity" (p. 81). On p. 95 we are told "aspirational forgiveness is the choice not to demand that she [the offender] improve." But this is simply acceptance of the facts of the matter.

promoted, and is repairing the causes and results of wrong-doing; and finally that the regime within, to borrow a phrase from Plato, is harmed if one withholds forgiveness under these (admittedly paradigmatic) conditions. Forgiveness is a virtue that both expresses and promotes the ethical excellence of its possessor.

To elaborate on this last point: one reason to let go of resentment is that its continuing presence can damage one's capacities for love, compassion, and sympathy with others. Something similar might be said of the continuing presence of guilt. These points are offered not primarily as therapeutic but as ethical ones. Deliberate anger, as well as guilt, can be the ethically appropriate emotions, and their absence an ethical failure. But as Butler and many others have noted, resentment is also an emotion that holds danger for its owner. The ethical benefits of forgiveness have nothing in common with the benefits of the "closure" about which we hear so much, at least insofar as that comes to something like forgetting, or to putting it away so that the issue is no longer felt as a live one. Closure has no necessary connection with the moral and spiritual gravity of forgiveness, and indeed is perfectly compatible with a decision not to seek (or grant) forgiveness. One could achieve closure by managing a way not to feel guilt, for example.

One could readily understand that the victim may be unable to overcome resentment; and as I will discuss below (in the context of considering "the unforgivable"), there is one circumstance in which a sympathetic observer would go along, the result being that the offender is rightly *unforgiven*. But that is very different from a case in which the injured person happens to be the sort of person who, for reasons dating back to childhood, cannot forgive others. Perhaps she is a hardhearted and vindictive person, or suffers from low self-esteem and "needs" the resentment in order to prop herself up. By stipulation, this occurs under conditions when the resentment is no longer warranted (because the offender has taken the appropriate steps and the wrong done is not in principle unforgivable). In such cases, the victim is either in the grip of one of the "abuses" of resentment specified by Butler, or suffers from a related shortcoming of character. One reason that forgiveness would be commendable would concern, then, the desirability of being a certain sort of person, of having a praiseworthy character that is not (by definition) in the grip of these "abuses."

Still other considerations speak in favor of forgiveness as well. Forgiveness rests in part, I argued above, on trust that the projected narratives about the offender, as well as oneself, will become true. Forgiveness is, so to speak, a vote for the victory of such values as respect, growth and renewal, harmony of self and reconciliation, affection, and love. It is not that every act of forgiveness will lead to all of these; but forgiveness will embody some of them, and stands by the principle that the door to the others should be kept open.[30] Acting on the basis of these ideals may also have a constitutive character, such that treating oneself and the other as capable of ethical growth may in itself help to promote that growth.[31]

The narrative underlying forgiveness expresses these ideals too, and thereby makes the assumption that standing by them is not an exercise in futility. Perhaps one should say: that broad scope narrative seeks to make these ideals credible, and successfully acting on them bears out that trust.

The forward-looking character of trust leads to a final question: is it possible to obligate oneself to forgive by promising to do so? The statement would take the form of: "if you (the offender) fulfill conditions one through six, I promise that I shall forgive you." If "forgive" is taken in its "perfect tense" sense – as an accomplished act – then I do not think one could promise it, for one cannot promise that which one might be unable to accomplish, namely to let go of all resentment (the injury the offender did may turn out to be humanly impossible to forgive, or one may simply be personally unable to shed the lingering resentment). If "forgive" is taken in its "imperfect tense" sense – as something one is in the process of accomplishing, specifically with respect to letting go of lingering resentment once one has already forsworn revenge and re-envisioned the offender – the question is trickier. The promise would be to commit to letting go of lingering resentment. Such a promise would seem conceptually doubtful; for a promise to commit to X before knowing whether or not X is possible seems not to be a promise to which anybody could be bound. Even if that argument is refuted, I would argue that the offender is in no position to request such a promise, for the reasons already given (the offender shows her respect for her victim in part by refraining from demanding forgiveness, and soliciting a promise to forgive is a way of demanding it). I would also argue that the injured party ought make no such promise, because doing so effectively subsumes a commitment to forgiveness under a "perfect" duty for whose violation

---

[30] Kolnai notes that forgiveness "expresses that attitude of *trust* in the world which, unless it is vitiated by hare-brained optimism and dangerous irresponsibility, may be looked upon, not to be sure as the starting-point and the very basis, but perhaps as the epitome and culmination of morality." "Forgiveness," p. 105.

[31] Kolnai remarks: "Offering trust 'in advance' *may* increase the *objective trustworthiness* of the recipient." "Forgiveness," p. 105.

one is rightly sanctioned. The motivation for forgiving ought not be that one has promised to forgive, but that it is the praiseworthy, appropriate, and timely expression of the disposition of forgivingness. It is also worth noting that for those who take forgiveness to be supererogatory, a promise to forgive would change its deontological status.

[vi] MORAL MONSTERS, SHARED HUMANITY, AND SYMPATHY

while we still remain among human beings, let us cultivate our humanity. Let us not bring fear or danger upon any one. Let us look down on damages and wrongs, insults and carping criticisms. Let us bear with greatness of mind our short-lived troubles. As they say, we have only to look back, only to turn round – quick now, here comes death!   Seneca, *De Ira* III.43

The reasons for giving up resentment will differ depending on whether forgiveness is granted in the "ideal" context or a non-ideal case (discussed at the start of Chapter 3). In this subsection I return to a point on which Butler insisted: viz., that one is to forgive, in the sense of forswear revenge and moderate resentment, in part out of love of one's enemy, in part in recognition of shared humanity, and from a sense of compassion. We need better to understand these ideas, so often mentioned along with forgiveness, and to examine the equally popular impulse to characterize the wrong-doer as inhuman, as a "monster."

Butler sees love of one's enemy not as a particular feeling but as avoidance of the "abuses" of resentment. I take this to mean that to love one's enemy is, among other things, to refuse the impulse to picture the wrong-doer as *only* that; that is, to refuse to demonize the wrong-doer. This leads quickly to the second idea, viz., the recognition of shared humanity. As Butler says, the "obligations of good will" do not arise only from our injurer being a social creature, "much less his being a moral agent," but from "an obligation to it prior to either of these, arising from his being a sensible creature, that is, capable of happiness or misery" (p. 159). Butler does not explain here why that fact would obligate us not to treat a person in certain ways.

Let me suggest a somewhat different way of looking at the notions Butler mentions. Given the religious background of "love your enemy," and the confusions that naturally arise when the word "love" is used in that context, I shall drop that language and speak instead of compassion and of recognizing our shared humanity. I approach the matter by examining (a) the problem of the "moral monster" and (b) the relevant sense of "shared humanity."

[vi.a] Moral Monsters

Butler suggests that when we see a wrong-doer as "monstrous," we no longer recognize "any thing right or human in him" (p. 163). Now, if that were indeed the bottom-line truth about the wrong-doer, forgiveness would surely be misdirected. What do the just-quoted phrases mean?

Such language is meant to capture a quality of actions and agents, namely that of being so profoundly wrong, or evil, as to be "incomprehensible" or "inhuman" (terms we also throw around loosely). The phenomenology of moral wrong and evil is vast and complicated: think of the spectrum from the sadist to the professional torturer, to a person who "snaps" and shoots his co-workers, to the sexual predator, to bland functionaries who from behind the efficient orderliness of their desks cause the death of millions. As it is not my purpose to analyze "evil," my response to the question I have posed will be selective.

On one interpretation, to say that X is a "monster" is to say X became, for such and such a reason, an automaton, or completely and criminally insane, or no longer able to exercise agency. As Strawson notes, our attitude toward such a person is "objective" rather than one of "involvement or participation in a human relationship."[32] In such a case, we are pointed to considerations of explanation and excuse rather than forgiveness. The label "moral monster" distracts and misleads here.

On a second interpretation, what we mean when referring to someone as a "monster" is that while the wrong-doer has many of the characteristics we would ascribe to any person, including the level of sanity and rationality required to plan the evil deeds, we see nothing morally good in that person; he or she is ongoingly and habitually given either to deliberately injuring others or to injuring others without giving it a second thought. For the first sort of case, imagine a thoroughly sadistic and cruel character. One way we might characterize this person would be as constitutionally incapable of moral sympathy and appreciation of the place and point of view of another.[33] Presumably we ourselves would in

---

[32] Strawson, *Freedom and Resentment*, p. 9. He also says there: "The objective attitude...cannot include the range of reactive feelings and attitudes which belong to involvement or participation with others in inter-personal relationships; it cannot include resentment...," which suggests that the "objective" attitude is not a reactive feeling.

[33] With reference to taking delight in inflicting misery for its own sake, B. Blanshard helpfully writes "On our own theory we should expect that most such cases would be explicable in other ways than as examples of mere 'motiveless malignity,' for example, as instances of love of power accompanied by relative lack of fellow-feeling and imagination; and

turn find such a person humanly unintelligible, in the sense of inaccessible to our sympathy. At this juncture let us underline that what makes such a person capable of so much evil is his or her agency, including the capacity to make and carry out plans, to organize a set of activities over time, and thereby prioritize ends and apply remembered lessons from the past. Such a person feels not just pleasure and pain, but recognizes his own and the other's happiness and misery. He may, for example, inflict cruelty precisely by recognizing that his victim feels love for his children; or might recognize enough of the moral concerns of another accurately enough to thwart their deepest intentions.[34]

A psychopath might serve as an example of an evil person who habitually injures others not for the pleasure of doing so but simply because she doesn't care and never gives them a second thought. This person too fails to sympathize with the victims of her maneuverings and manipulations, but in a different way than does the sadist, for she doesn't credit them with a point of view that matters to her, while the sadist enters into the other's world in order to derive pleasure from the violating of it.[35]

Even if such a person has *no* moral relations of his own – no attachments of any sort toward other human beings (such as children, kin, fellow gang

we should regard a man who took delight in inflicting misery when there was nothing to gain by it as not merely morally bad but as abnormally or inhumanly constructed, a monster lacking natural perception and sympathy. That, I think, is how we do feel. Furthermore, we should regard pure moral badness, the attitude that took as its motto, 'Evil, be thou my good,' as not really possible." *Reason and Goodness* (London: George Allen & Unwin Ltd, 1961), p. 341. Like Solzhenitsyn, he thinks that "choices of evil" turn out to be "sub specie boni" (p. 342), a view that goes back to Socrates.

34 I am grateful to Ed Delattre for discussion of the "moral monster" issue. Some of the phrasing in this paragraph is his, and is included with his permission. A. Morton points out another reason to resist thinking of wrong-doers as simply evil: "thinking in terms of evil can give us the same attitudes as evil-doers. They often think their victims deserve what they get, that they are worthless scum, inferior beings, or dangerously alien. They often think, in fact, that their victims are evil. Thinking in terms of evil can, if we are not careful, make us accomplices in atrocity." See Morton's *On Evil* (London: Routledge, 2004), p. 6. The dangers of the language of the "moral monster" are, quite obviously, magnified when one moves from the interpersonal to the political level.

35 For a discussion of the sociopath that draws on the American Psychiatric Association's *Diagnostic and Statistical Manual of Mental Disorders* (1980) see Morton's *On Evil*, pp. 47–53. Morton argues that while sociopaths "have no need to humiliate others" (for they do not care enough about them to bother; p. 51), their defining condition is marked by the lack of "sympathetic pleasure at another's happiness, dismay at another's sorrow, remorse at having brought trouble to another" (p. 48). For helpful remarks about the connection between the psychopath and the (lack of) sympathy see J. Deigh's "Empathy and Universalizability," *Ethics* 105 (1995): 743–763.

members), such that he would feel sentiments of care for their welfare on their account – he enters into the world of another sufficiently to recognize that the other's pain belongs to that other. As a sadist, he does not experience the other's pain as a bad for that other person in a way that has any claim on him to stop inflicting it; on the contrary, he experiences it as pleasurable to himself, and takes that as a reason to continue the torture. Twisted though this "sympathy" and exercise of agency is, he is not "monstrous" in the sense of no longer being human. In fact, part of what is so disturbing is that he is recognizably human. The language of monstrosity occludes this distressing and perplexing thought, and therefore is misleading. As Primo Levi remarks – somewhat shockingly given the ease with which we deploy terms such as "monster" – of the concentration camp guards at Auschwitz:

These were not monsters. I didn't see a single monster in my time in the camp. Instead I saw people like you and I who were acting in that way because there was Fascism, Nazism in Germany. Were some form of Fascism or Nazism to return, there would be people, like us, who would act in the same way, everywhere. And the same goes for the victims, for the particular behaviour of the victims about which so much has been said, mostly typically by young Israelis who object 'but we would never act that way.' They're right. They would not act that way. But if they had been born forty years earlier, they would have. They would have behaved exactly as the deported Jews – and, it's worth adding, the deported Russians and Italians and the rest.[36]

---

[36] P. Levi, "Interview with Primo Levi (1979)," conducted by G. Segrè. In *The Voice of Memory: Interviews 1961–1987*, ed. M. Belpoliti and R. Gordon, trans. R. Gordon (New York: The New Press, 2001), p. 270. For a similar statement, see Levi's *The Drowned and the Saved*, trans. R. Rosenthal (New York: Vintage Books, 1989), p. 202: "the term *torturers* alludes to our ex-guardians, the SS, and is in my opinion inappropriate: it brings to mind twisted individuals, ill-born, sadists, afflicted by an original flaw. Instead, they were made of the same cloth as we, they were average human beings, averagely intelligent, averagely wicked: save the exceptions, they were not monsters, they had our faces, but they had been reared badly." Consider also the case of Eugene de Kock, the head of South Africa's dreaded Vlakplaas unit (a secret police unit and de facto death squad), now in prison serving several life sentences. His crimes are horrific, as is suggested by the nickname given him by the media, "Prime Evil." And yet it appears that he was devoted to his family, and does not fit the profile of the sadistic narcissist either before or after the collapse of apartheid. While testifying before the TRC, he requested forgiveness of those he injured, and showed what looks like genuine sympathy for them. One member of the TRC, Dr. Pumla Gobodo-Madikizela, writes that de Kock received permission to request forgiveness in person from widows of those he killed – having detailed truthfully how they were killed – and received not only that but their forgiveness. His decision to provide truthful information about the police apparatus is credited with forcing "most of the security police and all of the police generals" to apply for amnesty and therefore

I conclude that we are better off without the language of "the moral monster."

The conclusion is supported by the fact that such accusatory phrases also feed much too easily into the tendency, natural to a rapidly accelerating sense of resentment, to dehumanize an offender and thereby to justify inappropriately harsh retaliation. The dangerous potential of this rhetoric is all the more evident at the political level, where it may be woven into narratives of innocence and "justified" revenge that sustain violence for generations.[37] And this holds a fortiori in the context of *self*-forgiveness. Self-dehumanization holds moral as well as psychological danger for oneself; threatening the possibility of agency and moral improvement on the one hand, and of psychic unity on the other.

We need not infer that abolishing labels such as "moral monster" entails that all offenders are forgivable. It might be impossible to forgive a non-monstrous offender. In the following discussion of such topics as "shared humanity" and "the unforgivable," I am concerned with wrong-doers who are not constitutionally incapable, at least in some corner of their lives, of sympathy with others. For I know of no way to prove definitively that a person is permanently incapable of at least that much. But I am not assuming that just because the wrong-doer retains tinctures of humanity, there is always reason to believe that he or she will change for the better; the dominant evil streak may well be incorrigible. In denying

to divulge truth. See her book on de Kock, the TRC, revenge and forgiveness: *A Human Being Died that Night* (New York: Houghton Mifflin, 2003), pp. 14–15, 137. Unlike many other high-ranking South African officers and politicians, de Kock detailed his crimes and without shirking responsibility. See also de Kock's book (written with J. Gordin) *Long Night's Damage: Working for the Apartheid State* (Saxonwold, South Africa: Contra Press, 1998).

37 The contrast between the human and the "monster," and the idea that the former can degenerate into latter, is undoubtedly ancient. So too with the characterization of the enemy as a non-human animal; e.g., see Achilles on Hector at *Iliad* 22.263, 346–348, as well as the dehumanization his furious vengefulness inflicts on him (Achilles). See also *Medea* 1340–1345, 1358–1359. But neither there nor anywhere else in Greek literature is the hated enemy characterized as beastly in a way that is supposed to legitimize excluding them from the human race, let alone exterminating them (a study of the history of the connection between notions of dehumanization and justifications of revenge would be fascinating). Closer to Butler, language connecting monstrosity and immorality can be found in Shaftesbury's *An Inquiry Concerning Virtue or Merit* I.ii.1, and especially toward the end of II. ii, 1; and *Moralists* I. iii. See his *Characteristics of Men, Manners, Opinions, Times*, ed. L. E. Klein (Cambridge: Cambridge University Press, 1999), pp. 167–170, 215, and 244 respectively (I am indebted to Laurent Jaffro for pointing me toward these passages). "Moral monster" is a common phrase in many contemporary discussions of evil.

that there are "moral monsters" I am not affirming that everyone is in fact able to mend their ways.

[vi.b] Shared Humanity and Fallibility, Compassion, and Pity

> Yet I pity
> His wretchedness, though he is my enemy,
> For the terrible yoke of blindness that is on him.
> I think of him, yet also of myself;
> For I see the true state of all us that live –
> We are dim shapes, no more, and weightless shadow.
> Sophocles, *Ajax* 121–126[38]

In the course of my discussion of *sungnômê* in Chapter 1, I remarked that sympathy, common humanity, understanding the other, and fallibility are intuitively and classically clustered together. The encounter between Achilles and Priam is one of the most compelling depictions in all of Western literature of the recognition of shared humanity. They are of course mortal enemies: Priam's city is doomed to be utterly destroyed by Achilles and the Greeks; Achilles has killed Priam's son Hector, and in his overwhelming rage has attempted to defile his corpse. Priam must do the seemingly impossible, as he himself says, namely to kiss the hand that slew his beloved sons (*Iliad* 24.506). They have every reason to hate, and to kill each other on sight. Both have been badly injured by the opposing side; it is a cycle of revenge well along in the making.

Instead, they weep, dine, converse together. There is no question of forgiveness or reconciliation, no talk about who is right or wrong, no talk about injury or justice. Yet they do recognize each other's humanity. First, each is reminded by the other of loved ones; Priam puts Achilles in mind of his own father, and he weeps for him; Achilles reminds Priam of Hector, and he too grieves. They participate in analogous webs of human attachment and recognize that as the case: just as you are a father, so I have a father; as I am a father, you have a father; just as I am a son, so you have a son. We may not care for each other, but we each care for our kin, and know what care is. There are analogous ties of concern, of misery, of rootedness in and love of one's homeland. In throwing himself at his feet, Priam asks for pity – a complex moral act understood as such by Achilles (and a request which, uncharacteristically, he grants). Achilles

---

[38] Trans. J. Moore, in *Sophocles II*, ed. D. Grene and R. Lattimore (Chicago: University of Chicago Press, 1969), p. 13.

explicitly recognizes Priam's pitiable plight, and his role in bringing it about (24.517–521, 542). Having "put aside their desire for eating and drinking" – breaking bread together also underlines what they have in common – they gaze upon each other with wonder (24.629–634).

Second, Achilles contrasts the human lot with that of the gods (24.525–551), and tells the famous story of the two urns of Zeus. We are both mortals, and therefore fated to unhappiness and misery; the relevant contrast is not between us, but between us and the gods. The fortunate lots dispensed by Zeus do not differ much from the miserable lots; regardless of which one receives we all suffer and then end in the grave. (Achilles knows well that he will die young; 1.415–417; 18.96.) This story provides a detached perspective on their lives, allowing them to grasp even more clearly their shared humanity (of course it helps here that they share the same gods). Achilles speaks almost neutrally of the destruction wrought on the Trojans by the Greeks (24.547), as well as of the misfortunes of his own family in spite of his half-divine parentage. He is even able, from this removed perspective, to say that Hector will be "much lamented" (24.620; not by him, to be sure); so he is able to look beyond his famous anger and desire for revenge, and see that his bitterly resented enemy too is a man like himself. Still further, he makes several comments that indicate his ability to see himself from the viewpoint of the other, as when he characterizes himself as far from his fatherland and a grief to Priam and his children (24.541–551). And he takes care that Priam not see Hector's corpse until it is washed and prepared, lest Priam involuntarily rage, in turn re-igniting Achilles' own rage (24.581–586). Achilles has acquired the ability to see the situation from multiple perspectives and to relate the perspectives. He evinces a certain self-knowledge as well.

The analogies of situatedness and kinship, and the contrast of mortals and gods, implicitly invite a sympathetic recognition of the enemy as one-like-us. The facts of our shared interdependence, embodiment, finitude, emotive make-up, subjection to forces beyond our control – in short, facts about our imperfection – allow us commiseration with one another, or at least to imagine the world from the other's point of view. (To be sure, Achilles and Priam are helped in this effort by the fact that both are of similar social status, a crucial factor in the world Homer depicts.) Having broken bread together – an act that again underlines their common embodiment and humanity – Priam departs with Hector's corpse, and there follows an agreed-upon truce during which he buries his son. Then the war resumes: as tradition completes the story, Priam and all that is dear to him are annihilated, and Achilles too is killed.

The audience of this extraordinary scene is also, through sympathy, brought into the web of the character's humanity. The resentment we felt at Achilles is modulated with fellow feeling as well as a certain admiration of his present high-mindedness. We recognize his ties of affection to his kin; and his words about our shared finitude, as compared with the lot of the divine, ring true. Not that Achilles has simply transcended his anger; neither perhaps has Priam. As already noted, Achilles has Hector's body washed out of sight of them both, lest Priam in his sorrow become angry, and Achilles in turn be "shaken to anger" (24.581–586; cf. 559–570). Achilles has forsworn revenge against Priam, and controlled his anger – for now.

I want to suggest that recognition of shared humanity by the injured party is a necessary step on the way to forgiveness (whether in our paradigm sense of forgiveness or not), though it is not a sufficient for it. It will also require some minimal acquaintance with the injurer's "story."

This may sound like an appeal to *compassion*. Butler speaks of the injury that the wrong-doer does himself, presumably by degrading himself through the doing of wrong (though Butler may also have in mind the consequences of the wrong-doer's action, such as the resentment he incurs), and of the compassion therefore appropriate to the wrong-doer (p. 165). He cites as the "perfection" of compassion Christ's behest that God forgive his tormentors. At least in contemporary usage, "compassion" is a stronger term than sympathy (again, in the Smithean sense), in that it connotes a level of care *for* the person and a willingness to take steps to promote his or her welfare. So understood, compassion by the injured for the injurer is not a necessary condition of forgiveness, except in an attenuated sense to be outlined below.[39] And while forgiveness does require sympathy, being able to grasp the situation and point of view of the other is not a sufficient condition for forgiveness for the compelling reason that – as already noted – having sympathetically entered into the situation and motives of the offender, one may justifiably experience even greater resentment.

---

[39] Cf. M. Holmgren, "Forgiveness and the Intrinsic Value of Persons," p. 349: "compassion is called for in response to her [the unrepentant offender's] sentience;" this seems to carry with it the recognition that the offender "is a fellow member of the human race who struggles with the same pressures we struggle with, and she is vulnerable to error just like the rest of us" (p. 350). The second point strikes me as different from and broader than the sentience point; both ideas are involved with compassion, but are not the same as it. I voice skepticism about the shared-fallibility notion below. I discuss the attenuated role for the injurer's compassion for the injured in the section on "sympathy."

Butler's sense of the term is close to *pity*; specifically, to God's pity for Christ's torturers (not Christ's pity; Christ does not himself forgive or pity them, while he is on the cross, but asks God to do so and offers the rationale). In Butler's English, this may simply be synonymous with compassion; and in some contexts the word is still used in that way. In the ancient sense of the term, pity was mostly reserved for *undeserved* suffering.[40] The modern sense seems largely indifferent to the question of desert. We find pitiable the suffering of a person, even when that suffering is deserved, if (a) we have nothing to fear from that person; (b) we do not resent the sufferer; (c) we are not undergoing the same suffering for the same reason; (d) we are sufficiently removed from the suffering person (we do not pity the suffering of our beloved child); (e) we are not so far removed from the person that their suffering makes little impact on us (we must be able to some extent to identify and go along with it); and (f) the suffering is significant (you do not pity someone who has stubbed their toe). If we "take pity" we incline to show mercy or to help out. Yet the term may also carry a negative tone; nobody wants to be pitied. In contemporary usage, the one who pities is in some way superior to the pitied; to be pitied is to be put in an abject position – that of someone who has lost much, or is seriously diminished, or has fallen down in some serious way, or is vulnerable, or is in some way at your mercy. Indeed, the term can also describe a person who is "pathetic," such that "I pity you" is to say "I find you a miserable and worthless person, regardless of how pleased you feel about yourself." Such a person is *not worth* resenting; in this most negative sense, to pity is to disrespect, and to dismiss from further consideration. A person who exhibits "self-pity" is thought to disrespect herself; thus to characterize someone as "self-pitying" is hardly to pay a compliment. Someone who has a disposition to pity others is not necessarily the more virtuous on that account, for we suspect her of attributing to herself a superior station, as though god-like she is exempted from the lot that befalls the common run of folk. At the same time, someone who is dispositionally "pitiless" is morally lacking as well.

Granting the complexity of the notion let us venture this: except when it is a sentiment of reproach, pity requires sympathy (in the sense of the minimal capacity to grasp through imagination the situation of another, not in the sense that we reproduce in ourselves the sufferer's emotion). But neither in this nor in its other senses is it a necessary condition for

---

[40] See D. Konstan, *Pity Transformed*, p. 43.

forgiveness, let alone equivalent to it. Indeed, pity and forgiveness are mutually exclusive, even though both may forswear revenge and resentment (pity may be felt for whom someone one bears no resentment toward, of course, in which case the disanalogy with forgiveness is all the more marked). When I forgive you, in response to steps you are taking, I do not pity you. I am instead engaged in a very different project of changing my moral relations to you and my sentiments about you. And if I pity you even when you have done me injury, I cannot forgive you, for I have concluded that you are beneath resentment and unworthy of the reciprocal moral project that is forgiveness.

One commentator has argued that "one does not ask forgiveness of those about whom one does not care." The offender must certainly care about being forgiven by the person he injured; and if her request is to carry moral weight, he must certainly care (in the sense of truly feel regret) about having caused this harm to this person. The forgiver will care about the offender, and about herself, in a symmetrical way. If "care" is taken in a stronger sense, then it does not seem to me to be apposite. The view just quoted seems to be a result of mistakenly holding that "the precondition for forgiveness, then, is the existence of a positive relation which is disturbed and often brought to awareness by the offense itself."[41] In many cases there was no prior positive relation, or indeed any relation except that of fellow human beings obligated not to cause each other injury.

If the argument of this chapter is correct, forgiveness does depend on a cluster of notions associated with *sungnômê*, such as sympathy, understanding the other, and common humanity. But given the element of *commitment* involved in forgiveness – specifically, commitment on the part of the forgiver to forswear resentment – forgiveness also incorporates a thought suggested by the New Testament word for forgiveness (*aphiêmi*), namely that resentment must be *let go* or *sent away*. Given that the conditions for granting forgiveness have been met, that revenge has been forsworn and resentment moderated, the offender seen "in a new light" for good reason, and that the wrong is not in principle unforgivable, a feeling of anger is likely to linger on. The emotion is not just a judgment. This psychological process of letting go of resentment strikes me as a combination of repeated suasion (including of the sort one addresses to oneself), of the resolve to stick with the commitment, and of the passing of time. One can imagine that the performance of (what amounts to)

---

[41] Both quotations are from Beatty, "Forgiveness," p. 247.

rituals or ceremonies would help – say, where the offender is an unfaithful spouse, resuming a family tradition of breaking bread together, in spite of the fact that the sentiments that earlier motivated it have not all returned. One can also imagine cases in which the injured party may require therapy, should unrelated past experiences play a role in blocking dismissal of the lingering resentment. Luck will no doubt play a role in determining how easily the remaining resentment – the affect that "sticks" even after the cognitive changes described above have taken place – can diminish. In any case, it is crucial for my account that "sending away" kicks in only in conjunction with the commitment to forgiveness, itself warranted in ways already described.

Finally, I have mentioned the issue of *shared fallibility*. We are imperfect creatures, authors of wrongs as well as the sufferers thereof. Supported by passages from the New Testament and elsewhere, it is often said that X ought to forgive Y in view of the fact that X too has been guilty of causing injury. Stated in that way, the argument is not convincing, and indeed would seem to lead to across the board excusing or condoning (none of us is really responsible for causing injury because we're all fallible creatures liable to doing that sort of thing). But looked at in a different light, the thought that our shared fallibility is relevant to my forgiving you may be supported by two considerations.

The first is that of reasonableness (itself closely tied to consistency in the logical sense): if I expect to be forgiven (either by myself, or by others) for injuring others, I ought to forgive the injuries caused by others (assuming comparability between the injuries, etc.). I should not make claims of others that I am unwilling to make of myself. A story about shared fallibility would naturally enter into the explanation of the wrong-doing. Secondly, in order to see the offender in a new light, it would normally help to recognize that he or she is embodied, imperfect, and fallible, just as you are, and that his wrong-doing can be understood (not excused, but rather be made intelligible) in part by reference to his fallibility as distinguished from, say, by imputation of a permanently rotten or monstrous character. Disabusing yourself of the conviction that you are decidedly superior – not fallible or flawed in related ways – is a way of gaining truer perspective on the offender (compare Seneca's remarks on anger and humility at *De Ira* II.28). Falsely thinking that you are better than you are distorts your understanding of the other, as it almost always implies that they are worse than they are. Further, it pretends to a moral standard nobody can in fact attain, and provides a self-congratulatory "justification" for resentment. Right judgment and the appropriate attunement of the sentiments should be sensible to the context – the ineliminable imperfection of the human world.

[vi.c] Sympathy

I have referred repeatedly to "sympathy." The meanings of the term are multiple and confused – not only with each other, but with those of "empathy." This is as true in philosophical and scientific parlance as it is in ordinary language. While both terms derive from perfectly good Greek, the modern use of "empathy" is quite recent. It was coined in 1907 by E. Titchener, as a way of translating *Einfühlung* (literally, feeling at one with, but meaning for Theodor Lipps, among other German psychologists and aestheticians, something like "feeling oneself into" a work of art or the mind of another). The term has also carried the range of meanings from "motor empathy" (reflexively duplicating facial expressions one sees in others, for example) to projecting oneself into the perspective or situation of the other. Yet all of these meanings have also attached to "sympathy." The history of the usage of the terms is, correspondingly, frustratingly tangled at both semantic and conceptual levels.[42]

Another book would be required to untangle this knot, let alone defend a theory of sympathy or empathy. My purpose in discussing the matter is solely to distinguish a specific sense of "sympathy" at play in forgiveness (I have referred to it as the "Smithean" sense). For the sake of clarity, in this book I have avoided use of "empathy" and cognates. I distinguish between five senses of sympathy, as follows:

1) Sympathy as Simple Contagion. Hume associated the term "contagion" in connection with sympathy. He has in mind the way in which an emotion gets transmitted, by means of the psychological mechanism he describes in the *Treatise,* from one person to another.[43] In this first case of sympathy,

---

[42] See L. Wispé's "History of the Concept of Empathy," in *Empathy and its Development*, ed. N. Eisenberg and J. Strayer (Cambridge: Cambridge University Press, 1990), pp. 17–37. See also L. Wispé's *The Psychology of Sympathy* (New York: Plenum Press, 1991), chs. 1 and 2 (Hume, Smith, Schopenhauer, Darwin, McDougall). For the confusing history of the meanings of "sympathy" and "empathy," the *Oxford English Dictionary* entries are enlightening as well. A detailed discussion of Adam Smith's influential notion of "sympathy" may be found in my *Adam Smith and the Virtues of Enlightenment* (Cambridge: Cambridge University Press, 1999a), ch. 2.

[43] See D. Hume's *A Treatise of Human Nature*, ed. D. F. Norton and M. J. Norton (Oxford: Oxford University Press, 2000), 2.1.11.2 (p. 206); and the second of his *Enquiries Concerning Human Understanding and Concerning the Principles of Morals*, ed. P. H. Nidditch

I have in mind the simplest possible version of that phenomenon (hence my calling it "simple contagion"), as when an infant catches the mood or feeling conveyed by, say, another's weeping (the infant may cry when it hears crying).[44] Only affectivity and little or no cognition is at work here, which is to say that no distinction between self and other is recognized by the sympathizer, and that there need be no sense of why the other is weeping and no judgment as to the appropriateness of weeping. I referred in Chapter 1 to Aristotle's *Problems* vii, where similar phenomena are catalogued (one example given is that of a yawn migrating from one person to the next).

Some forms of motor mimicry seem to fall into what I am calling the "simple" form sympathy as contagion, as when a smile in one person is reproduced in the onlooker (possibly making the latter experience a sense of happiness as well). Wispé notes that "innate motor mimicry" happens even among neonates.[45]

2) *Sympathy as Complex Contagion.* Contagious sympathy may both involve some cognitive activity and assume that the sympathizer is aware of the distinction between self and other, thus qualifying as "complex." Associations between behavioral markers and emotions may occur here. I have in mind the research showing that facial cues can carry affective as well as cognitive information, at times instantaneously (the precise neurological mechanism seems not yet understood). As L. Wispé puts it, there is "abundant empirical evidence that facial appearances that reflect feelings of anger, pain, sadness, and grief, among others, are different from positive faces, in that they appear to be salient, accurately recognized, and angular; they are also prepotent stimuli capable of forming enduring associative bonds with fearlike responses in the presence of aversive conditioning stimuli. There are mutually related findings, and they have come from different laboratories, using different methods and different subjects; thus our confidence in them is strengthened." Wispé adds that with respect to "negative" facial expressions "the 'message' being conveyed is not 'help me,' or anything about the 'meaning' of the situation, but

---

(Oxford: Oxford University Press, 1990), Sect. VII, p. 251 ("others enter into the same humour, and catch the sentiment, by a contagion or natural sympathy"). My quotations from these texts are from these editions.

[44] See M. A. Barnett, "Empathy and Related Responses in Children," in *Empathy and its Development*, p. 149.

[45] L. Wispé, *The Psychology of Sympathy*, p. 149. Further references to Wispé advert to this book and are included directly in my text.

'I am a person like you, and you can feel that I am in difficulty'" (pp. 119–120).

As the level of complexity rises, the sympathetic response comes to be "about" something – fear about the fearsome, for example. While cognition is involved here, "changing places" with the other seems not to be, even though there is a recognition of difference of self and other. Again, infants are capable of tracking another's gaze; later, the operation becomes ever more complicated. As one philosopher puts it: "... if the other is frightening, we look for something that is frightening. If pleased, we look for something pleasing. That is, we look for something that is startling, or frightening, or pleasing *to us.* To do this, we engage our own system for generating emotions out of our perceptions."[46] But of course the point is to understand why the other is responding to X in the way she is.

Hume's notion of sympathy as "contagion" fits in this spectrum of "complex" cases. On his view, even instantaneous transmission of an emotion involves inference, and therefore is to some degree cognitive:

> When any affection is infus'd by sympathy, it is at first known only by its effects, and by those external signs in the countenance and conversation, which convey an idea of it. This idea is presently converted into an impression, and acquires such a degree of force and vivacity, as to become the very passion itself, and produce an equal emotion, as any original affection. However instantaneous this change of idea into an impression may be, it proceeds from certain views and reflections, which will not escape the strict scrutiny of a philosopher, tho' they may the person himself, who makes them. (*Treatise* 2.1.11.3)

What is absent from this view is any idea of "changing places" with the other. Note that one could feel the other's feelings (thanks to whatever the mechanism is) and not care at all about the other, or even enjoy – maliciously, or sadistically – the other's feelings of misery.

Some cases of mimicry involve cognition, and perhaps imaginative changing of places. Adam Smith's opening examples in the *Theory of Moral Sentiments* of bystanders twisting this way and that as they watch the tight-rope walker, or drawing back their leg as they see a stroke about to fall on someone else's leg, describe the mimicking of actual or potential responses. His explanation is that the spectators' response results from their "conceiving what they themselves would suffer, if they really were the wretches whom they are looking upon" (*TMS* I.i.1.3), or again, "conceiving what we ourselves should feel in the like situation" (I.i.1.2). The

---

[46] R. M. Gordon, "Sympathy, Simulation, and the Impartial Spectator," *Ethics* 105 (1995), p. 731. On p. 730 he notes that gaze-following "emerges in the child's first year."

two formulations are not identical, though they are found in adjoining paragraphs. Smith does not distinguish here between (a) imagining oneself as the other person (primarily an affective move) or (b) imagining oneself in that person's situation (and thus as responding to situational influences, a more cognitive response). Presumably Smith holds that (a) is impossible without (b). Some form of projective understanding is present, on his view, even in cases where the response looks to be automatic and instantaneous.

Smith's view is the accepted explanation, though some empirical psychologists argue that a particular experiment shows that his view cannot be correct, at least not in all cases (mirroring someone's movements as you face them, you lean to your left as they lean to their right, which is to say that you have not put yourself in their place and then react as they do or would).[47] Their thesis is that "the observer is not having the other's reaction but is portraying it" (p. 329), and that the purpose is to convey "a message that is of vital importance to our relationships with others: I can feel as you do; I am like you." On this account, mimicry does not require that the spectator fully understand the other's situation or "first experience the other person's feelings him/herself" (p. 332). As Darwall puts it: "In these instances, we mimic, not by stepping into others' shoes so much as by stepping into shoes that will mirror to them their expressive behavior in their shoes. This suggests a more interesting and satisfying mimetic basis for reciprocity (and, thus, reciprocal altruism) than mere copying."[48] We have moved to the far end of the spectrum of complex contagion.

Even if this is the correct interpretation of mimicry in these instances, though, there is room for sympathy understood as putting oneself in the shoes of another.

3) Sympathy as Putting Oneself in the Shoes or Situation of the Other; as Bringing the Other's Situation Home to Oneself. As already remarked, sympathy so understood is partly a cognitive enterprise. It assumes both that the spectator does not forget herself when sympathizing, unlike a case of very strong emotional identification – the difference between self and other remains present – and does not absorb the other into self (as one might when substituting one's own biography, say, for that of the person

[47] See J. Bavelas, A. Black, C. R. Lemery, and J. Mullett, "Motor Mimicry as Primitive Empathy," in *Empathy and its Development*, p. 325.

[48] S. Darwall, "Empathy, Sympathy, Care," ch. 3 of *Welfare and Rational Care* (Princeton, NJ: Princeton University Press, 2002), p. 57.

with whom one is attempting to sympathize). I am going to assume, with Smith, that projective sympathy is not simply about replicating the other's feelings in oneself, and that it includes an understanding of what it would mean to occupy the agent's situation or circumstances (that in turn both ties the agent's perspective to the situation, and permits a comparison between the agent's response to the situation and what any one of us would feel in that situation). That given, the process could be understood in several different ways, and these may be arranged along a spectrum:

a. The spectator could construct *by analogy* what you (the agent) would feel in your situation. You have lost a child; I grasp the signif-icance for you by remembering what it was like when I lost some-thing of great value to me, and by drawing on what I take to be a resemblance between the cases. While we may in fact proceed in this sort of way in some instances, the problem is that the sympathy is still felt as from the observer's standpoint, even if it is about the other. Further, not only do all analogies have limits, in many cases they may have severe limits due to inexperience, in the relevant case, on the spectator's part (what if I have never lost anything of great value?).

b. Alternatively, putting myself in your shoes could mean taking on your persona, through an act of projective imagination, and look-ing at the situation from your point of view, just as an actor might when becoming a character. This would be a kind of vicarious emotion, a simulation of the agent-as-situated.[49] This is full blown Smithean sympathy. As Smith puts it:

> When I sympathize with your sorrow or your indignation, it may be pre-tended, indeed, that my emotion is founded in self-love, because it arises from bringing your case home to myself, from putting myself in your situ-ation, and thence conceiving what I should feel in the like circumstances. But though sympathy is very properly said to arise from an imaginary change of situations with the person principally concerned, yet this imag-inary change is not supposed to happen to me in my own person and character, but in that of the person with whom I sympathize. When I con-dole with you for the loss of your only son, in order to enter into your grief I do not consider what I, a person of such a character and profession, should suffer, if I had a son, and if that son was unfortunately to die: but I consider what I should suffer if I was really you, and not only change circumstances with you, but I change persons and characters.... A man may sympathize with a woman in child-bed; though it is impossible that he

---

[49] See Gordon, "Sympathy, Simulation, and the Impartial Spectator," pp. 734–735.

should conceive himself as suffering her pains in his own proper person and character. (*TMS* VII.iii.1.4)

This passage draws the distinction between (a) and (b), and insists that sympathy proper is (b). This leads naturally to a further step.

c. Sympathy as not just a taking up of the other's perspective and imagining their sorrow, indignation, or what have you; but also understanding the other's purposes as generating reasons for feeling and action, reasons as independent of one's own. Here the other is seen as a separate, autonomous agent. We have definitively advanced beyond an egocentric point of view, and have imaginative participation in the perspective and situation of the other, without falling into the sort of emotional identification that leads to a loss of self.

4) Sympathy and Assessment. The distinction between the agent's perspective and the agent's situation, as well as the perceived tie-in between the two (the perspective as a response to as well as expression of the situation), provides logical space needed for assessment or evaluation. Entering into your situation along the lines of steps 3.b and 3.c just outlined, I may understand what it would be like for you to lose your son, and may disapprove of your reaction to your losing your son (perhaps you lament too much, too long, or too little), on the basis of my understanding of what it would mean for any one us to lose a son. Smith refers to this as an assessment of "propriety."[50] To be sure, there is a vexing ambiguity in his various formulations as to whether this means (i) that if we cannot "enter into" the sentiments of the other, then we find them improper; or (ii) that we enter into them but find them out of proportion with the situation and *then* find them improper. "Enter into" can mean approve, or imaginatively simulate. On balance, Smith's theory points to the latter.

And if we both "understand" the other's perspective or affection sympathetically – as from her standpoint – and find her standpoint appropriate, and are not ourselves blocked by inappropriate envy, anxiety, resentment, or the like, we shall feel sympathetic in the sense of wishing to help alleviate misery, or prolong joy. In putting it this way, I am following Smith

---

[50] "In the suitableness or unsuitableness, in the proportion or disproportion which the affection seems to bear to the cause or object which excites it, consists the propriety or impropriety, the decency or ungracefulness of the consequent action" (*TMS* I.i.3.6; Smith almost immediately includes "affections" as possible objects of assessment as well).

in allowing that it may also apply to fellow feeling with their joy, though admittedly that stretches ordinary usage (*TMS* I.i.1.5, I.iii.1.1).

5) Sympathy as Compassion and Care. This constitutes the last distinction I will draw in this all too brief discussion. "Sympathy" is often used synonymously with "compassion," that is, fellow feeling with the sorrow of others. The essential point is that the spectator enters into the situation of the other and experiences *concern* for the other. As Darwall puts the point, with the agent's suffering in view, sympathy "is a feeling or emotion that (i) responds to some apparent obstacle to an individual's welfare, (ii) has that individual himself as object, and (iii) involves concern for him, and thus for his welfare, for his sake. Seeing the child on the verge of falling, one is concerned for his safety, not just for its (his safety's) sake, but for *his* sake. One is concerned for *him*. Sympathy for the child is a way of caring for (and about) him."[51] To care for the agent is to conclude that the agent is to be cared for; it is to feel that anyone else, similarly situated (e.g., who sees the child on the verge of falling), should care. Note that our caring is not contingent on the agent's caring; the child may have no idea that it is about to fall, or what the fall will mean. Sympathetically entering into its situation in such a way as to care is very far from simply reproducing in oneself the agent's sentiments; or even feeling what the agent would feel were she able to feel appropriately.

I have argued that the offender must "sympathetically" grasp the perspective of the victim on the injuries the offender caused her. In the terms just sketched, this requires sympathy in senses 3b and 3c. For purposes of this discussion, I am stipulating that the victim's response to the injuries is appropriate; the offender is not called upon to adjudicate the "propriety" of that response. In an attenuated sense, though, the offender is to sympathize in the sense of feel compassion (not pity) in order to qualify for forgiveness. It is not that the offender is required to attempt directly to alleviate the victim's suffering (that would be to presume the role of a friend) but rather, by taking the steps required, including that of changing oneself and showing one is worthy of trust, to manifest respect for her victim, as well as provide the victim reasons requisite to the latter's forswearing resentment. That is an indirect and limited form of care, and far short of the "compassion and care" that is the fifth form of sympathy

---

[51] Darwall, "Sympathy, Empathy, Care," p. 51.

I have listed. But it is substantive nonetheless, with real implications for the disposition of the victim.

And the victim too must sympathize in analogous ways with the offender – entering into her narrative, understanding why she did wrong, why the promised steps are worthy of trust, why the offender should be worthy of forgiveness. Strangely, this too is an indirect form of sympathetic care (contrast it, for example, with dismissive pity, or the resolve to take revenge, or continued hatred). The alleviation of guilt that may follow from forgiveness may have enormous consequences for the offender's well-being, as may the re-admission to the moral community signaled by warranted forgiveness.

I noted that the core idea in the Smithean theory of sympathy is that self-understanding is socially mediated, and that acceptance in community is desired (see *TMS* III.1.1–6). The offender cannot help but consider the view in which she is held by others. In Smith's Humean metaphor, we are mirrors to each other (*TMS* III.1.3; Hume, *Treatise* 2.2.5.21). We are also aware that the mirror can distort, in which case we endeavor to view ourselves (or others) as they would, were they in the know (*TMS* III.2.9).

[vii] THE UNFORGIVABLE AND THE UNFORGIVEN

Are some acts, and therefore actors, unforgivable? Let us distinguish between two senses of the term: (a) beyond one's ability to forgive and (b) not to be forgiven in principle. The question addresses sense (b); but the answer turns out to have a subterranean connection with (a).[52]

Someone could be unforgivable in principle either (b.i) until certain conditions are met (such as those for which I have argued), or (b.ii) even if all the stipulated conditions are met. In the next chapter, I will consider cases of (b.i), as for example, when the wrong-doer is dead, and the conditions for forgiveness are impossible to meet. I have not yet argued that failure to meet these conditions entails that the wrong-doer is unforgivable; I have set out conditions for the paradigm case. At this juncture, I would like to consider the possibility of (b.ii). I continue to focus on what I have called the paradigm case of forgiveness.

---

[52] J. Derrida rhetorically asks: "is this [the unforgivable] not, in truth, the only thing to forgive?" *Cosmopolitanism and Forgiveness*, p. 32. He assumes, without argument, an affirmative answer; whence the paradoxical air of his assertions throughout (e.g., forgiveness is the "madness of the impossible," p. 45). By contrast, I answer his question in the negative.

The issue of "unforgivability" arises with respect to levels of evil that elicit resentment so deep as to be accompanied by rage, indeed outrage. I sketched previously one candidate for the label: the sadistic torturer who injures another in almost inconceivable ways. Imagine that such a person inflicts the damage in question on just one person; the "scale" in that sense would be small, but the damage to the victim may be incalculably large. Or to take a second sort of case: that of someone who, while not necessarily sadistic, injures others on such a massive scale – so many people injured so profoundly – as to be guilty of crimes against humanity (Eichmann as described by Arendt comes to mind). For purposes of the present discussion, I will not distinguish among other sorts of cases.[53]

Most of us contemplate the second case from outside the circle of those immediately affected, in which event ours would be third-party forgiveness. And even those who contemplate it from within that circle presumably speak for themselves, first and foremost, when contemplating forgiveness.[54] For present purposes I will ignore the differences between kinds of malevolence in posing my question about the unforgivable, as well as between third-party forgiveness and forgiveness by the injured party. For we are seeking to understand whether there is such a thing as the unforgivable, and that is a philosophical question. I grant that the act of forgiveness properly belongs to the injured party to offer (though I have not yet discussed whether or not it belongs *only* to that party). In deciding whether or not to forgive, the injured person must decide what forgiveness is, and thus must decide the question under discussion here.

---

[53] Note that these may include the kind represented in Matthew 12.32: "and whoever speaks a word against the Son of Man, it will be forgiven him (*aphethêsetai*); but whoever speaks against the Holy Spirit, it will not be forgiven him, either in this age or in the age to come." Even the "religion of forgiveness" sets in-principle limits to forgiveness. St. Augustine holds that the unforgivable disposition toward God "is to be understood as nothing other than continuing in wickedness and maliciousness with despair of the kindness and mercy of God." See his *Unfinished Commentary on the Epistle to the Romans*, in *Augustine on Romans*, text and trans. by P. Fredriksen Landes (Chico, CA: Scholars Press, 1982), 22.3 (cf. 14.2).

[54] S. Wiesenthal's famous *The Sunflower* (New York: Schocken Books, 1969) records a case in which an S.S. officer asks him for forgiveness for the evils he had done to Jews. The example is complicated by the fact that it is one of third-party forgiveness. Among the contributors to the volume who insist that the S.S. officer is unforgivable are S. Shachnow (pp. 242–243; note the language of the officer as a "foul beast") and Rabbi Telushkin (p. 264). Consider the recent case of Elie Wiesel's remarks at the White House on April 19, 1985, when receiving the Congressional Gold Medal from President Reagan; he all but said that the S.S. were unforgivable, never to be reconciled with. See *Bitburg in Moral and Political Perspective*, ed. G. Hartman (Bloomington: Indiana University Press, 1986), pp. 241–244.

We are saturated with the language of and pleas for forgiveness. At the same time, it is not at all uncommon that such and such is pronounced to be unforgivable. Consider the case of Margaret Hassan, a British-Iraqi aid official murdered in Iraq in November of 2004 while carrying on her life-long humanitarian and non-political work. She was director of the Iraqi branch of CARE International when she was kidnapped. As reported in the *New York Times*, a videotape showed her being executed while blindfolded.[55] With supreme cynicism, her captors had earlier broadcast her desperate and tearful appeals for her life. She was treated as a means merely. Her deliberate and cold-blooded murder led to the withdrawal from Iraq of CARE, the International Rescue Committee, and of Doctors Without Borders. The same story quotes Ms. Hassan's family as follows:

Nobody can justify this. Margaret was against sanctions and the war. To commit such a crime against anyone is unforgivable. But we cannot believe how anybody could do this to our kind, compassionate sister.

An irresistible and intense sympathetic resentment flows through one's veins as one enters into the case, and with it an endorsement of her family's judgment.

But imagine that her murderers came forward and convincingly fulfilled all of the conditions for forgiveness; assume that there are no moral monsters. Are her murderers forgivable? Once again it is crucial to keep forgiveness, pardon, and mercy separate; and to recall that forgiven or not, some evil doers may deserve punishment. My analysis of forgiveness as a virtue, and as the expression of a disposition of character I called "forgivingness," does not decide the question; the broadly Aristotelian notion of virtue as a "mean" between excess and deficiency is compatible with the idea that some wrongs are absolutely unforgivable, but does not require that conclusion.

One commentator argues that a negative answer would come to the view that the offenders ought be the subject of resentment forever.[56] One could reply that while the offenders are not forgivable, the injured should let go of as much anger as possible for other reasons, including peace of mind. Nonetheless it would be true that a person who is in principle

---

[55] *New York Times* Nov. 16, 2004, on-line edition, "Family of Kidnapped Aid Worker in Iraq Mourns after New Video."

[56] Govier, *Forgiveness and Revenge*, p. 102.

unforgivable *warrants* resentment forever. Similarly, it would also be a mistake to hold that, given the frequency with which humans have treated each other cruelly and brutally, the thesis that such behavior is unforgivable "offers a blueprint for lasting hatred, ongoing conflict, and sagas of revenge."[57] As I shall argue in the next section, forgiveness is not a sufficient or even necessary condition of reconciliation understood minimally as non-interference (as the acceptance required for basic *modus vivendi*). Even if the just-quoted statement were true, it would give us a reason of the wrong sort to claim that no one should be considered unforgivable. It would instead establish that it is useful to treat people *as though* they are in principle forgivable.

The same author argues that

> to regard people as absolutely unforgivable on the grounds that what they have done is atrocious is to extend attitudes, unwarrantedly, from acts to persons, to argue from acts to character in such a way as to mark an irrecoverable stain on the agents. The line of reasoning is mistaken: logically, metaphysically, and psychologically, the act is not the agent. To claim that because he has committed terrible deeds a moral agent is reducible to those deeds and is thus absolutely unforgivable is to ignore the human capacity for remorse, choice, and moral transformation.

The key idea here is that to judge an offender to be unforgivable is to assert that she "is no longer deemed to be a human being, and thus to violate the norms of respect for persons." For to respect them qua human is to refuse to reduce them to their wrong-doing and to hold open "their capacity for reflection and transformation."[58]

It seems to me that a generous reading of Govier's argument at best establishes that no agent is absolutely and forever unforgivable. In a different formulation: it is indeed impossible to rule out a priori the possibility that the agent could not only change, but also satisfy all the conditions required of the offender if she is to qualify for forgiveness. However, it does not follow that all evil doers are in principle forgivable. First, it is possible – indeed it is the case – that some offenders turn out to be incapable of remorse, choice, and moral transformation, an incapacity confirmed a posteriori as it were, when they have lived their life accordingly. I would not infer, with Govier, that in such a case the offender is

---

[57] Govier, *Forgiveness and Revenge*, p. 106.

[58] Govier, *Forgiveness and Revenge*, pp. 112 (the long quotation) and 118 (the two shorter quotations).

"no longer deemed to be a human being," for being human in this sense is a status, not an achievement. Such a person might be contemptible, but human all the same. I have argued against the "moral monster" characterization.[59]

Second, even in the case in which the offender has shown a capacity for reflection and transformation, and has fulfilled the other conditions I have specified, the magnitude of the wrong done generates doubt that anything could *ever* "make up for" a *truly* atrocious wrong whose effects on you are permanent. The doubts are not dispelled by the argument that acknowledgment of our humanity is a sufficient reason for forgiveness. The "common frailty" thesis might just as well lead to the view that it is all the more important – just because we are so frail – to hold ourselves and each other accountable by *not* forgiving.

I have sought to specify the standards that must be met if X is forgivable; they include the commitment by the injured party to let go of resentment. But given the principle that ought implies can, we face a problem: some injuries may be so profound that it seems humanly impossible, at least for now, that resentment should be sent away. If it is the case that, the victim *as well as* those who have entered into the case sympathetically and knowledgeably (the "moral community") judge it to be impossible to commit to letting go of resentment – given appropriate efforts to reduce resentment, and all other conditions pertaining to offender and injured having been met – then the injurer is *unforgiven*.[60] But as to whether the offender could *ever* be properly forgiven, one must suspend judgment. Concerning an end-of-the-day case of this sort, in other words, my position is aporetic; from which it follows that I cannot assert or deny, in the abstract, that *every* wrong-doer is in practice forgivable. It also follows that end-of-the-day judgments in any particular case can be revised in the new light of another day. This argument underlines my view that even as forgiveness responds to one aspect of imperfection – moral

---

[59] E. Garrard comments: "But even if Govier is right in thinking that respect for the capacity for moral choice and change gives us reason to regard the perpetrators as members of the moral community, this does not by itself amount to a reason to forgive them. Forgiving someone certainly involves regarding them as a member of the moral community, but then so does refusing to forgive them." "Forgiveness and the Holocaust," in *Moral Philosophy and the Holocaust*, ed. E. Garrard and G. Scarre (Aldershot: Ashgate, 2003), p. 238.

[60] Does this imply that there is no such thing as "radical evil"? The complexities inherent in the matter are many (they start with the definition of "evil"). Fortunately, the present investigation does not require an answer to this query.

evil – it remains bound to the imperfect context out of which it itself arises.[61]

In contrast with the Hassan case, consider that of Amy Biehl, murdered by a group of South African youths on August 25, 1993. She was a white Stanford graduate whose adult life was devoted to ameliorating the lot of black South Africans. She was in the impoverished Guguletu township at the time, "helping to register black voters for the country's first free election." The four ringleaders appeared before the TRC and "detailed their parts in the killing and apologized to the Biehl family."[62] Two who served five years in prison eventually met Biehl's parents, asked for and received their forgiveness, and joined the staff of the Foundation set up by the parents to improve the lot of the poor in South Africa. Several of their daughter's murderers soon felt themselves to be part of the extended family, and the family evidently reciprocated the sentiment. This is a compelling demonstration of the transformative power of forgiveness – assuming one is willing to count it as a case of forgiveness.

When a wrong reaches epic proportions, it is easy to declare it unforgivable. And yet there are cases not complicated by third party considerations (as is the Biehl case) that warrant our taking a cautious stance on the matter. Eric Lomax's gripping story of his torture, intense desire to take revenge, and eventual forgiveness of one of his tormentors, is one such example.[63] Lomax was a British POW, captured in Singapore in

---

[61] J. Améry writes in *At the Mind's Limits: Contemplations by a Survivor on Auschwitz and its Realities* (Bloomington: Indiana University Press, 1980) that after being tortured in Auschwitz, "I preserved my resentments. And since I neither can nor want to get rid of them, I must live with them…"(p. 67). He agrees that "resentment is not only an unnatural but also a logically inconsistent condition. It nails every one of us onto the cross of his ruined past. Absurdly, it demands that the irreversible be turned around, that the event be undone. Resentment blocks the exit to the genuine human dimension, the future" (p. 68). His argument for hanging onto his resentment is difficult to counter, given what he suffered. However, when he says that "forgiving and forgetting induced by social pressure is immoral" (p. 72), we can agree, but note that forgiveness may have other motivations, and that it is neither forgetting nor approval of the evil that is forgiven.

[62] For the quotations, see "Why Do They Forgive Us?," by B. English, *Boston Globe*, April 23, 2003, pp. C1, C4. For the 1997 transcript of the TRC proceedings, see http://www.doj.gov.za/trc/hrvtrans/index.htm; the decision, also reproduced there, was announced in 1998. A revealing interview with the parties concerned, and description of the steps they have gone through to reach this point, may be found at http://www.theforgivenessproject.com/stories/linda-biehl-easy-nofemela.

[63] E. Lomax, *The Railway Man: A True Story of War, Remembrance, and Forgiveness* (New York: Random House, 1995). The railway and the bridge were portrayed in the film *Bridge over the River Kwai*. My page references to Lomax advert to that edition. Over 10,000 Allied troops died building this "pointless" and never finished project (pp. 230, 268).

1942 and forced to help build the notorious Burma-Siam railroad. When caught with diagrams of the railroad, as well as a home-made radio, he was subjected to torture for several years. He came to detest the Japanese translator (Nagase Takashi) who was present during the torture and, in Lomax's eyes, became its most significant and hated participant. Lomax's inability to talk about his terrible experiences took a horrendous toll on him over the decades. Learning through an amazing sequence of events fifty years later that Takashi was still alive, he corresponded with him in order to seek information about his torture, but also to request an explanation as to how the translator could dare to forgive himself given that the victims of his military unit's torture had not done so (pp. 251–252). Takashi recounted in an interview Lomax read that he had had a quasi-religious experience, after decades of his own moral agony, in which he felt himself "pardoned." Significantly, he did not know that Lomax, about whom he also wrote with enormous regret and compassion, was still alive. Takashi had exercised a form of non-paradigmatic forgiveness, viz., self-forgiveness. Indignation as well as fantasies of violent revenge were very much on Lomax's mind, even those decades later:

> Physical revenge seemed the only adequate recompense for the anger I carried. I thought often about the young interpreter at Kanburi. There was no single dominant figure at Outram Road on whom I could focus my general hatred, but because of his command of my language, the interpreter was the link; he was center-stage in my memories; he was my private obsession. . . . he stood in for all the worst horrors. (pp. 225–226; cf. 210, 241–242)

Ultimately they arranged a meeting (it took place at the bridge, as it turned out), accompanied by their spouses.

Takashi not only begged forgiveness, but showed that he had had lived in moral agony over his conduct during the war, and had devoted himself to the cause of reconciliation, atonement, and anti-militarism (p. 273). This devotion was public, sustained, politically engaged, and followed by such deeds as erecting a Buddhist temple at the site of the bridge. In his writing he specifically remembered Lomax and felt remorse over what was done to him (p. 263), unambiguously accepting responsibility for his own role for the conduct of his country's military toward POWs (p. 239). He become a deeply committed Buddhist (p. 255), and made great efforts to understand the suffering of the POWs – all this in the midst of recurring ill health of his own. In short, "he decided [after the War] to dedicate the rest of his life to the memory of those who died constructing the railroad" (p. 238). His sincerity was unimpeachable.

When he met Lomax, he listened sympathetically to Lomax's narrative of his own suffering during and after the war. Having learned that Lomax was alive, it became essential to Takashi that Lomax forgive him; self-forgiveness was no longer enough. In sum, Takashi had in effect met all of the conditions for forgiveness that were in his power to meet.

Takashi had made himself morally as well as well as physically vulnerable to Lomax – for it was not entirely clear to him until the last moments together alone in a hotel room, as requested by Lomax, that he would not be harmed or killed. Instead, Lomax had arranged a formal if private ceremony, presenting him with a letter of forgiveness:

> I read my short letter out to him, stopping and checking that he understood each paragraph. I felt he deserved this careful formality. In the letter I said that the war had been over for almost fifty years; that I had suffered much; and that I knew that although he too had suffered throughout this time, he had been most courageous and brave in arguing against militarism and working for reconciliation. I told him that while I could not forget what happened in Kanburi in 1943, I assured him of my total forgiveness. (p. 275)

Takashi was deeply moved, and in his conclusion to the book Lomax notes that "meeting Nagase has turned him from a hated enemy, with whom friendship would have been unthinkable, into a blood-brother" (p. 276). Lomax's moral hatred has all but evaporated. Both were liberated, for different reasons, from related kinds of suffering.

As the just-quoted sentence indicates, their time together clearly showed Lomax something essential: Takashi was not a monster, but a human being like him, located in an analogous web of kin relations, believer in a religion (not the same as Lomax's, but recognizable by analogy), capable of moral sentiments and of suffering. Lomax reframed his view of Takashi, and thereby of himself. In a way the real drama of the book lies in Lomax's own developing narrative: "stuck" for decades in anger and hatred he could not express, Lomax was finally able to experience and envision a different way of interpreting his past, such that his suffering could take on meaning "beyond that of the emptiness of cruelty" (to adapt Lomax's phrase, p. 269). He found a new and far better way of continuing his "story" – and this involved in part *telling* his narrative, even publicly (prior to meeting Takashi, precisely that began to occur; p. 242).

Once one is acquainted with Lomax's narrative, entering into its details, noting the thoughtfulness, sobriety, and honesty of its tone, the truthfulness of its assertions, and the steps that Takashi took after the war as well as after meeting Lomax, it is impossible to withhold the judgment that the forgiveness Lomax grants him is genuine and warranted. The case to that effect cannot be made, or rejected, a priori; it is the result of a sympathetic and informed engagement with the narrative in its full detail and complexity. Lomax's story shows that even injuries that for all the world seem unforgivable, may not be so.

[viii] FORGIVENESS, NARRATIVE, AND IDEALS

I have suggested that in various ways, narrative plays an important part in forgiveness. In this section, I will expand on the notion of narrative, with the aim of fleshing out the diachronic and perspectival dimensions of forgiveness, as well as the role of background ideals about which I have just commented. Forgiveness understood as a process, rather than simply as the end result, is much concerned with the temporalization of relations (to action, to other agents, to the actual and ideal self, to ideals as such). Of course, ordinary life, and certainly ordinary moral life, teem with story telling, and given that human life unfolds in time, the narration is on-going.[64] The interpenetration of narrative and perspective on and understanding of one's life is no doubt multi-layered; which is not to say, that human life *is* a narrative. My concern here is only with narrative as it arises in the context of human lives that suffer or inflict injury and consider the seeking or granting of forgiveness in response. Narrative theory is a sprawling and contested landscape; I am entering into it in a very limited way, in keeping with the purposes of this chapter.[65] And quite obviously, I am not thinking of narrative simply as confined to texts, let alone as fiction; but as a notion that helps to make sense of how both parties to the scene of forgiveness may fulfill certain requirements. I am not arguing that all thinking has a narrative structure – that is a much more comprehensive thesis lying well beyond the limits of this inquiry.

[64] A. MacIntyre writes: "man in his actions and practice, as well as in his fictions, is essentially a story-telling animal. He is not essentially, but becomes through his history, a teller of stories that aspire to truth." *After Virtue* (Notre Dame, IN: University of Notre Dame Press, 1984), p. 216.

[65] I am grateful to Christine McBride for her very helpful comments on an earlier draft of this discussion, including her definition of story as "content abstracted from viewpoint" and her conceptualization of the three "matrices" dividing up the territory within the "internal" as well as the "external" perspectives (see below). I also thank Peter Goldie for his comments on a draft of this section.

Let us begin by distinguishing between the "story" and "narrative." I shall stipulate that the former refers to the bare facts: say, that X injured Y in manner Z at time T. By referring to "facts" I mean to keep the door open not just to events, but reactions to events (say, that Y hit X at time T, and X felt angry). Notionally, story is content abstracted from viewpoint. Normally there will be different ways of trying to convey the story, the content; but notionally, just one content to be conveyed. Narration does the conveying or the telling; it organizes events into some sort of pattern – say, a temporal pattern, a causal one, or one that supplies insight into motivations (this is not a complete list, and these could hold concurrently) – *and* implies one or more perspectives. Narrative does not aspire to be non-perspectival in the way that a mathematical treatise or logical proof does.

The basic ideas of narrative include (i) the organization of events into a pattern or whole with beginning, middle, and end – plot, in short; and (ii) the perspective of the narrator on events and on the perspectives of the agents or actors – a point of view implicit or explicit in the telling. A narrative is normally a unifying – and in that way meaning making – discursive enterprise.[66]

The line between story and narrative is not hygienic; how could one say what the story is – tell the story – without narrating in any way whatever? Yet one cannot infer that a story "just is" a narrative, let alone that every narrative is a fiction.[67] The narrative *characterizes* what is happening or happened; in so doing it reshapes it, or remembers it, or re-imagines it, but does not thereby fabricate it out of thin air. So narrative here claims to represent, in some sense, how things are (or were), what happened, and why – not just causally "why," but why from the perspective of the agent. The narratives of forgiveness under discussion make claims to truth, and can be evaluated in that regard, to begin with in respect of

---

[66] This is a long established view of the "organic unity" of narrative; see Plato's *Phaedrus* 264b3-c5 and Aristotle's *Poetics* 1450b25–1451a6 (cf. *Parts of Animals* I.5, 645a10–645b1). Aristotle's word for "plot" is *mythos*, which can also be translated "story." The terminology for the basic distinctions at play is at times confusing and contested. I am not assuming that unity alone confers meaning or that disunity precludes it – though everything depends on how "unity" is defined.

[67] For some helpful comments on both points, see P. Goldie's "Narrative and Perspective; Values and Appropriate Emotions," in *Philosophy and the Emotions*, ed. A. Hatzimoysis (Cambridge: Cambridge University Press, 2003), pp. 215–218. References in my text to Goldie advert to this essay. Drawing on M. White, D. Velleman discusses a sliding scale stretching from annals, to chronicles, to narrative: "Narrative Explanation," *Philosophical Review* 112 (2003), pp. 1–4.

their consistency with the facts of the matter – i.e., with (what I am calling) the story. If your narrative includes resentment against an individual for causing you great injury, and it turns out that you have misidentified the responsible individual, your narrative is in part premised on a mistake about the basics of the story. If "story" is stretched to include facts about sentiments, intentions, and motivations, the room for error grows even further. There remains a relation of "aboutness" between the narrative and a life, such that one's perspective could be false in important ways. And as argued above, with reference to Butler's list of "abuses," one's response to injury could be disproportionate; hence a narrative "justifying" that response would be faulty. In sum, the distinction between story and narrative does not have to commit to "perspectivalism" in a sense that makes the telling "merely subjective." Some perspectives are more adequate to the facts than are others; some are more adequate to defensible ideals than are others.

I noted in the Prologue that forgiveness (whether interpersonal, or in the form of apology and its acceptance in the political realm) confronts in a particular way the brute metaphysical fact that the past cannot be changed. The idea of narrative helps to explain just how the past can nonetheless change without pretense to undoing it, or ignoring, avoiding, rationalizing, or forgetting it. One may adopt a different *perspective* on it, attach a different meaning to it, respond to it in a different way, adapt it to one's evolving life "story" (as we say, using the term loosely). In this restricted but crucial sense, the narrative of forgiveness is a solution to what Arendt aptly called (to quote her phrase once again) the "predicament of irreversibility."[68] It should be clear by now that I do not mean that narrative alone can accomplish this end, independent of sentiments, norms met in deed by both parties, and ethical ideals. It is however an essential part of the mix; consequently, it is important to understand something of its structure.

Let us next distinguish between two aspects of narrative. The first concerns the narrative's subject; this includes the story, but also the perspectives of the characters in the story-world. Their perspectives may include their judgments, beliefs, evaluations, and sentiments; the narrative seeks to represent them. The viewpoint of a character within the story world is – to borrow Goldie's terminology – an *internal* one. It can stem from participating in the action, or being spatio-temporally continuous with

---

[68] Arendt, *The Human Condition*, p. 237.

the story-world. That is, it could be first personal or third personal, so long as the latter is within the story-world.

The second aspect of narrative is, by contrast, the *external* perspective, one held from outside the story-world. In one way or another, this perspective is detached from that world. Roughly, it is the perspective of the narrator (and by extension, that of her audience) on the internal perspective(s) of the story-world.

"Outside the story-world" can mean (i) outside temporally, i.e., after it is over (or before it happens, in cases where one is imaginatively narrating a projected story); or (ii) outside spatially (contemporaneously with the events, but not placed in them); or (iii) detached from the relevant events in such a way that the telling of the events is different from what it is to live through them on the ground, however imaginatively the story is told; or (iv) as from the perspective of a detached party who simply reports it all (something like the perspective of a police report). The third of these modulations allows for the possibility that the external perspective may nonetheless seek to engage the story world sympathetically, to see it as though from within (obviously, great story tellers excel in that). Something like "simulation," or imaginative changing of places and identification with the other, will presumably be required here. At the same time, this sympathetic perspective piggy-backs on a viewpoint of the actors, or of one within the story-world, in such a way as to convey a further viewpoint (in effect, a commentary or interpretation that may be, say, ironic, satiric, tragic, etc.).[69]

A still different, and radical case of "outsideness" or external perspective is represented by some of the Platonic cosmological myths, for they are told from a perspective that beholds the cosmos itself (a "view from nowhere"). In effect, that is the perspective of synoptic omniscience that purports to "tell it like it is." We might dub this the entirely "objective," or "philosophical" narration. In effect, it aspires to transcend narration and tell the story un-narrated. It is not surprising that this impossible feat is sometimes characterized in these myths as a moment of vision. Admittedly the matter is complicated, since such myths tend to report

[69] For a wonderfully complex example of the narrator moving from an external standpoint to the internal, see the very start of ch. 29 of G. Eliot's *Middlemarch*, where the voice of the narrator speaks to the reader, interrupts herself in mid-sentence ("was her [Dorothea's] point of view the only possible one with regard to this marriage?" – the narrator's answer is negative), conveys a great deal of external perspective on the character's and her own narration thereof, and then takes up Casaubon's perspective on the marriage, though not in his voice.

that there is a view from nowhere, rather than to be that very view. And then it is not the myth itself, but the vision the theorist described within and by the myth, that is the moment of a-perspectival knowing.[70]

The matrices dividing up the territory *within* the "internal" as well as the "external" perspectives are, then, those of spatio-temporal relation; of participating in the action or not (the distinction between agent and spectator, first person and third person); and of affective relation.

The external perspective may be offered in the first person – as in autobiography – or in the third person. I want to claim that so long as there is a difference between the perspective had by the person living the life (or episode thereof), and that expressed in giving an account of that life, the internal/external distinction remains valid.[71] Further, I want to claim that with one possible exception, the external perspective is always present in narrative, given the logical difference between being the participant in an experience and interpreting that experience. It is from the latter standpoint that *any* narrative is told. The possible exception is that of a present-time stream-of-consciousness narration flowing from the agent in the story-world. Of course a narrator could tell the story *as though* present-tense, stream-of-consciousness, as seen from the moment by moment experiences of the agent as we imagine she is undergoing them. I would argue that in such a case the narrator's voice is inexplicit but still present – even when the narrator is the agent at a later time, attempting to recapture what it was like to be her past-self as the subject of that experience. The narration is not the same thing as being the subject of that experience at that time, it is a perspective on it shaped by time, filtered by memory, informed by the knowledge of what happened next, and targeted at an audience. Almost always, then, the external perspective is one that has not forgotten what happened next, and that views the story spectatorially rather than *just* as from the person living through it. This is so even in autobiography.

The telling of the narrative is typically, in the cases under consideration, a telling *to* someone; it seeks to convey how things really stood, and why one's responses and perspective were or are appropriate. The narrative telling is in that way *rhetorical* (which is not to say, a matter of

---

[70] I have discussed the problem of myth as a-perspectival telling (and of the telling of an a-perspectival seeing) in my *Self-Knowledge in Plato's Phaedrus* (rpt. University Park: Pennsylvania State University Press, 1996), ch. 4.

[71] I am once again in agreement with P. Goldie; see his "One's Remembered Past: Narrative Thinking, Emotion, and the External Perspective," in *Philosophical Papers* 32 (2003), p. 310.

"mere persuasion"). This connects with the point made in Chapter 1.ii.a to the effect that narratives of resentment and forgiveness typically seek a public.

Let us now bring this to bear on the scene of forgiveness, as imagined in our paradigm case. Consider first the person who has suffered the injury; the event over, her resentment seeks to make itself heard, understood, accepted. Perhaps it prompts its owner to contemplate getting even. She develops a narrative, thus adopting an "external," first-person perspective on her own earlier "internal" perspective. The sentiments of her self-past are communicated ever more forcibly and vividly to her self-now, and the narrative expands its justificatory ambitions. As her resentment is a reactive sentiment, she is also narrating a story about the offender who, let us imagine, at first appears as monstrously bad. Now suppose, with our paradigm case in view, she begins to moderate her resentment and desire for revenge. It is not just that "time brings perspective" but that the offender has begun to take emendatory steps; and the victim begins to "put the injury in context." Suppose that she is encouraged in this by friends, whose indignation is of a lower pitch than her anger was originally. Her narrative had not persuaded them to view things entirely in the light her sentiments suggested. Those who matter to her do not altogether share her feelings. She begins to narrate her story differently, as she looks at self-past and self-now from a different "external" perspective, viz., one resonant with that of others who were not part of the story-world. The different perspectives are brought into focus, compared, and weighed – diachronically of course. Cognizant that the offender is meeting the conditions for forgiveness, and that it would be appropriate for her to do so as well (after all, she has also read and agrees with this chapter!), she sets down the path, seeing herself and the offender in a new light, letting go of revenge, moderating her resentment, and seeking to let the resentment go altogether. Notice that the *story* has not changed.

The forgiver must not only see the injurer in a new light, but see herself in a new light. We are describing a change of heart, and in such a change not just the target of the sentiments (here, the offender) but their possessor necessarily change their aspect. Prospectively considered by the agent, the possibility of that change comes to projecting forward a story about the self one wants to be – that is, the self one wants to be in relation both to self-now and to the vicissitudes of self-past (to repeat, we are not considering amnesia as the route to "moving forward"). Does one hold onto the resentment, with all of the moral and psychological implications thereof, or not? Letting go of resentment could be a complicated process if one has identified, at least in part, and even if unwillingly, with the injured self. That injury – suppose it to be a great one comparable, say, to the incarceration borne by Nelson Mandela – is a central part of who you are, and thus of your story.[72] Especially if the injury is significant, the account of it is part of your presentation to yourself as well as to others of "who you are." Giving up the resentment naturally provoked by the injury, and forgiving the offender, would also become another central chapter, discontinuous in some ways with the one presently unfolding. It will stand in a relation, as mentioned, to self-now and self-past, but as well in a different relation to others. The injurer was an opponent, and therefore one against whom you defined yourself; forgiveness gives that up, and along with it identification as the self opposed to that offender.

The victim's change of narrative of self thereby encompasses three other aspects I would like briefly to discuss in turn: first, it expands to include the offender's narrative; second, it projects her own narrative into the future; and third, it incorporates a view about the sort of person one would want to be, about the "ideals" one wishes to live out.

Concerning the first point: in a way that formally parallels the narrative developed by the victim, the offender who addresses a request for forgiveness presents a narrative explaining how she came to do the injury, describes the moral sentiments that ensued (sentiments such as guilt, regret, and remorse), and convincingly depicts a change of ways that will unfold over time. She will have to show that she is not *just* a wrong-doer; that wrong-doing is not "all" of her, and indeed that she is becoming her "better self." This is a narrative of change. The offender re-frames her earlier self, as it were, in the context of a newly (re-)fashioned account, grounded in deeds, about the whole person and her future, and seeks to persuade the victim of its credibility. The injured party will need to enter "sympathetically" into the narrative, and thus into both the situation and the offender's past, current, and prospective responses to it – this process plays out in several different temporal modalities. This means, among things, trying to understand how the other could have made sense of her actions at the time, how the reasons she gave herself could have been reasons for her then. This imaginative engagement does not of course require endorsing those reasons, let alone substituting one's own biography for that of the other (which would amount to a confusing of self and other).

---

[72] About which see Mandela's autobiography, *Long Walk to Freedom* (New York: Little, Brown and Company, 1995).

In the paradigm sense of forgiveness discussed in this book, then, *two* narratives develop in tandem; their interplay may be referred to as a *dialogical narrative* between the offender and injured. As I have described the process, it is asymmetrical – the narratives each side offers express different conditions. This would of course change if each party had injured the other. Nonetheless they encompass each other, as each side comes to "understand," from its external standpoint, the perspective of the other. The hope is that they will meet and forgiveness be achieved, and that the same set of ideals is affirmed.

By contrast, the giving and exchanging of accounts, and the giving and receiving of forgiveness are diminished or impossible in the derivative or non-paradigmatic cases of forgiveness. For example, if the offender is unwilling or unable to request forgiveness, then the injured party's narrative is *monological* whether or not she forgives; so too if the injured party is unwilling or unable to receive a request for forgiveness. Its monological character is an expression of its deficiency as a modulation of forgiveness.[73] But narrative still remains crucial to whatever forgiveness is possible in non-paradigmatic cases.

Both the dialogical and monological narratives share, as I have already indicated, a common starting point, viz., the recognition of the humanity common to offender and victim. From the side of the victim, the narrative will include the thought that injured though I am, I too have injured; my oppressor is not a monster, I am not a saint; the offender's situation, character, motivations, are more or less intelligible, albeit reprehensibly expressed on this occasion. Were the two unable to recognize each other as akin subjects of experience, the narratives would sustain the asking for or granting of forgiveness only with difficulty and indirectly, if at all. Of course there are other reasons why the external perspective each party has on the other may make it very difficult or impossible to simulate imaginatively, or somehow to understand, the other's viewpoint, and therewith consider forgiveness.

I paint in broad strokes here; the precise character of narratives of both paradigmatic and non-paradigmatic forgiveness will depend on the

---

[73] "Monological" serves to underline that the injured and offender are not in dialogue, but is not meant to preclude the possibility that the injured person is in conversation with others; as mentioned, resentment is a story-telling passion that seeks an audience, and the overcoming of resentment may also, depending on the particulars, involve quite extensive exchange – except with, in the "monological" case, the offender. Even so, qua reactive it will be conditioned by the offender's action, and is at the very least likely to characterize the offender's motives and demeanor.

particulars of the situation. The indefinitely many textures the narrative may take are best left to literary description. I offer one more general observation. At the borderline between cases possibly eligible for non-paradigmatic forgiveness and those in which forgiveness seems out of reach for now, the reframing of one's view of oneself would perhaps amount to some version of this: having been massively injured, I defy the offender. I shall not be diminished or destroyed; I am a person who has not succumbed, shall not do so. In similar marginal cases where a reason for forgiving, however threadbare, presents itself, the narrative of self may evolve in a direction that casts the injury as an occasion for growth ("resisting and overcoming made me stronger"). However imperfect, both stances offer *some* movement forward.

By contrast, consider a rather extreme case in which the narrative reframing of one's view of other and especially of self is blocked. Where the trauma has been sufficiently great, it may be impossible for the victim to simulate imaginatively her own viewpoint, and that "block" seems to go along with an inability to integrate the trauma into one's life or to achieve "closure" with respect to it. Dori Laub argues in his study of Holocaust testimonies that "there is, in each survivor, an imperative need to *tell* and thus to come to *know* one's story, unimpeded by ghosts from the past against which one has to protect oneself," and yet that "no amount of telling seems ever to do justice to this inner compulsion." This chimes with the point I have made above about the indispensable role of narrative. Of a traumatized survivor of the camps he writes:

Hers is a story that could never be told in the way she chose to tell it, that is by structuring her whole life as a substitution for the mourned past, because there could not be an audience (even in her family) that was generous, sensitive, and self-effacing enough to obliterate its own existence and be nothing but the substitutive actors of her unexplicated memory.[74]

Unable to tell her story at the time, this person's identity and with it her narrative of self disintegrated in a combination of false self-perception and diachronic disunity. She even began to perceive herself as responsible for the atrocities in question (because she was unable to stop them at the time – presumably this is a desperate way of making sense of what happened) and as a result could no longer "be an authentic witness to herself." Laub argues that a peculiarity of the Holocaust was that it was

---

[74] D. Laub, "Truth and Testimony: The Process and the Struggle," *American Imago: Studies in Psychoanalysis and Culture* 48 (1991), pp. 77–78.

designed to be impossible to be witnessed; not just because witnesses were exterminated but because all those involved were presented with an event that was both incomprehensible and structured so as to insist on the utter "otherness" or "inhumanity" of the victims. The terms of the dehumanization were internalized even by its victims, with the result that they were unable to speak their narrative (pp. 80–81). The process is self-reinforcing. The possibility of truth telling about suffering, even to oneself, depends on the possibility of *address*, and thus of an interlocutor as well as speaker capable of seeing themselves and the other in the requisite way. The consequence was disbelief in the existence of a "you" available to be addressed and a "me" whose experience is narrated. The experiences were "secrets" and incommunicable, they never took place. And yet, they did.

The consequence seems to be a sort of obsessive repetition but not narration, perhaps mixed with deep conceptual confusion about responsibility for the evil deeds. In the terms used here, the victim has no *perspective* on the traumatic events, and thus no way to incorporate them into an on-going or unfolding account of self; her affective standpoint on this chapter of self-past is *internal*, and thus relives or reiterates the trauma. The "story" is repeated non-narratively, as it were. The impossibility of emotional closure means that the events are not integrated discursively (in a narrative that offers meaning-making unity, and recognizes both speaker and audience) or affectively (by means of the appropriate reactive sentiments and, possibly, the moderating and forswearing of them through forgiveness). So the victim is unable to reframe her view of herself.

This excruciating dialectic of rage, of grief yearning for a voice, and a conspiracy of silence, finds hope in a particular kind of narrative, viz., that of "testimony":

the testimony aspires to recapture the lost truth of that reality [of the Holocaust] . . . it is this very commitment to truth, in a dialogic context and with an authentic listener, which allows for a reconciliation with the broken promise [of 'testimony as a realization of the truth'], and which makes the resumption of life, in spite of the failed promise, at all possible. . . . It [testimony] is a dialogical process of exploration and reconciliation of two worlds – the one that was brutally destroyed and the one that is – that are different and will always remain so. (p. 90)

What Laub is calling "dialogical" narrative is not directed to the wrongdoers – presumably they are unable or unwilling to hear, so there is no dialogue with them – but nonetheless allows the victim to take an "external"

enough perspective on her experience that she can both tell it, and tell
it to someone. One of the most striking features of this sort of narrative
is that it expresses as well as promotes the victim's ability to re-envision
or reframe her view of herself, as well as perhaps of the offender (picture
this as happening in turns and by degrees). Laub once more:

> The testimony is, therefore, the process by which the narrator (the survivor)
> reclaims his position as a witness: reconstitutes the internal 'thou,' and thus the
> possibility of a witness or a listener inside himself. (p. 85)

So the telling not only helps give perspective, but in so doing recognizes
the moral standing of narrator as well as both the self-past who is narrated
and of the narration's addressee. We see again the interdependence of
self-conception, conception of one's self by the other, and one's conception of the other, that are part and parcel of "sympathy."[75]

Let me now turn to the second related feature of narrative, viz., its
future-oriented dimension. The narratives that the parties in our paradigmatic scene tell are both backward looking and forward looking – they
involve a commitment to make certain changes such that one's life story
will unfold in the ways desired. Narratives of forgiveness will be projective
as well as recollective, so to speak. In the instant case, this would come to
thinking of the changes I plan to make, the specific ways in which I am
re-envisioning myself and the offender (or the injured party, as the case
may be). The forward looking perspective from which I do this has two
modalities. On the one hand, I must be imagining my self-to-be from an

---

[75] In her *Aftermath: Violence and the Remaking of a Self*, philosopher S. J. Brison notes
that in one phase of her own recovery from violence she had trouble speaking at all
(p. 114). Crucial to her recovery was what she calls "narrative therapy" (p. 77), by which
she evidently means not only the telling and retelling of her story, but also listening to
the stories of others in such a way that the survivor can "feel empathy for her traumatized self (by first feeling it for another who experienced a similar trauma)" (p. 73).
"Narrative . . . facilitates the ability to go on by opening up possibilities for the future
through retelling the stories of the past. It does this not by reestablishing the illusions
of coherence of the past, control over the present, and predictability of the future, but
by making it possible to carry on without these illusions" (p. 104). She concludes that
in the final analysis recovery "no longer seems to consist of picking up the pieces of a
shattered self (or fractured narrative). It's facing the fact that there never was a coherent
self (or story) there to begin with" (p. 116); so it is a matter of shaping a new self. In
her case, the arrival of her child provided hope and trust in the world (pp. 112, 116);
"contingent" events such as that may of course play a pivotal role in the creation of
the new, life-giving narrative. As Brison's autobiographical account makes clear, telling
a narrative will not by itself bring about growth and stability; other events that helped
her rewrite her narrative included taking a self-defense class. I note that her book is not
about forgiveness.

internal perspective; for how could I adopt an external perspective on a viewpoint that does not yet exist? And yet, on the other hand, precisely because I am not yet that person, *and* can imagine in some detail that person's perspective (that of the "person I hope to become"), I may be as different from my self-to-be as I am from my self-past, and able to adopt an *external* perspective on my future self. (Goldie makes this sort of point on p. 206, n.7, suggesting that if the self-to-be is imagined as sufficiently different from self-now, then one's perspective on one's future self is external.)

Turning to the third feature of the narrative of forgiveness, I suggest that one key theme both the forgiven and forgiver affirm is that of *growth*. This expresses an *ideal* one seeks to realize in oneself. The significant change I am imagining each party must undergo is positively marked; and it is not simply a rupture with the past, let alone its obliteration, but its reinterpretation and integration into a larger narrative – that of a life as a whole. An underlying theme is reflected in the decision not to be determined by the past alone. In its future-looking dimension, forgiveness must commit to the idea that as yet undetermined and desirable possibilities lie ahead. The hoped-for growth or renewal may be compared to that represented by a new circle in the trunk of a tree; it surrounds what came before, and in a sense builds on it so as to develop new life. So one seeks to author (or perhaps co-author) a narrative that includes both "reversal" (a new perspective on the injury) and continuity (one remains the same subject of the various chapters of the narrative).[76] My purpose in saying this is not to "justify" suffering or wrong-doing – on my account, forgiveness is decidedly not an exercise in Panglossian optimism – but to get at a feature of the narrative for oneself that the choice to forgive (and to request forgiveness) involves.

As I suggested at the end of the discussion of "praiseworthy conditional forgiveness?" (II.v.c), there are other background ideals implicit in the narrative expressed by forgiveness, namely those of respect, harmony of self and reconciliation with others, affection, and love. Forgiving acts on the assumption that these ideals are not "mere ideals," in spite of the fractured state of the world.

---

[76] As P. Ricoeur observes: "When I interpret myself in terms of a life story, am I all three at once, as in the autobiographical narrative? Narrator and character, perhaps, but of a life of which, unlike the creatures of fiction, I am not the author but at most, to use Aristotle's expression, the coauthor, the *sunaistion*." In *Oneself as Another*, trans. K. Blamey (Chicago: University of Chicago Press, p. 1992), p. 160 (part of ch. 6, "The Self and Narrative Identity").

Of course these ideals themselves can be told from an external perspective that is still further detached. That perspective is, so to speak, bi-focal: we see, first, the character and attraction of those ideals. In contrast to them, second, we also see the many ways in which the world *is* fractured or broken, and far from ideal. The distance between the two might easily give rise to a "tragic sense of life," to borrow Miguel de Unamuno's phrase, and thus to any number of responses including Stoic resignation, Epicurean withdrawal, and the Platonic flight to another world. In contrast to what I have elsewhere called the Platonic "narrative of nostalgia," however, that in which forgiveness finds a place attempts to repair what is broken and thereby to stick with it rather than to detach or flee or insulate oneself.[77] The "perfectionist" narrative – whether Platonic or Stoic or Epicurean – makes no room for forgiveness in part because it valorizes the (perfected) person who stands outside the circle of sympathy, whose identification is first and foremost with his or her own excellence rather than with the equivalent of "the moral community." Forgiveness points toward a contrasting notion of transcendence within time and the circle of sympathy. It assumes a background picture of human life as temporal and mortal, embodied, emotive, and interdependent or social, recognizes the pervasiveness of suffering – most often unmerited where it is intentionally inflicted – and expresses the value of the sorts of ideals I have sketched. Forgiveness is a model virtue for the project of reconciliation with imperfection. As to the political expression of forgiveness and reconciliation – and thus of ideals such as "progress," hope, as well as the disappointment in ideals that is expressed in quietism – a separate discussion is required.

[ix] FORGIVENESS, RECONCILIATION, AND FRIENDSHIP

In my paradigm case of forgiveness, the two parties establish a moral relationship and, in the manner I have indicated, intertwine their narratives. Both commit to change – the one to reform her ways, the other to forswear resentment. At a minimum, the commitment to forgiveness entails that neither will interfere with the other again as they go forward. In the Prologue to this book I distinguished between various senses of "reconciliation." If "reconciliation" is taken to mean "acceptance," in the minimal sense of non-interference, then we may say that forgiveness may lead to

---

[77] For "narrative of nostalgia," see my "Longing for the Best: Plato on Reconciliation with Imperfection," *Arion* 11 (2003): p. 124.

it. But if reconciliation means "affirmation" – the relevant sense of which here would be something like friendship and support or a renewal of any previous ties of affection – then there is no reason to think that forgiveness *must* lead to "affirmative reconciliation" as one might call it. Such an outcome might be neither warranted nor desirable. For example, one could forgive one's partner for infidelity but no longer wish to remain together as a couple; forgiveness does not necessarily restore the love that was destroyed by infidelity, even if it does restore a certain level of mutual respect, and dissipate resentment and guilt. As noted above, I am not arguing that forgiveness obviates every negative sentiment about the offender (one might forgive the infidelity, but still feel disappointed or sorrowful that it occurred). I do not claim that the past act has no bearing on present relations, even when forgiveness obtains. In other interpersonal contexts, reconciliation in the stronger sense may be appropriate and desirable (one thinks of cases of relations between parents and their children).

Interpersonal forgiveness is a necessary condition of reconciliation in the stronger sense of affirmation and friendship; but not of mere acceptance in the minimal sense of the term. One could reach acceptance by other means. For reasons of psychological or social survival, for example, one might decide to refrain from violence or revenge, to put aside guilt and resentment as best one can, and cooperate with what self-preservation requires.

Affirmative reconciliation through forgiveness is not an appropriate political goal, or so I shall argue. Political reconciliation as mutual support, collaboration, solidarity, and even friendship also requires much more than forgiveness, including quite possibly the changing of institutional structures, social practices, and reparations. Severe injury is likely to lead, at least on the part of the injured, to a long term sense of loss, and therefore to present a challenge that in a religious context would be called a "crisis of faith," but that in a secular context raises the issue not just of forgiveness but of "metaphysical forgiveness," as I called it in the Prologue. How could the world be such that so terrible a thing was done?[78] We are particularly familiar with this question after the mass

---

[78] See Améry's chapter on torture in his *At the Mind's Limits.* He writes "Whoever has succumbed to torture can no longer feel at home in the world. The shame of destruction cannot be erased. Trust in the world, which already collapsed in part at the first blow, but in the end, under torture, fully, will not be regained. That one's fellow man was experienced as the antiman remains in the tortured person as accumulated horror. It blocks the view into a world in which the principle of hope rules. One who was martyred

slaughters of the last century, but it has certainly been asked repeatedly throughout humankind's extraordinarily bloody history. I do not claim that interpersonal forgiveness somehow "solves" this problem. But it does contribute to a viable response.

is a defenseless prisoner of fear. It is *fear* that henceforth reigns over him. Fear – and also what is called resentments. They remain, and have scarcely a chance to concentrate into a seething, purifying thirst for revenge" (p. 40; see also p. 28). Améry was tortured by the SS and then sent to Auschwitz. Sadly, in 1978 Améry committed suicide.

3

Imperfect Forgiveness

In the Prologue, I mentioned five examples of non-paradigmatic or imperfect forgiveness in which one or more of the logical features defining forgiveness is absent. Because I am focusing on secular forgiveness, I am ignoring the problem of the forgiveness of God. The first three types – forgiving wrongs done to others (including victims no longer living), i.e., "third-party forgiveness," forgiving the dead or unrepentant, and self-forgiveness – admit of myriad shades and textures, depending on the circumstances. The notion of imperfect instances of a virtue or moral quality raises a complex metaphysical question, which I will begin by sketching briefly, before turning to each of the three types of imperfect forgiveness. The puzzle centers on the idea of "degrees" of forgiveness.

[i] IDEAL AND NON-IDEAL FORGIVENESS: AN INCLUSIVE OR EXCLUSIVE RELATION?

I have argued that forgiveness is a virtue especially important in an outlook that underlines our irremediable human imperfection. It both responds to an aspect of imperfection – wrongdoing and evil – and expresses our imperfection (our vulnerability, embodiment, finitude, and affective nature). I have set out a theory of paradigmatic forgiveness – of what forgiveness would have to be in order to be perfectly accomplished. It is a safe assumption that in the world as we have it, all of the conditions required by the paradigm case will not always obtain (though sometimes they will). Do the non-paradigmatic cases of forgiveness still count as instances of forgiveness, or does their logical deficiency defeat forgiveness? This is not a semantic question. The old Platonic problem of making sense of the relation between the ideal or perfect and the imperfect seems to have reiterated itself – this time in an outlook at odds with Platonic perfectionism.

If non-paradigmatic cases of forgiveness were like being a little bit pregnant, then obviously a high percentage of cases we would want to call forgiveness are actually cases of something else, and for the most part, forgiveness would remain a distant "Platonic" ideal. But if non-paradigmatic cases of forgiveness can count as forgiveness, then we need a view as to how qualities can be approximated or shared in to some degree. The alternatives here would not be comparable to "pregnant or not" but, say, to "lit brightly, or lit dimly, or somewhere in between – but in each case, sharing in light." The metaphysical puzzles that arise here are as ancient as they are difficult. The context of my brief discussion remains interpersonal forgiveness, and not other members of the related family of concepts (such as nations accepting apologies from each other, judicial pardon, and so forth).

I have argued that even under "ideal" conditions, forgiveness requires a commitment that may not yield its intended result; forgiveness is a temporally bound process. In this sense even paradigmatic forgiveness may temporarily be incomplete, so to speak. Even when it is accomplished, it involves a balance of actions, dispositions, and sentiments; this is the completion of a quality that is not Platonically "form-like." In a moment I will argue that non-ideal senses of forgiveness can count as (imperfect instances of) forgiveness. The relation between ideal and non-ideal forgiveness is in that sense inclusive rather than exclusive. I am therefore subscribing to the view – whose metaphysics it is not my object to analyze in this book – that forgiveness admits of approximation or degree. Of course, it does so only to a degree. I do not have a precise rule for determining in every imaginable case when "enough" amounts to a qualitative difference, in part because, with Aristotle, I want to say that "the judgment depends on particular cases, and [we make it] by perception" (*NE*,1126b3–4). In practice this is true even in our paradigm case, as I have already underlined.

But this is not to deny – indeed, I wish to affirm – that "forgive" is a "success word" that comes with what one might call threshold conditions, applicable therefore to imperfect or non-paradigmatic forgiveness too: fail to achieve at least those conditions, and you are not engaged in forgiving, but doing something else.[1] Non-paradigmatic forgiveness does not encompass every form of reconciliation not encompassed by paradigmatic forgiveness. Rather, non-paradigmatic and paradigmatic forgiveness line on a spectrum above the threshold conditions required of any forgiveness whatever.

To illustrate with the standard example: if you take a drug and forget what the offender did to you, perhaps even feel positively benevolent toward him, you have not met the threshold conditions for forgiveness. Or again: if the injury is humanly unforgivable, then you are impeded from forgiving no matter what steps the offender takes. Or if the injury is humanly forgivable, contingent on the offender taking minimal steps – or at least, our being able to imagine that she would have done so had conditions been different, i.e., our being able to construct *some* sort of narrative that gives forgiveness a chance – and if the offender provides not even that much; then the threshold has not been attained. Or if the injury is humanly forgivable, and the offender meets takes the minimal steps to qualify for forgiveness, but the victim simply refuses to attempt to lower her resentment or even retributive impulse, then the threshold has not been crossed.

The baseline conditions include, then,

i. the willingness – whether in fact, or as imaginatively reconstructed by a suitably qualified third party – of the victim to try to lower her pitch of resentment, as well as her ability to do so to some minimal degree, and to forswear revenge (this of course assumes that the victim does or would feel resentment for the injury done; if not even that is felt, then of course (i) fails to come into play at all);

ii. the willingness – whether in fact, or as imaginatively reconstructed by the victim (picture the victim being presented with the offender's death-bed letter of contrition, for example, that supplies a basis for reframing her view of the offender) – of the offender to take minimal steps to qualify for forgiveness;

iii. that the injury be humanly forgivable.

Only when all three are met does forgiveness come off at all. The threshold conditions are interpersonal in that they involve both parties. To

---

[1] For discussion of "success" or "achievement" words (as distinguished from "task" words), see G. Ryle, *The Concept of Mind* (London: Hutchinson & Co., 1963), ch. 5, section 5, pp. 149–153.

repeat, judgment and sympathetic engagement will be needed in order to determine when that has taken place, as is especially obvious from my formulation of (i) and (ii). Below the threshold may lie excuse, or condonation, or explanation, or any of a number of psychological strategies from rationalization to amnesia. Above the threshold lies a spectrum of possibilities for forgiveness, from the tentative and questionable to the accomplished. When presented with the chance that all rather than some of the conditions for forgiveness I have set forth be met, we would wish for them to be so, indeed we would insist that they be so. That is one way in which we recognize that there *is* a spectrum containing more and less accomplished cases, or degrees of the moral relation in question. "Forgive" behaves a bit like "rebut": one has not rebutted an argument if one waves one's hands or utters magic spells or throws something at one's opponent. Having met the threshold conditions for rebutting, however, one may or may not succeed, or may succeed in various degrees, in that which rebuttal aims for: refutation. Refutation is the *telos* of rebuttal. Similarly, the *telos* of non-paradigmatic forgiveness is paradigmatic or model forgiveness.[2]

It follows that *just* being in the psychic state of no longer feeling resentment at the agent who caused the injury is not an imperfect form of forgiveness, whether that state is induced by medication, therapy, an astonishing act of will, an ostensible religious revelation, or what have you. Per se, being in this state falls below the threshold of forgiveness if (as I am assuming) it is not a response to the sorts of reasons that, on my account, are necessary for even imperfect forgiveness. Above the threshold, and well toward the "imperfect" or non-paradigmatic end of the spectrum, there does exist a form of unilateral forgiveness (as when, say, one forgives the dead), which I will explore in a moment. But it is responsive to certain reasons that are missing from the mere state of no longer feeling resentment (however it was motivated). I emphasize this point because of the widespread proclivity, especially among both religious authors and pop psychologists, to count as "forgiveness" – indeed, perfected forgiveness – the unilateral giving up of resentment *tout court* (perhaps on the mistaken theory that forgiveness is a "gift" or "unconditional," as discussed

---

[2] I am grateful to Walter Hopp and Lisa Griswold for extended discussion of these issues. Hopp suggested to me the rebut-refute analogy, the "telos" language, and the helpful formulation to the effect that if conditions were favorable for paradigmatic forgiveness, then we would insist that they be met – that being part of what makes a non-paradigmatic case derivative from the paradigmatic case.

at length in Chapter 2). Achieving an inner state of peace in response to injury is necessary but not sufficient for accomplished forgiveness.

[ii] THIRD-PARTY FORGIVENESS

The question of third-party forgiveness comes up ongoingly and naturally, for several reasons. To begin with, we share sympathetically in the resentment of people whose narratives we enter into (recall Butler's example of a fictional narrative), and particularly of those we care about. We identify to varying degrees with the victim, with what we take to be (or even imagine to be) her resentment, and experience both indignation and a retributive impulse. The question of forgiveness by third parties – of foreswearing retribution, moderating and working toward the elimination of resentment, inter alia – therefore arises. So does a great deal of confusion about what this would mean, and whether it is legitimate.

In the very cases under discussion, we often are personally affected in the sense that we experience an injury of our own. The murder of a loved one injures you, and the question of forgiveness presents itself to you in light of your loss. This sort of case is not a matter of third-party forgiveness. It may or may not lend itself to forgiveness in our model sense; either way, it is a matter between victim and offender – even though the offense involved another person. (The same would hold with the mirror image case, in which the offender requested forgiveness from you for the injury done to you by means of injury to the other person.) It is contrasted with a situation in which the question of forgiveness arises in light of your indignation at the loss suffered by another person, thanks to someone else's actions: here the matter concerns your forgiving their offender on their behalf for the harm done to them (not to you). The "mirror image case" holds as well. Our intuitions about this "third-party" forgiveness are conflicting.

Especially where the injured party is no longer capable of responding to the offender, those intimately affected often assume they have a right to forgive or to refuse to forgive. Yet it is nonetheless taken for granted by almost all authors on the subject that *only* the injured party may forgive (and correlatively, that only the offender may request forgiveness), in which case talk of forgiveness (or the withholding of it) by third parties (including family and friends of the victims), on account of the wrong done to the victim, is illegitimate. Yet consider a case in which the offender is in principle forgivable (or not), but the injured party simply refuses to forgive (or alternatively insists on forgiving) for reasons that are not defensible: the common hypothesis would prohibit any third parties from doing what the injured party ought to have done. Or again, consider that if the victim alone has standing to forgive, that person's murderer could never be forgiven for the wrong in question; and that an offender who does wrong that is in principle forgivable is doomed to the status of the unforgiven should her victim so declare. These consequences seem counter-intuitive, and lead one to question their premises. Let us ask, then: why think that the actual granting of forgiveness is the privilege of the victim alone?

The answer has two sides. The first stems from the fact that forgiveness, as I have defined it, involves forswearing resentment, and the injured party's resentment is something that only the injured party can possess or shed. The second comes to what one might call common-sense moral individualism: individuals are the basic moral units; to them is ascribed responsibility for good or wrong-doing, responsibility for contrition and forgiveness. Properly speaking it is individuals who are injured; the moral harm in injuring an individual lies – even if the effects are widely felt (as in the case when, say, the legitimate president of a nation is assassinated) – in the wrong done to that particular agent. And so, the intuition goes, one can no more forgive on behalf of the injured person than one could tender a request for forgiveness on behalf of the offender. An impartial spectator may declare the act an injury; but the injury in question was not done to us all, at least not in the same sense.

If this were the last word, however, then the unforgiving resentment of a sympathetic third party, such as Hassan's family, or the tendering of forgiveness, as in the case of Biehls' family, would be acceptable only with respect to the injury done *to them* as relatives of the deceased. They could not forgive (or withhold forgiveness) on behalf of the victim for the injury done to the victim. Given the sometimes counter-intuitive consequences this "hard-line" position generates, I propose to soften its force, as follows.

Suppose again that there is a distinction between the injury done to the victim, and the injury done to oneself by the victim's injury, and cor-relatively that there are two separate reasons, as it were, for resentment of the offender. At stake here is the first of these injuries – that to the victim. Suppose that the victim is for indefensible reasons unwilling to forgive, or alternatively is unable to forgive, the offender for the injury done to her. Further, suppose that the offender has met all of the requisite criteria it is possible to meet given the victim's condition, such that as third parties we judge that it would be appropriate and humanly possible to forgive the offender. I suggest that a third party may forgive on behalf of the victim, but only if that third person also has *standing* to do so. Standing would seem to presuppose not only justifiable indignation (sympathetic resentment), but also something else: identification with the victim.[3] Indignation alone is too impersonal to grant the requisite standing. Identification, however, must be warranted; one cannot simply bestow it on oneself. It is warranted by the combination of at least two things: first, ties of care for the victim; second, reasonably detailed knowledge not only of the offender's wrong-doing and contrition, but especially of the victim. As a suitably well-informed, sympathetic, concerned third party, we would then be in a position to render the forgiveness due to the suitably qualifying offender, as we imagine the victim would and should – were she willing or able. Third-party forgiveness requires the development of a credible narrative about what one of the parties in the original scene would have done under different circumstances (forgive, or ask for forgiveness). It is possible that no such narrative could take place: the victim, say, never gave us (the third party who knew her well and cared for her) any reason for entertaining the slightest hope that she would, under any conditions whatever, forgive; nothing in her character suggested any such wish for reconciliation. Should that conclusively be the case, then we cannot offer or accept forgiveness in the name of that person. The offender may be forgivable, but is not forgiven; or the victim deserves contrition, but is fated to live without it.

Even when it does come off, third-party forgiveness is unquestionably imperfect. Were it possible for the conditions of the model case to be fulfilled, and in particular for the victim to reflect on the matter herself (or, alternatively, for the offender to reflect on asking for forgiveness), we should certainly wish for them to be. Unfortunately, the familiar truisms are quite correct: the imperfect world in which we find ourselves is often not as we would wish.

---

[3] I have referred to "identification" several times in my discussion of "sympathy" (Chapter 2). The notion, and the philosophical literature on it, are complex. For a very helpful discussion, see D. Velleman's "Identification and Identity," ch. 6 of *Self to Self* (Cambridge: Cambridge University Press, 2006). As in the case of a certain sense of "sympathy," what I have in mind is, as Velleman puts it there, "imagining the world as experienced by him – as seen through his eyes and traveled in his shoes" (p. 350). As in the relevant sense of sympathy, a great deal of intimate knowledge may be required to identify with another in this way.

[iii] UNILATERAL FORGIVENESS: THE DEAD AND THE UNREPENTANT

An analogous and familiar problem arises when the offender is unable or unwilling to meet the conditions required of her for forgiveness. As the cases of "unable" and "unwilling" have different implications, let us examine them separately.

[iii.a] Forgiving the Dead

While there are multiple conditions under which the offender might be unable to ask for forgiveness, let us simply focus on the most obvious and common one. Can one forgive an offender who is dead? For the sake of simplicity, assume that she took no steps at all down the path of qualifying for forgiveness. Having committed the dreadful injury, she died.

Victims of deceased offenders are faced with a dilemma: the scene of forgiveness seems both permanently withdrawn and urgently necessary. The necessity derives in part from the continuing goad of "settled anger"; the wish to be recognized and respected as one who ought not have been thus treated; the urge to understand how the offender could have done such a thing; and the sense of being captive to the past and blocked from growing. It is a maddening and perplexing situation.

The logic of third-party forgiveness applies here as well, and so too the conclusion that the only mode of forgiveness available to the injured is in the subjunctive. The injured party may work out a simulacrum of forgiveness by gathering data that help explain why the offender acted so badly; she may even find indications in the offender's past (supposing she learns all about her) that amounted to "cries of help"; she may reflect on their common humanity, and cease to see the offender as a monster. Perhaps with time, this provides reasons for letting go of much of the resentment. Suppose that unbeknownst to her, the offender wrote, in moving detail, a death-bed recantation and apology of unimpeachable sincerity. The document reaches her hands; she is now able to construct a narrative from which reasons to forgive may be drawn. The injured party is still deprived of the full measure of such satisfaction built into the paradigm case, and therefore is fated to live with a limited measure of moral satisfaction, of anger forsworn (for reasons related to forgiveness), and reconciliation. Just how far even that is possible will depend on the relevant particulars of the situation. The variations are many, as is obvious when one contemplates, say, the shades of meaning the offender's death-bed recantation might embody. Much will hinge on just what words are chosen, why contrition was expressed at all, and so forth. Moral philosophy cannot provide guidance at that level of detail, and literature is much better suited to describing the particulars and their context.

[iii.b] Forgiving the Unrepentant

It is hard to deny that where the offender is simply unwilling to ask for forgiveness, offering it anyway would likely be interpreted by the offender (and possibly third parties as well) as condonation or excuse making – either amounting to collusion with wrong-doing. Obviously this would compromise the moral point of the act. For the injured person, this would reduce it to the letting go of resentment for other moral and psychological reasons (say, in order to protect one's capacity to love; or, to allow one to "move on").[4] The case is very similar to that of forgiving the dead, with the obvious difference that death forecloses what must otherwise remain a possibility, namely that the offender might undergo a change of heart.

One could argue that an excellent way to encourage the offender to repent is precisely to forgive her even if she is unrepentant; bestowing this "gift" opens a moral door for the offender and leads the way through it. Now, it is possible that the offender will see the light streaming in through that door, and that the conditions for true forgiveness will be enacted backwards, as it were. One can imagine conditions under which "prospective forgiving" is based on a reasonable hunch about the person's ability to change, if shown the way.[5] My claim is that whatever it is that the injured party is doing proleptically, it is not forgiving, but something else

---

[4] H. McGary discusses the idea that "oppressed and powerless people may be motivated to forgive for reasons that might be quite different from those of free and powerful persons." The reasons he has in mind are "self-pertaining" ones, in particular, reasons of psychic self-preservation in the face of sustained injustice and the bitter resentment it arouses. Forgiveness offers a way to resolve the "dilemma": either hold onto the resentment, or give it up and lose your self-respect. "Forgiveness and Slavery," in *Between Slavery and Freedom: Philosophy and American Slavery*, ed. H. McGary and B. E. Lawson (Bloomington: Indiana University Press, 1992), pp. 108 and 110. My quarrel with this view is that the conditions to met by the offender have dropped out of the picture as though they are of no consequence.

[5] Something like this happens in V. Hugo's *Les Misérables*, bk. II, ch. 12, when the Bishop in effect forgives Jean Valjean for stealing the rectory's silver even though Valjean (just apprehended and presented by the police) has taken no steps whatsoever to warrant forgiveness.

that seeks to become forgiveness but has not yet crossed the threshold as defined at the start of this chapter.

[iv] SELF-FORGIVENESS

Self-forgiveness is rightly suspected of abuse. The spectacle of preachers of the faith caught in flagrante and forgiving themselves with lightening speed naturally feeds cynicism about the whole concept. It all too easily degenerates into self-interested condonation or excuse making. And yet it deserves serious consideration. We observe occasions on which it strikes us that a failure or inability to forgive oneself is problematic morally and psychologically. It seems possible to be overly hard hearted toward oneself. Indeed we sometimes wonder whether a person's refusal to forgive herself betrays an objectionable sort of pride in being outstandingly principled, in never buckling under the weight of one's humanity. A failure to forgive oneself, when self-forgiveness is due, may lead to a destruction of one's own capacity for agency, and even to self-annihilation. It is certainly as intelligible to reproach someone for failing to forgive herself when she ought as it is to reproach her for forgiving herself when she ought not. If the one makes sense, so does the other; and in both, we perceive a failure on the agent's part to assess her past appropriately. Such thoughts lend credence to the claim that self-forgiveness can be appropriate, even if unusually open to abuse. As in the case of forgiveness generally, there exists a huge pop-psychology literature on the subject. I take it that where there is so much smoke, there must be fire. The issue is humanly important; it is also complex philosophically.[6]

One might forgive oneself for injuries one has done to others; or for injuries one has done to oneself. Let us examine these in turn. I am of course assuming in what follows that the wrongs done are not unforgivable in principle.

---

[6] Arendt denies that the notion is even coherent, but her reasons are elusive and therefore difficult to assess: "But the fact that the same *who*, revealed in action and speech, remains also the subject of forgiving is the deepest reason why nobody can forgive himself; here, as in action and speech generally, we are dependent upon others, to whom we appear in a distinctness which we ourselves are unable to perceive. Closed within ourselves, we would never be able to forgive ourselves any failing or transgression because we would lack the experience of the person for the sake of whom one can forgive." Her view does not consider the possibility of our viewing ourselves "from the outside," in the mirror of a notional "other." *The Human Condition*, p. 243 (see also p. 186). For one of the best discussions, see R. S. Dillon, "Self-Forgiveness and Self-Respect," *Ethics* 112 (2001): 53–83.

[iv.a] Self-Forgiveness for Injuries to Others

Self-forgiveness for injuries done to others is peculiarly similar to third party forgiveness, even though just two parties are involved. As the territory is complicated here, I discuss *seriatim* three sorts of cases, viz., when an injury is done to a person who is

1. unwilling to forgive, even if the offender meets the necessary conditions
2. unable to forgive, even if the offender meets the necessary conditions
3. willing to forgive, if the necessary conditions are met

To begin with (1): if the injured party does not grant forgiveness, for reasons that are not defensible, and if the offender has met the threshold conditions for forgiveness and made every effort to meet the remainder, then may self-forgiveness be in order? It seems objectionable to make forgiveness altogether hostage to the injured party, in such a case; yet the remedy seems once again to be an approximation of forgiveness. One forgives oneself in the name of the person one injured; the possibilities for abuse are great. This suggests that the offender must first of all examine herself, and the injury she did as well as the remedial steps taken, from the standpoint of "any one of us" – that of a detached and impartial spectator. The offender should also feel the victim's warranted resentment against him, vicariously or sympathetically. Next, if the offender is to forgive himself in the victim's voice – if she is entitled to this species of vicarious forgiveness – she must manifest a sort of care for and knowledge of the victim analogous to that required in cases of third-party forgiveness. It is possible that in temporal terms, both will come after the offense itself. Neither may be available to the offender, whether for reasons of the offender's limitations, or because there is no credible narrative as to what the victim would have done in such a situation. In such a case, self-forgiveness is ruled out, even if one is in principle forgivable.

The same holds true of (2), and is relevant in such cases as when the injured party has gone mad, or for psychological reasons refuses to forgive, or is deceased. The last of these is, strangely, a case of being forgiven by the dead, rather than forgiving the dead. The story one tells about the dead will of course affect how one construes this not uncommon situation; the framework here is secular, which in some respects creates greater obstacles here to forgiveness (if it were the case that God could intervene as a representative of the deceased, or if the souls of the deceased could speak from the afterlife, the account would change). As in case (1), the offender would in effect have to sympathetically put herself in the position of the injured party, "as any one of us," express the requisite care and knowledge, and forgive herself on behalf of the injured. Forgiveness under circumstances where the injured person is dead or otherwise unable to react appropriately is irremediably imperfect, because all of the conditions we would wish to have met cannot be.

Given the attractions of self-love, and the respect due the victim, it is particularly important that in cases of type (3), where the injured party is capable of receiving and considering a request for forgiveness, the offender's self-forgiveness waits upon the forgiveness of the injured party. Else one of the conditions for asking for forgiveness has been violated, viz., that the offender address her victim in the ways described and ask for something she has not yet received, viz., forgiveness. If self-forgiveness has already lifted the burden of guilt, the address to the injured party looks to be a formality, and a form of disrespect.

If the injured party does grant forgiveness, all of the conditions I have specified being fulfilled, does there remain a place for self-forgiveness? It seems to me that the answer is affirmative, and this constitutes a transitional moment to the topic of self-forgiveness for injuries done to oneself. One would think that self-forgiveness would follow unproblematically (from a conceptual and even existential standpoint) from forgiveness for injuries done to others. If your victim has quite properly forgiven you, how could you be warranted in not forgiving yourself? In such a case, does not forgiveness entail self-forgiveness? Would we not suspect a negative answer of betraying a bit of rigoristic moralizing ("I have even higher standards for forgiveness than does my victim, so dutiful am I"), secret pride, or self-hatred, as the case may be?

It does seem that all the conditions for forgiveness having been fulfilled, there are no further norms to be met by oneself or anybody else, *with respect to the injury to the other*. Admittedly, the phenomenology of the subject includes familiar cases in which a person is forgiven but continues to struggle with the burden of guilt, even to the point of being unable to fulfill optimally the commitment to change her ways. Tempting though it is to speak of the need for "self-forgiveness" here, though, it would be more accurate to speak of the need to *accept* the forgiveness one has rightly been offered. Should pathology of one sort or another (secret pride, or what have you) prevent it, then the answer to it is not so much self-forgiveness as it is some sort of self-examination and therapy that brings the sentiments into harmony with the moral facts of the matter.

However, *with respect to the injury one has done to oneself* – precisely in injuring another – there remains a role for self-forgiveness. So forgiveness and self-forgiveness are distinct at both conceptual and existential levels. In the latter case, the forgiving and forgiven parties are in some sense the same.

[iv.b] Self-Forgiveness for Injuries to Oneself

Is it possible to injure oneself? The answer is plainly affirmative. Indeed, we may distinguish two ways one may do so; first, as just noted, when one does wrong to others, one also injures oneself (say, by becoming the sort of person who does wrong, by betraying one's moral principles, and so forth). Second, one can injure oneself in all sorts of obvious ways without necessarily involving others – though others may indirectly and unintentionally suffer as well. For example, drug abuse, or frittering away large amounts of time, may count as self-injury. We speak without a sense of paradox of self-hatred, of being angry with or reproaching oneself for doing such and such to oneself, self-recrimination, disgust with or contempt for self, and of self-doubt. We accept the notion of having compassion for oneself, sympathizing with oneself, grasping one's own limitations and fallibility (to that extent, one's humanity), and even of punishing oneself. So self-forgiveness for injury caused by oneself to oneself does not seem incoherent. And yet the idea is puzzling in at least two ways.

First, it would seem that the injured party – oneself – does not *resent* the injury done. The notion of resentment of self, with its Butlerian "abuses" led by the retributive desire for revenge, makes little sense here (something similar would hold, say, with respect to the idea of envying oneself). Because forgiveness is the moderation of resentment, and ultimately the forswearing thereof, it seems that there is no such thing as forgiving oneself for injuries one has done to oneself. One does not normally feel outraged by one's injuries to oneself.

Presumably we speak of hating but not resenting oneself because of the retributive impulse embedded in resentment. "Settled anger" has so strong a tendency to objectify the injurer, to picture the offender as so thoroughly "other" and therefore not-oneself, to wish for massive retaliation, that talk of resenting oneself – even when one hates oneself – sounds inappropriate. Self-forgiveness for injuries done to oneself seems better understood as the moderation and then letting go of self-hatred rather than of self-resentment.

Admittedly, the phenomenology is complex. For we do speak of self-punishment, and in extreme cases speak of ourselves as less than human, as not worthy of being alive, and such. Our earlier discussion of the "moral monster" problem is relevant here. Self-hatred may shade into self-demonization, and that self-conception is (with rare exceptions, perhaps) no more accurate than the conception of another wrong-doer as monstrous. Like the "abuses" of resentment about which Butler warned, self-reproach too is liable to unwarranted expression, from which it follows that extreme self-hatred may itself express a kind of vice (and not just be the warranted affective recognition of vice). If the wrong-doing "part" of oneself is imagined as a monster, an enemy or ogre, the result is likely not only self-alienation but self-contempt, and therewith the impossibility of self-forgiveness, indeed of any kind of moral self-improvement. For on the one hand, one's self qua wrong-doer is being viewed as evil incarnate, as incapable of taking any of the steps requisite for becoming a candidate for forgiveness, and hence as irredeemable. In one's own eyes, one no longer possesses dignity or basic moral worth. Self-forgiveness could not restore basic dignity; rather, it assumes a perspective from which the self already possesses it. On the other hand, one's demonized self is being viewed, in this extreme instance of self-hatred, as "other" – as somehow not oneself. But then, forgiveness of *oneself* is impossible. While the moral problem to which self-forgiveness responds undoubtedly involves self-redemption, it would seem impossible to take the requisite steps unless there is sufficient psychic unity present to make sense of such notions as "taking responsibility for oneself." Morally successful self-forgiveness does not excuse, condone, or forget. It acts in view of a hope for reconciliation with self that over time may be experienced as wholeness.

This brings us to the second way in which the idea of self-forgiveness is puzzling, viz., with respect to the old problem of identity of self through time. A true case of multiple personalities would present a very different sort of question here (in such a case, self-forgiveness would not be an issue, because by stipulation there would be no unitary self to forgive and be forgiven). If anything like injuring oneself is to make sense, there has to be a distinction between aspects of self, but one that does not come to positing multiple personalities – between injured and injuring self, even as both identify themselves as (parts of) the same self. In the discussion of interpersonal forgiveness, I argued that narrative plays an important part. Although I will not develop the point here, narrative may also help to explain the identity of self through time, or at least more narrowly, the sense in which self-now can both identify with self-past and benefit from the perspective of distance in a way that makes self-forgiveness possible.

Fortunately it is not my present purpose to attempt to sort out the metaphysical issues, so I shall simply note that it is a striking feature of self-relation that the injuring self can change itself for the worse when causing the injury. As a person slips into drug abuse, for example, whatever part of self it is that inflicts the injury on the whole self augments its proclivity to continue inflicting the injury in question. Butler's point holds even here, or especially here: the offender injures himself in doing wrong. At the same time, because in the instant case one is both offender and victim, the prospect of a sort of living unity of the two may hold greater promise for moral transformation and redemption than is normally the case in the scene of interpersonal forgiveness. I have quoted Arendt's comment about forgiveness as "the possible redemption from the predicament of irreversibility"; perhaps self-forgiveness is an exemplary case of this possibility because both offender and victim are the same self, or of the same self.

The reciprocal moral exchange that is forgiveness fits imperfectly into the scene of self-forgiveness, then, but it does fit in part (again, this is why it is a non-paradigmatic form of forgiveness). One must reframe one's view of oneself and see oneself in a new light; make a commitment to change one's ways; confront honestly and fully the injury one has done to oneself; have compassion for oneself, and refrain from objectifying oneself as though one were a "moral monster"; develop a narrative that explains how one came to do wrong, what emendatory steps one will take, and that expresses how one "re-frames" one's view of oneself. As in the interpersonal case, a narrative of oneself as injured and accusing will also be called for. Crucially, one must take responsibility for oneself. The target of forgiveness remains the agent, not the deed. Self-forgiveness too is subject to criteria, just as is interpersonal forgiveness. Because the agent is oneself, and because one sees oneself qua wrong-doer as having failed to live up to the norms one accepts, a loss of self-respect is undoubtedly part of the self-conception addressed by self-forgiveness.[7] A moral case for self-forgiveness, finally, does not assume that self-reproach is always

---

[7] On this point, I am in agreement with M. R. Holmgren, "Self-forgiveness and Responsible Moral Agency," *Journal of Value Inquiry* 32 (1998), p. 76: "The wrong-doer's self-forgiveness may be incompatible with respect for her victim, herself, and her moral obligations if it is undertaken before the process is complete. In that case her self-forgiveness would also not be genuine." For very helpful discussion, see R. S. Dillon's "Self-Forgiveness and Self-Respect."

unjustified – on the contrary, it assumes that it may be justified and then –
for good reasons – cease to be.

With this in mind, let me return to Butler's point that wrong-doing does
"a much greater" injury to the wrong-doer than it does the victim (Butler,
p. 165). Putting aside "much greater," and stipulating that injury to self is
different in character from the victim's injury, the point is persuasive. If
you injure another by cheating her, you do not thereby cheat yourself but
you do debase yourself. From this it would follow that if you are forgiven
for cheating her, there is a related but distinct injury you have also caused
yourself for which you also require forgiveness. Fortunately, in changing
your ways as part of the reciprocal moral relation with the person you
cheated, you are already doing some of what is required in order to be
forgiven yourself. But there may be much more to do with respect to
yourself, such as to mend a habit of rationalizing, or of deceiving yourself
about wrong courses of action, as the case may be.

Indeed, overcoming whatever moral or intellectual vices led you to
cheat – and thus living up to the terms of the forgiveness your victim
granted you – would seem to be impossible unless you forgive yourself as
well. Consider the difficulties you would encounter were you to continue –
after your victim has forgiven you – to regard yourself with moral hatred
for injuries you did *to yourself* when injuring her.[8] There is truth, then,
to the popular view that the self-renewal intrinsic to forgiveness requires
self-forgiveness.

[iv.c] Self-Forgiveness for Injuries One Could Not Help Inflicting

I would like to conclude this discussion of self-forgiveness by returning
to a thought mentioned when we discussed Aristotle: "there is pardon
(*sungnômê*), whenever someone does a wrong action because of conditions of a sort that overstrain human nature, and that no one would
endure" (*NE* 1110a24–26). Aristotle is not talking about self-forgiveness,
and we are not talking here about continence. But it does seem that suc-
cumbing to excessive pain in a way that injures others as well as, possibly,
oneself, can give rise to guilt, a loss of self-respect, and a question as to
whether one can forgive oneself. I have in mind the victims of torture

---

[8] C. Card argues that self-forgiveness makes sense "as renunciation of self-blame," and
that "some self-forgiveness may be requisite to that sense of self-worth"; without self-
forgiveness, wrong-doers might not bother to emend their ways. *The Atrocity Paradigm: A
Theory of Evil* (Oxford: Oxford University Press, 2002), p. 176.

who "break" and give damaging information to the enemy. Sympathetic third parties would no doubt react along the lines of the *NE* passage just quoted. But the victim of torture may have a much harder path to follow, never being quite sure whether she could have held out just a little longer, whether it is forgivable to have broken at all. In discussing what he takes to be the severest form of guilt, James Stockdale writes:

> ours was the Epictetus guilt of self-betrayal: we had not anticipated our fragility, did not know that the cultivated gentleman of confidence could be, with the right techniques and the right violence, reduced to a self-loathing wreck in a period of minutes. In the darkness of our isolation we repeated to ourselves endlessly: 'I could have hung on longer before I submitted; I could have kept silent if I had just had more courage.' 'I can never face my friends again.'

Stockdale recounts that he instructed his fellow captives of the North Vietnamese that they would retain their self-respect as well as be forgiven if each suffered torture before giving in, but suffered only to the point where he retained his wits for the next interrogation. In addition, they communicated about what they had divulged to the enemy; this served both a strategic purpose (helping each face the next round of torture more effectively) and prevented each from feeling isolated in guilt and shame. In effect it made one's injurious deeds public, and submitted them to the relevant moral community. Stockdale himself recognized in the late goings that he had reached his limit, and attempted suicide. A doctor somehow saved him, and not long after he and the other inmates of the "Hanoi Hilton" were released. On the whole, the officers who followed his counsel did retain their self-respect in spite of the pain, humiliation, and degradation to which they were subjected.[9]

My suggestion is that under these extreme circumstances, where one does injury solely because one is injured in ways beyond what is endurable, self-forgiveness is necessary, though unavoidably imperfect. It is the latter because the tie here to responsibility for one's actions is nebulous at best. Strictly speaking, it makes no sense to forgive oneself for something for which one is not responsible. Yet in the case under consideration,

---

9 The lines just quoted are from his *Thoughts of a Philosophical Fighter Pilot* (Stanford: Hoover Institution Press, 1995), p. 181 (see also p. 7). On p. 196 he discusses the strategies for maintaining self-respect in the face of torture, and on p. 200 his attempted suicide. See also *In Love and War* by J. Stockdale and S. Stockdale (New York: Harper and Row, 1984) for their extensive account of his saga (e.g., see p. 252 on communicating to fellow prisoners on what they divulged). It is noteworthy that Stockdale and his comrades did not forgive those few officers who collaborated with the enemy, and unsuccessfully attempted to have them prosecuted later.

talk of "excusing" or "pardoning" oneself does not do credit to the sentiment of guilt one is likely to feel, or to the sense in which one *takes* responsibility.[10] Allowing that we may speak of self-forgiveness here, certain standards obtain, namely those of the sort Stockdale promulgated: a recognition of one's own humanity and therefore limits, the refusal to "sell out" in light of pleasurable inducements, the decision to keep going for as long as possible in ways consistent with the preservation of life as well as honor, and a clear as well as public recognition of what wrong one has done (in this case, what one has divulged). Self-forgiveness in such a case does not meet all the criteria I have set out. But like the other imperfect instance of forgiveness I have discussed, it is nonetheless worth understanding and accepting, at least in instances where exculpatory excuse is not unquestionably the correct and sole response.

[v] FORGIVENESS AND MORAL LUCK

Fortune, which governs the world, has some influence where we should be least willing to allow her any, and directs in some measure the sentiments of mankind, with regard to the character and conduct both of themselves and others.... Every body agrees to the general maxim, that as the event does not depend on the agent, it ought to have no influence upon our sentiments, with regard to the merit or propriety of his conduct. But when we come to particulars, we find that our sentiments are scarce in any one instance exactly conformable to what this equitable maxim would direct.   Adam Smith, *Theory of Moral Sentiments* II.iii.3.1.

As I have analyzed the virtue of forgivingness, it is peculiarly intertwined with the vagaries of fortune and accident, at several different levels. To a large extent this is arguably true of all the virtues: absent possession of the appropriate material goods, for example, it is difficult to exercise the virtue of beneficence. Or imagine that a child born to a mother addicted to cocaine may be doomed to a difficult struggle to control her own subsequent intake on the drug. Self-control or temperance may be affected by such events. A person who has world class gifts as a pianist

---

[10] As J. Blustein rather nicely puts it, "One cannot forgive oneself for what one has done if one is not prepared to take responsibility for it, and the explanation of the failure to take responsibility for some problematic part of one's past might be that one cannot or will not forgive oneself for it." "On Taking Responsibility for One's Past," *Journal of Applied Philosophy* 17 (2000), p. 17. Blustein distinguishes useful between responsibility for one's past and *taking* responsibility (which has a distinctly forward-looking dimension, and commits itself to emendatory action; pp. 7–8). He also ties the idea of taking responsibility for one's past to *narrative*, with an emphasis on the ideas of retrospective creation of unity, meaning, and on "thematisation."

may never be able to develop them fully, if arthritis or some other such misfortune strikes. It comes as no surprise that forgiveness too is affected by fortune, though this fact has not been discussed in the literature on the subject. The surprising vulnerability of forgiveness to luck, as well as the particular points of vulnerability, are worth analyzing. The imperfection of the human world forms the backdrop of my discussion of forgiveness; and as contingency is one aspect thereof, a brief discussion of luck offers further specificity to our theme.

Bernard Williams proposed the intentionally paradoxical sounding notion of "moral luck" in order to draw attention to the pervasive influence of luck in moral life.[11] The immediate target of the idea is Kant's thesis that, as Nagel puts it in the just-cited piece, "there cannot be moral risk" (p. 24); the moral lies entirely within the scope of the voluntary. Of course he also recognizes the antiquity of the idea. We saw in Chapter 1 that several major philosophical views rejected forgiveness as a virtue in good part because of their perfectionist thrust. They developed pictures of the perfectly virtuous person – the Sage, the noble soul – whose self-assessment and happiness are insulated from contingency. And yet we also recognize in common life that much of what we do, and much of who we become, does depend on luck; our moral assessments have as their object intentions, states of affairs, or relations in the world that are in one way or another affected by luck. Consequently our assessments are themselves affected by luck.

It is not my purpose to address the comprehensive themes at stake in the Williams or Nagel articles or the disagreements between the two. I do want to recall several of their distinctions between *kinds* of moral luck, and to see how they bear on the scene of forgiveness. These are as follows:

a. "incident luck," which is what we often mean by "luck" – those unanticipated events we take to be unforeseeable that "happen" to us for good or ill, and that define one's circumstances (in Nagel's terms, this is "circumstantial luck," and concerns "the kind of problems and situations one faces"; p. 28);

---

[11] B. Williams, "Moral Luck," in his *Moral Luck* (Cambridge: Cambridge University Press, 1993): pp. 20–39. At the start of his "Moral Luck: a Postscript," Williams notes that when he introduced the expression he "expected it to suggest an oxymoron." In *Making Sense of Humanity* (Cambridge: Cambridge University Press, 1995), p. 241. Williams' original paper was responded to by T. Nagel's "Moral Luck," reprinted in *Mortal Questions* (Cambridge: Cambridge University Press, 1988), pp. 24–38. My paginal references from Williams and Nagel advert to these texts.

   b. "constitutive luck," those events outside of our control that help
      make us who we are (this would include what sort of family and
      culture one is born in to, what historical period, what early educa-
      tion one had, one's health, and such (as Nagel puts it, p. 28, luck
      concerning "your inclinations, capacities, and temperament"));
   c. "luck in the way one's actions and projects turn out" (Nagel, p. 28).

It goes without saying that these three kinds of luck are mutually implicated. For example, the sorts of problems and situations you face will
affect the sort of person you are.

From the standpoint of the injured person, forgiveness is obviously
responsive to (a); for the injury itself was, presumably, unwilled, and
in its specificity at least unanticipated. For all one knew, things might
have been otherwise. Perhaps if one had been in a different place at a
different time, the injury would not have taken place. It is possible to tell
a story according to which the offender too is subject to circumstantial
luck.

Forgiveness is also responsive to (b), on the parts of both the offender
and injured. The capacities of the one to do wrong, and then to ask for
forgiveness, have a history that is subject to constitutive luck; and so too
the capacity to extend forgiveness. "There but for the grace of God go
I" is a commonly noted sentiment. The injured party may be unable, for
reasons deeply embedded in her character, or by reason of the profound
damage done by the wrong, ever to let go of lingering resentment. Further, the willingness of the injured party to attempt to forgive hinges in
part on the ability of the offender to take the appropriate steps. And the
ability of the offender to release herself from guilt depends in part on
the victim's ability to take the appropriate steps. The dyadic character of
interpersonal forgiveness entwines two lines of luck, so to speak. Each
party's vulnerability to luck is augmented by the independence required
for the completed moral exchange.

So too with (c): had the offender's bullet missed, and the victim not
been badly injured, things would have been very different. Once forgiveness is entered into, both parties make commitments to change in
certain ways; but these projects are subject to luck, and may not yield fruit.
I remarked in Chapter 1 that the degree of resentment the victim feels
ought to be in proportion to the degree of the wrong intended; and yet as
Butler also noted, we resent the evil deed more than we do the intention
to do the deed. And I would agree that the standard of proportionality is
to be consistent with the phenomenology of the sentiments, that is, it will

go along with ascribing greater weight to the deed than to the intention alone. In this way too, moral assessment is influenced by luck.

Adam Smith referred to the pervasive influence of luck in the judgments of common moral life as an "irregularity" of the moral sentiments (see *TMS* II.iii.intro.6, II.iii.3.2). It is an irregularity that very much affects the sentiments of anger and resentment, and correlatively, judgments as to what to forgive and when. Smith "justifies" (if that is the right word) the irregularity, and its huge effects on human life, with utilitarian arguments as well as with dire predictions of the consequences were we to assess character and conduct from the standpoint of reason alone (e.g., *TMS* II.iii.3.2–4). Such arguments help him to accept, rather than seek to emend, "so weak and imperfect a creature as man" (*TMS* II.i.5.10) of the moral world. It is not my present purpose to offer any such justification. But I do point out that the irregularity in question befits the picture of the imperfection of the human world to which forgiveness seeks to respond. That forgiveness itself turns out to share "irregular" features of that to which it responds is not surprising.[12]

---

[12] I am grateful to Aaron Garrett for his comments on a draft of my discussion of moral luck.

4

Political Apology, Forgiveness, and Reconciliation

We have thus far considered interpersonal forgiveness and its modulations. The focus has been on forgiveness in what one might call a private context. Can forgiveness be conceived of as a public, civic, or political virtue as well? The term is certainly used today in a political context, but its meaning is vague and its legitimacy disputed. At times "political forgiveness" seems to describe exchanges that look rather like the giving or the appeal for pardon, clemency, debt relief, or reconciliation.[1]

The backdrop to our inquiry continues to be the fact of imperfection, as well as a critique of the impulse to respond to imperfection by fleeing, in one way or another, from the world. What would reconciliation with the moral imperfections of the political and social world look

---

[1] "Political forgiveness" is now a widely used phrase (indeed it is the title of a major book on the subject by Digeser). I shall be using the term "political" in an extremely broad sense, to indicate a sphere of relations that is public, and governed (at least notionally) by the community's norms. Consider C. G. Flood's *Political Myth: a Theoretical Introduction* (New York: Garland, 1996), p. 5. He defines "political" as "referring to either (a) the spheres of social organization and action covered by the principal fields of political science as an academic discipline – namely, government, public administration, political behaviour, political theory, and international relations; or (b) other spheres of social organization and action, such as the economic, the juridical, the religious, the educational, the ethnic, matters of gender, and the artistic, insofar as they are pertinent to the political as defined under (a); or (c) the historical dimension of any of the areas figuring in (a) or (b)." This is rough and ready, but pretty well captures what I shall mean by "political," including when it modifies "apology." For a succinct overview of the debate about the meaning of "political" see R. Dahl, *Modern Political Analysis*, 3rd ed. (Englewood Cliffs, NJ: Prentice-Hall, 1976). On p. 3 he defines "a political system as any persistent pattern of human relationships that involves, to a significant extent, control, influence, power, or authority." Again, this definition serves my present purposes well enough. (My thanks to Barnabas Malnay for discussion of these points.)

like? Perhaps the chief reason for despairing that anything like forgiveness or apology could provide the answer is the sheer magnitude, pervasiveness, and on-goingness of wrong-doing and injury. The chronicle of peoples devouring each other and themselves is almost too painful to contemplate. The incalculable extent of suffering that humans have caused throughout their short history, the immense mountains that the bones of the unjustly killed would form, the vast lakes their blood would fill, not to mention the evidence that the rate of slaughter is increasing rather than decreasing, encourage the judgment that collective human life is irredeemable. Slivers of hope would hang on the chance that an individual soul may somehow escape the wheel of suffering.

Yet any such conclusion overlooks the real and qualitative difference between degrees of moral evil that societies habitually inflict, as well as the fact that reconciliation and something resembling forgiveness can and do take place at the political level. It is the purpose of this chapter to achieve clarity about these notions. As to how far they may contribute to any optimism about the emendability of collective life, and as to the analysis of the social and political conditions under which these rays of hope are encouraged, it is not the aim of this chapter to discuss.

[i] APOLOGY AND FORGIVENESS WRIT LARGE: QUESTIONS AND DISTINCTIONS

Do forgiveness and apology have a political dimension? A moment's reflection on several of the examples cited in previous chapters – those of Margaret Hassan (murdered in Iraq), Amy Biehl and Eugene de Kock (a victim and a murderer, respectively, in South Africa), and of Jean Améry (a victim of the Holocaust) – certainly suggest an affirmative answer. Violence rarely takes place in a political vacuum; it normally is conditioned by the political and social context, and even in some sense motivated by it (de Kock, for example, was a paid agent of the apartheid state, carrying out its orders). Something similar could be said of a less blatantly political example, such as spousal abuse – its political and social dimensions have been much discussed. The narratives of the individuals involved in interpersonal forgiveness (whether in the model case, or nonparadigmatic cases) may very well have an explicitly political dimension (all of those just mentioned certainly do, or would). So this is one sense in which we might speak of forgiveness as "political." But in this broad sense, just about every moral notion is political (think of courage, for example), and we have not isolated a distinctive political role for forgiveness. And while nothing I have said in previous chapters is intended to deny the relevance and importance of the political aspect of interpersonal injury and forgiveness, the distinction I drew (following Bishop Butler) between forgiveness and the administration of justice was intended to carve out a separate space for each (such that, for example, one could forgive some-one while also affirming the justice of their punishment as specified by the legal system).

The paradigmatically dyadic character of interpersonal forgiveness may, however, be tied to the political and legal in another more robust way. At some historical junctures, interpersonal considerations of forgive-ness may carry explicit political weight (e.g., through their symbolism), and possibly have political as well as judicial consequences. I am thinking of moments when regimes and conceptions of justice change, and the scene of forgiveness is public and political. Eugene de Kock's request for forgiveness from the widows of several people he killed was made in an open session of the South African Truth and Reconciliation Commission (TRC). While the request itself was made in relative privacy (with attor-neys and presumably prison guards present), the results were very widely broadcast (see footnote 36, ch. 2). Though I have no reason to doubt the genuineness of his appeal, de Kock was hoping to qualify for amnesty (which would have been considered under a separate but related TRC proceeding). Requesting forgiveness before the TRC was not required, but to repeat, the moment was nonetheless inextricably bound up with the political revolution the TRC was designed to further. Now, this sort of example begins to touch upon a sense of "political forgiveness" I have in mind – for it is just the sort of scene Archbishop Tutu, among oth-ers, wished to encourage at that stage of South Africa's history – and in a moment I shall discuss the thesis that forgiveness is to be publicly encouraged on account of its civic benefits. It is certainly the case that forgiveness is here extended into the political realm.

Is there a species of forgiveness that is appropriate to an explicitly political setting, and is tied to the political goal of reconciliation? Is there a coherent concept of "political forgiveness" distinct from pardon, clemency, mercy, the dismissal of debt, and interpersonal forgiveness?

Let us recall that in the Prologue, I drew a distinction between con-cepts bearing a Wittgensteinian "family resemblance" to one another. To reiterate, these siblings of forgiveness include:

   a. *political apology*: this encompasses a cluster of phenomena con-
      cerned with the giving and accepting acknowledgment of

wrong-doing, always in relation to some political entity (be it a state, corporation, church, or other institution or organization in civil society).

b. *economic forgiveness*, i.e., the forgiveness of debts.

c. *political pardon*: this encompasses a cluster of phenomena, including prominently the pardon that a duly recognized member of a non-judicial branch of government may grant (in the American system, an "executive pardon" issued by the President); the granting of amnesty, either by an individual or a group, either to an individual or a group; the decision by the victorious state or its leader not to punish the defeated, for any of a number of reasons including strategic or political advantage, or a sense of humanity (this last easily shades into "mercy"). Executive pardon may amount to a grant of immunity, without necessarily implying guilt or that a set punishment is suspended.

d. *judicial pardon*: the exercise of mercy or clemency by a court of law, in view of extenuating circumstances, such as the suffering already undergone by the guilty party. Normally this would come to obviating a set (the expected, or already determined) punishment. As in (b), the pardoner must have recognized standing to issue the pardon, and the pardoned has, at least in some cases of (b) and in all of (c), committed offences as defined by the law of the land.

As should by now be clear from my extensive analysis of the model case of interpersonal forgiveness, sense (b) is not really about "forgiveness," in spite of the ancient use of the word in this context. (I have also argued that forgiveness is not to be understood on analogy with the "forgiveness" of debts.) Further, while a response to wrongdoing is at issue in contexts (c) and (d), they too are not about forgiveness in the paradigmatic or moral sense. In neither of them is the individual *forgiven* for his or her wrongdoing, even though a response to wrongdoing is at issue. Normally the pardoner, in cases (c) and (d), will not be the person who was injured, or at least not have been intentionally singled out to be wronged. To reiterate: in (b), (c), and (d) there is no necessary tie to any specific sentiment; in particular, pardon does not necessarily require the giving up of resentment on the part of the injured, and does not necessarily require contrition on the part of the offender. In all three of these cases, any mix of economic, legal, political, and even military considerations may motivate the request for or granting of the dismissal of debt, pardon, or mercy. But what is at stake is neither forgiveness nor apology, and consequently I have not analyzed them in this book.[2]

Ought we to be speaking of "forgiveness" as functioning within a political context, and not just as having a political context (in roughly the way that every moral concept and exchange has a political context)? There are certainly phenomena – such as the apologies issued by states to those they have injured – that look like forgiveness in some respects. And what is an apology (one might think) if not a request for forgiveness? As my use of the term "apology" rather than "forgiveness" suggests, however, there are disanalogies too. By way of sorting this out, let us compare the conditions to be met by the offender and the injured party if forgiveness is to come about, to the conditions for apology relevant to the political level. In effect, I am inquiring about the relation between a moral concept at home at the interpersonal level, and its kindred concept (for it will turn out to be kindred, and not exactly the same) at the public level.

In framing the inquiry in this way, I mean to preserve the idea that political apology is not to be analyzed as a modulation of interpersonal forgiveness – as one of its non-paradigmatic or (logically) deficient modes – but as a member of the same family of concepts. It will share some characteristics but not others with interpersonal forgiveness. A chief goal of this chapter is to map out that "complicated network of similarities" (to quote Wittgenstein once again). It will turn out that some features of deficient or non-paradigmatic interpersonal forgiveness – specifically the third-party, or proxy structure of forgiveness – are deeply pertinent to political apology.[3] Even there, however, the characteristics of proxy or substitution or representation differ from their relatives in the private realm. Political apology is not a species of non-paradigmatic forgiveness. What explains these differences between forgiveness and public apology?

The answer is that the political sphere possesses structural characteristics, tensions, and dynamics that in relevant and significant ways differ from those present in the interpersonal context upon which I have thus far focused. It will not be surprising if interpersonal and political apology map onto each other only imperfectly. The one may bring with it

---

[2] For an excellent philosophical discussion of political and judicial pardon see Moore's *Pardons: Justice, Mercy, and the Public Interest.* I noted in Chapter 1 that the problem of the relation of justice, mercy, and clemency is ancient, having been discussed by Seneca among others.

[3] Unless otherwise noted, by "apology" I shall mean, in this chapter, only political apology, not interpersonal or private apology.

tensions – say, between forgiveness and justice – that were not pertinent at the other level.[4]

First, I note the sheer complexity of the public realm, evident in the inevitable conflict and multiplicity of perspectives, interests, and passions; in the multiplicity of civic and governmental organizations or "bodies"; and in its past. Every offer of apology, and acceptance or rejection thereof, will likely involve or have involved dispute at both ends, when more than one person is involved. It is quite unlikely that a single self-same sentiment (such as resentment, sorrow, regret) will animate all parties concerned. Further, the historical narrative of a society records as well as represents the movement of complexity over time, and will itself be as complex as it is liable to controversy. The question as to whose narrative it is, and under whose control it lies, is ever-present. This level of complexity does not present itself at the level of interpersonal forgiveness.

Second, the scene of political apology or forgiveness will be inflected by efforts to anticipate the consequences for the individual actors as well as relevant political entity, locally and perhaps internationally. Note that apologies offered at the political level may bring with them the possibility of legal liability, a threat that surely affects its formulation (typically, at the political level it is terse and guarded, whereas at the interpersonal level it tends to expand into a rhetorically forceful narrative). The giving or receiving of an apology may also entail financial consequences, such as restitution. In the public or political realm, then, the moral exchange that is apology mixes with money, liability, and power in a way that is not characteristic of interpersonal forgiveness. Still further, the consequences at the political level are inflected by the invisible hand effect, i.e., the "law of unintended consequences." The above-mentioned complexity makes it extremely difficult to determine the consequences, especially long-range consequences, of initiatives or actions, and in addition unintended outcomes are all but guaranteed.

Third, political authority is inseparable from representation, that is, from the notion that X acts in the name of (or by virtue of, or by grace of) Y. This is as true in a governmental organization as it is in a non-governmental one (such as a corporation or church). The "proxy" structure already mentioned is much more deeply embedded in politics than it is in exchanges between individuals in the private sphere. For the very idea of an organized group having an identity that allows it to exercise

[4] I am grateful to James Sheehan and Margaret Anderson for helpful discussion about these issues.

agency as though it were an individual – let alone to apologize or forgive – itself relies on a kind of substitution of the group for its members, or if you like, it relies on a metaphor (viz., that the group is an individual).

Political apologies are typically offered by persons not themselves injured, and on behalf of those who were. This vicarious expression of contrition speaks on behalf of individuals; strikingly, the individuals in question may never be identified. The reach of proxy or representation (that has an "on behalf of" structure) may exceed that which we discussed in connection with non-paradigmatic forgiveness. At the political level, the spokesperson for a political entity may apologize for an injury committed by that body even though neither the spokesperson nor any of its current members may personally be responsible for committing the wrong, the individuals injured may be long since deceased, and the political entity may itself be only distantly related to its offending ancestor.

Consequently, political apology and its acceptance will take a thoroughly *symbolic* form. The moral exchange is somehow to be accomplished primarily if not entirely through that medium; and this is quite unlike the dyadic exchange in interpersonal forgiveness, even in its non-paradigmatic forms.

Finally, while we do speak of political sentiments, it is not clear at the outset that they here play the same role as the sentiments ascribed to individuals. Some of the language associated with forgiveness is natural at the political level (e.g., we speak of "class resentment"), and some not (e.g., the notion of an institution or organization being "contrite" sounds hollow). Some is clearly metaphorical, as when we speak of "the nation" being angered, or proud, or what have you. All this makes it very doubtful that the close connection between the moderation and the forswearing of resentment and interpersonal forgiveness is reproducible at the political level.

It should by now be clearer why political apology cannot be conceptualized as a form of non-paradigmatic forgiveness. We may also bring out the point in this way: one can address a request for forgiveness to a victim who is dead and for whom there is no proxy representation except the notional moral community; but one could not address a political apology to nobody in particular. Either the victim must be capable of receiving the apology, or there must exist representatives thereof who are identifiable at least as a category (say, the descendants of the victim); there has to be at least one descendant, even not identified by name. And one can imagine, I argued, granting a request for forgiveness to someone who is unwilling or unable to request it, imperfect though that transaction would be. But one could not accept an apology from someone who is unwilling or unable to offer it.

The logic of political apology, unlike that of forgiveness, requires that the parties on both sides of the equation exist, even if the transaction occurs solely through proxies (they must of course have standing to count as proxies). So while it is true that non-paradigmatic forgiveness and political apology share a reliance on proxy (substitution, representation), political apology is more closely reliant conceptually on traceable links from the willingly involved parties to the parties originally concerned. And yet, unlike paradigmatic forgiveness, the parties involved need not be the individuals originally concerned (neither the offender nor victim), indeed they need not be *individuals* except in the metaphorical sense that a social or political body is an individual. Perhaps another way to put this is to note that there can be no "third-party" political apology. Third-party forgiveness dwells in the subjunctive mood (speaking of what X would have said or done, had that been possible, and as a consequence what one is warranted in saying or doing); apology by proxy dwells in the indicative mood, and there is rarely even a pretense concerning what the original offender or victim would have done or said under the circumstances.

I argued that non-paradigmatic forms of forgiveness would be logically and humanly completed by fulfillment of the conditions met in paradigmatic forgiveness; if it turned out that those conditions could be met, we would wish for them to be met. By contrast, we do not wish, and have no grounds for wishing, that political apology meet the conditions of paradigmatic interpersonal forgiveness. To do otherwise would be to misunderstand the categorial differences between the political and the interpersonal. This is yet another way of seeing why political apology is not an imperfect form or interpersonal forgiveness, even though it shares features with it.

As already noted, it has been argued that "political forgiveness" is characterized precisely by its lack of relation to sentiment.[5] Phrases such as "we regret" or "we apologize" when uttered in a political context are not reports of sentiments – at least not necessarily – but are speech acts aiming at some different purpose. (I do not deny that they may have an *effect* on

---

[5] Digeser, *Political Forgiveness*, pp. 21, 28. He admits that his use of the term forgiveness "runs headlong into ordinary uses of the word" (p. 21). Digeser also holds both that political forgiveness cannot succeed where conditions of (rectificatory) justice have not been met, and that it is not just a modulation of justice but a "supplement" to it (p. 6). I would certainly agree that if political forgiveness cannot be distinguished from rectificatory justice, it ought not be called "forgiveness."

the sentiments, however.) It would seem that the force of political apology
is independent of sentiment or motive. But then ought we to speak of
political *forgiveness* at all? My answer is negative. I am arguing that the use
of the term in this context is for the most part misleading, and that we
should speak of "apology" instead.

We saw that forgiveness is necessarily connected to the sentiments. I
briefly raised the question of their connection to political apology, and
return to that point now. It seems to me that one function of an official, ritual, or ceremonial expression of apology and regret, offered in a
political context, is precisely to communicate a moral point publicly and
impersonally. By this I mean that the person or entity (say, "The University of Alabama" or "The Aetna Life Insurance Company") can utter the
requisite phrases sincerely and meaningfully but not necessarily in a way
that reports the speaker's sentiments.[6] When the apology has the character of proxy or substitution – its speaker or author represents others,
speaks or writes in their name or in the name of the entity of which they
form or formed part – the point is even clearer. The spokesperson for the
corporation in question may experience no relevant personal feelings at
all; so too "the insurance company" as an abstract entity; and perhaps
none of its chief officers or current employees.

The presence of the sentiment of resentment in the person(s) or political entity to whom the "formal apology" is addressed is also a contingent
matter, so far as the normativity of the exchange is concerned. As noted,
the addressees may long since be deceased, and the wrongs in question
inflicted generations ago. The causal connection between the original
injury and the welfare of the descendants of the injured may be extremely
difficult if not impossible to document.

For such reasons that pertain both to the offender and the injured,
the offering of political apology should not be understood as a request

---

[6] Aetna apologized for "selling policies in the 1850's that reimbursed slave owners for financial losses when their slaves died." The company refused to consider paying reparations,
and apparently did not identify the addressee of its apology. Its spokesperson is quoted
as saying "we express our deep regret over any participation at all in this deplorable
practice." CBS News.com, March 10, 2000, at www.cbsnews.com/stories/2000/03/10/
null/main170356.shtml. In its own press release of March 10, 2000, the company
argues that "we have concluded that, beyond our apology, no further actions are
required, considering our strong, consistent commitment to diversity over many years
and the numerous philanthropic and workplace diversity initiatives we undertake and
for which we have been publicly recognized." See www.aetna.com/news/2000/prtpr_
20000310.htm. The first person plural pronoun functions here as a metaphor, but seems
entirely natural given our ability to picture the collectivity as an individual.

for forgiveness; in which case, the proper response to it is not forgiveness but something else, viz. acceptance. In diplomatic circles, acceptance is often signaled by stating that the apology is "noted"; this verb would mean something very different in the context of interpersonal forgiveness, as one would expect given the relevant differences between the political and private spheres.

My effort to distinguish between apology and forgiveness, and so to resist using the latter term when discussing its conceptual relatives in the public sphere, finds support in the by now enormous presence of the discourse of apology among Western political bodies. One author writes that

> We live in an age where it is nearly impossible to escape the plethora of public apologies made by corporations and politicians alike whether over the airwaves, on prime time television or on the front page of local newspapers. Apologies are common in the context of medical malpractice, attorney disciplinary actions, civil mediation, and victim/offender cases, to name a few. A large body of case law discusses the role of apology, and in addition, a number of legal articles discuss the role of apology in litigation and various forms of alternative dispute resolution.[7]

So far as I can tell, the language of forgiveness is uncommon in this legal literature. The same phenomenon evidently occurs at the level of international relations.[8]

If political apology and forgiveness are dissimilar in the ways indicated, in what ways are they similar (such as to form part of the same "family")?

Political apology will certainly share some of the basic assumptions of interpersonal forgiveness. Both apology and the request for forgiveness assume that an injury has been done; that its author can be identified; that its author takes responsibility for doing the wrong; and therefore that an *excuse* is not being offered. This supplies a basis for distinguishing between apology and the expression of regret; properly speaking, one can apologize only for something that it was within one's power to

---

[7] T. Fuchs-Burnett, "Mass Public Corporate Apology," *Dispute Resolution Journal,* published by the American Arbitration Association, 57 (2002), pp. 27–28; online at: www.findarticles.com/p/articles/mi_qa3923/is_200205/ai_n9060883. For examples of recent public apologies see M. Minow, *Between Vengeance and Forgiveness: Facing History after Genocide and Mass Violence* (Boston: Beacon Press, 1998), pp. 112–117. See also the examples offered by M. Cunningham in "Saying Sorry: The Politics of Apology," *Political Quarterly* 70 (1999): 285–294.

[8] See B. O'Neill, *Honor, Symbols, and War* (Ann Arbor: University of Michigan Press, 1999), ch. 11 ("Apologies") for a helpful discussion of political apology in the international sphere. As he notes, there have been many apologies (his classificatory scheme is useful), and *none* have been answered with statements of *forgiveness* (p. 181).

do otherwise. A well-intentioned mistake that a reasonable person (the stand-in for the moral community, the "impartial spectator" in Adam Smith's phrase) would have made is involuntary. Stipulatively, it is not an instance of culpable negligence. It is therefore an occasion for the expression of regret, but does not entail an apology. An apology will normally be accompanied by the expression of regret, but the obverse is not the case.

Recall Bernard Williams' distinction between agent-regret and regret. As he points out, "the constitutive thought of regret in general is something like 'how much better if it had been otherwise.'" Now this sense can be shared by anybody in possession of the relevant information, and can be directed at someone else's actions, by definition externally (since not from the perspective of the agent responsible for those actions, but from the perspective of a spectator). Note too that the events regretted may not have been done voluntarily, though they may have. By contrast, agent-regret not only has as its object the agent's own past actions (or those "in which he regards himself as a participant") but necessarily identifies them as one's own past actions. The perspective is that of the participant and not the spectator. As Williams says, this does not mean that the actions were voluntary, though they may have been. But even where the consequences of one's actions were not willed by the agent, such that no reasonable person would think her culpable, the agent's consciousness of somehow owning them is very different from the spectator's consciousness of the whole sequence. The agent's self-understanding and sentiments are very probably affected by moral luck (see Williams, *Moral Luck*, pp. 27–28). At the political level, the effect of both bad and good fortune on the popular estimation of a (corporate or individual) agent is notoriously great.

How does all this bear on political apology (the only species at stake here)? I have claimed that one can apologize for actions that were not involuntary; that an apology takes responsibility and therefore assumes agency and continuity of agency through time; and that it is typically the case that the person uttering or conveying the apology herself had nothing to do with the actions, but speaks as a representative of or proxy for a collectivity that exercised agency. So the expression of regret that accompanies apology is a peculiar form of agent-regret, necessarily expressed in the first person singular or plural (imagine the spokesperson for a corporation reporting, as a spectator, that "they" regret and apologize for X), but by a person whose own deeds are not an issue and on behalf of an entity that "acts" only in the way that a collectivity, as distinguished from an individual, acts.

Regret expressed without apology, on grounds that the wrong-doing was involuntary, must also be a form of agent-regret, and generally subject in the political realm to the impersonal structure just mentioned. Unapologetic regret implicitly appeals to an excuse or justification; but also concedes that, as in the cases of an individual's regret for the unintended and unforeseeable consequences of actions, an "irregularity of the sentiments" (Adam Smith's phrase again) nonetheless leads one to associate oneself with those consequences and to wish that things had not turned out thus.

Let us consider several additional points of resemblance between forgiveness and political apology. Like forgiveness, political apology is not a request for mercy or clemency; but it is an address to the party injured, and amounts to a request that the moral relationship between the parties involved be restored.

Further, political apology cannot be a mode of forgetting. There are numerous ways in which forgetting, or a resolve to forget, may come about. Unconditional amnesty, for example, may amount to amnesia (as their etymology suggests). Political apology is indissolubly tied to memory, but the obverse is not the case. As we will see in Chapter 5, it is possible to memorialize, even in a way that recognizes valor in a doubtful cause, without apologizing.

Political apology depends on truthful statement of the facts of the case, and is undercut by avoidance thereof. Correlatively, political apology aims to free its beneficiaries from the past in such a way as to promote a desirable future. Similarly, we noted that forgiveness attempts to free the future from being determined by the injuries and resentments of the past. What counts as desirable depends in part on the specification of ideals. These are not altogether the same as the ideals we discussed in connection with forgiveness, though there is overlap. And both the offering and receiving of political apology are responsive to reasons. There will be grounds for its exercise, and correspondingly there may be grounds for refusing to offer or receive an offer thereof, just as in the case of interpersonal forgiveness (these grounds will turn out to consist solely in the offender failing to meet the requirements of apology).

Political apology, then, is a norm-governed concept. An apology has not been offered, or accepted, simply because one declares that it has been. This is another crucial point it has in common with interpersonal or dyadic forgiveness. As a consequence, there are some political gestures, decisions, and initiatives that will *not* count as political apology, even though they may share its end of bringing about reconciliation.

For example, peace accords that simply reach a settlement and broker terms for the cessation of hostilities have nothing to do with apology. I have already mentioned another example, viz., *unconditional* amnesty that is unaccompanied by any public recognition of or accounting for the wrongs done.[9] Variations on the amnesty theme are many, stretching from the Athenian amnesty of 403 BCE, to the amnesty Chile's General Pinochet granted to himself and his cohort in 1978, to mention but two interesting and well studied examples.[10]

I am going to flesh out the conceptual structure of political apology by studying a series of candidates for apology. These examples also offer instructive lessons about the diversity of contexts for apology, as well as the complexities and nuances of the concept. This is a realm in which attention to the particulars provides the best avenue into grasping the topic.

[ii] POLITICAL APOLOGY AMONG THE ONE AND MANY

The first set of examples I should like to study may be understood as "many to many" exchanges. That is, they concern the acknowledgement of and

---

[9] If an amnesty is unconditional, then it cannot be the expression of forgiveness. But even if it is conditional (say, on the offender's contrition), and would obviate what otherwise would be just punishment, it is not the expression of forgiveness – for as I have argued, the spheres of forgiveness and politics move at different levels. Rather, it is a prudential judgment that all things considered civic peace requires the measure. Perhaps at a time of regime change, amnesty conditional on truth telling (as in the recent South African case) also serves the end of civic reconciliation by establishing a detailed public record of the injustices committed. But that is not to say that the amnesty is granted *because* the offenders are forgiven. For an argument against the idea that amnesty could express forgiveness, see C. Bennett's "Is Amnesty a Collective Act of Forgiveness?," *Contemporary Political Theory* 2 (2003): 67–76.

[10] The Amnesty of 403 BCE prevented another round of blood letting when the victorious democrats retook Athens from the oligarchs. It did not extend to the oligarchs themselves unless they passed a review of the way in which they had discharged their office, but gave amnesty to "those [supporters of the oligarchy] who had been convicted, or who faced trial, on a wide range of criminal and political charges." The amnesty also "proscribed the raising of any malicious references to past offences," as noted by J. Atkinson, "Truth and Reconciliation the Athenian Way," *Acta Classica* 42 (1999), p. 5. As Atkinson explains, complex provisions for the return of confiscated property were also instituted (pp. 8–9). Interestingly, while expressions of apology or contrition were not demanded, the reinstallation of the democrats in power was performed through a series of complex and powerful ceremonies and rituals. See B. Strauss, "Ritual, Social Drama and Politics in Classical Athens," *American Journal of Ancient History* 10 (1985): 67–83. Concerning the very complicated Chilean case, see A. Barahone de Brito, "Passion, Constraint, Law, and *Fortuna*: The Human Rights Challenge to Chilean Democracy," in *Burying the Past: Making Peace and Doing Justice after Civil Conflict*, ed. N. Biggar (Washington, DC: Georgetown University Press, 2007), pp. 150–183.

contrition for wrong-doing offered by the relevant political body, be it the state, an organized group, institution, or corporation. In such cases apology is offered by the appropriate official or spokesperson. Especially in cases where that person is the leader of a nation, the apology may sound as though it is offered by an individual rather than a collectivity. However, unless it is clearly a *personal* apology, the leader is speaking as representative for the collectivity, and thus for a "many." That an apology on behalf of a "many" is offered by a "one" does not remove it from the category of a many to many exchange. As to the addressee of the apology, it is here either an incorporated collectivity (a state, organized group, institution, corporation) or an unincorporated or non-organized number of individuals whose relevant distinctive shared characteristic is that they were subject to the injury in question, or have standing to represent those who were.

My chief examples of many to many apologies concern the University of Alabama; Archbishop Tutu and the South African Churches; King Hussein of Jordan; and the United States Senate. In discussing the first of these, I am led to the question of the conceptual relation between apology and reparations. The point is fleshed out by examining the apology and restitution offered to Japanese-Americans by the government of the United States.

The second subsection (ii.b) examines "one to many" apologies offered by individuals to a collectivity. My two examples are perhaps unusual in that they represent failures to offer apology where apology is due; but the failures are instructive.[11]

[ii.a] Many to Many Apology: Test Cases

• *The University of Alabama and the Legacy of Slavery.* Consider the recent apology for slavery offered by the University of Alabama, apparently the first of its kind in American history. The actions for which the University apologized – on recommendation of the Faculty Senate – all pertained to its ante-bellum ancestor. They included the fact that several of its

---

[11] The classificatory terminology of "many" and "one" is borrowed from Tavuchis, *Mea Culpa: A Sociology of Apology and Reconciliation*, ch. 4; and Digeser, *Political Forgiveness*, p. 110. "One" is being used here to denote an individual. Of course, a representative of a political body – say, the President of a nation – can apologize to her counterpart. If the matter is personal, then it is a case of interpersonal forgiveness. But if they speak qua holder of their office, then it is a one to one apology only in a metaphorical sense of "one"; given the potential for confusion, I shall consider it a many to many apology articulated by the appropriate spokespersons.

presidents, and faculty, owned slaves; that in at least one case a slave worked as a laboratory assistant; and that some of the bricks still present in its buildings had been made by slaves. The University agreed to mark the graves of two slaves, as well as to put plaques on three buildings where slaves had once lived. The text of the resolution states that the "University of Alabama recognizes and regrets that the University has benefited from the work of slaves" and "we apologize to the descendants of persons who were slaves at the University for such exploitation of human beings." I note that the word "forgiveness" is not used in the Resolution. While the apology was evidently well received in some quarters, as signaling that in spite of its ancient as well as modern history (recall Governor George Wallace's high profile efforts in 1963 to keep the University segregated) the University wishes to be inviting to African-American students, the minutes of the debate in the Faculty Senate record these objections:

the University as it existed before the Civil war is not representative of the University today. . . . To apologize is to accept responsibility. No member of this faculty, student body, or administration can legitimately claim responsibility for slavery. Therefore, an apology from this body for thoughts and actions of those long deceased, actions at least, which are criminal by modern standards, imputes the lives and reputations of the innocent as well as the guilty, and in that injustice compounds the negative effect of our greatest American tragedy.[12]

---

[12] See J. Reeves, "An Apology for Slavery," *The Decatur Daily*, April 21, 2004, p. C1. The Faculty Senate Minutes of April 20, 2004, from which I quote is available through the University of Alabama's website: http://facultysenate.ua.edu/04–05/mn042004.html. The speaker is identified as Professor Marvin Johnson. The text of the Resolution is available there as well, and reads: "Resolution Acknowledging and Apologizing for the History of Slavery at The University of Alabama: /Whereas, in the period from the opening of The University of Alabama in 1831 until the Civil War slaves made a significant contribution to The University of Alabama; and /Whereas, some faculty members of The University of Alabama owned slaves, supervised the labor and discipline of slaves, and in at least one case used a slave as a laboratory assistant; and /Whereas, the current Faculty Senate represents a link to the body of University faculty past, present, and future, /Therefore be it resolved that the Faculty Senate of The University of Alabama recognizes and regrets that the University has benefited from the work of slaves; and /Be it further resolved by the Faculty Senate of The University of Alabama that we apologize to the descendants of persons who were slaves at the University for such exploitation of human beings; and /Be it further resolved that the University recognize the cemetery where the slaves, a student, and the Pratt family are buried with a historical marker; and /Be it further resolved that the Faculty Senate endorses the actions taken by The University of Alabama President Robert Witt on April 15; and /Be it further resolved that the University take actions to atone for that history and to memorialize the contributions of slaves to the campus in some prominent fashion. – Proposed by Faculty Life Committee; Adopted by the Faculty Senate, April 20, 2004."

These objections would be fatal in the context of interpersonal forgiveness even in its non-paradigmatic form. Are they fatal with respect to political apology?

I am going to assume that the University is sufficiently self-identical through the relevant time period to be legitimately identified as the "same" institution.[13] Is it true that "to apologize is to accept responsibility"? It seems to me that the answer is certainly affirmative, else apology collapses into excuse. The next question is *whose* responsibility is being accepted; the author of the statement quoted assumes that it refers to the present members of the University, and then rightly denies that *they* individually are responsible. But this need not necessarily be the case; it is the abstract entity, "the University," as well as the individual employees who for example owned slaves, on whom responsibility devolves. Because the individuals in question are long-since deceased, in practice it is the abstract entity that is responsible. This answers another objection to the effect that the Faculty Senate's Resolution "imputes the lives and reputations of the innocent [current members of the University] as well as the guilty." For it is not individuals, but the abstract entity, whose guilt is imputed. The example illustrates in a rather extreme way the level of abstraction that political apology can reach, and the vicarious structure of the moral exchange inseparable from political apology.

Granting the continuity of identity through time, and granting that political entities can be held responsible for their actions (an assumption that is thoroughly inscribed in contemporary law), the proxy-structure of such an apology does seem intelligible as well as defensible. After all, even simple cases of corporate apology to identifiable victims for recent wrongs assume a proxy structure; the University of Alabama example is simply a limit case of the same phenomenon.

I set out six conditions that a candidate for forgiveness would have to meet:

1. acknowledge that she was the responsible agent
2. repudiate her deeds (by acknowledging their wrongness) and herself as their author

[13] I realize that the problem of identity through time is complex. For present purposes, though, rough and ready rules will do: the University of Alabama identifies itself as self-same through time, identifies with its tradition and offers a narrative of a history it claims as its own, and enjoys the legal status (in particular, with respect to property rights as well as tax status) that assumes its identity as the same entity from its founding through the present day. If the ante-bellum institution were not "the same" as its descendant in these ways, then the idea of the one apologizing for the actions of the other would of course be absurd.

3. express regret to the injured at having caused this particular injury to her

4. commit to becoming the sort of person who does not inflict injury; and show this commitment through deeds as well as words

5. show that she understands, from the injured person's perspective, the damage done by the injury (this requires Smithean "sympathy")

6. offer a narrative accounting for how she came to do wrong, how that wrongdoing does not express the totality of her person, and how she is becoming worthy of approbation

Brief though the University of Alabama's apology may be, it meets the first four of these conditions, though each in its own way. For example, the "agent" in (1) is the political entity, not the person who speaks on its behalf and not (necessarily) any current or even past members of the entity. Nonetheless, the Resolution is clear both in respect to the burden of responsibility, and in the specificity of what exactly is being apologized for. Condition (2) is met by definition. Compliance with condition (3) is accomplished by proxy, as none of the injured parties or immediate circle are alive; the addressees of the expression of regret are the unnamed descendants of the injured parties; and more broadly, the addressee is the moral community. Compliance with condition (4) is shown, in the instant case, by the grave markers and plaques on buildings, among other actions. And those are four of the necessary conditions a successful apology must meet. The Resolution also meets other expectations I set out for forgiveness: the expression of contrition is expressed, it is public, it is specific in indicating the wrongs done and remedial steps. Assuming that the wrongs in question are not of such a magnitude that apology is inappropriate – an issue analogous to that of the "unforgivable" to which I return below – the University has accomplished the act of apology.

The fifth and sixth steps required for forgiveness are not, therefore, required for political apology. The reason once again has to do with the fact that the agent is not an individual but a political entity. An entity does not sympathize, in Smith's sense or any other sense of the term. The inherent depersonalization of political apology – even when proper names are somewhere attached – is also reflected in the fact that it need not (and at a literal level, does not) express any sentiments (an abstract entity does not have sentiments). Further, the extensive narrative that is often appropriate to the scene of forgiveness is out of place in political apology. This is so not only because of its intrinsically impersonal character, and correlative abstraction from the sentiments of individuals, but also because it is much more centrally concerned than is forgiveness with putting truth "on the record." The "publicness" of the act is of its essence. And a public record is not served by a lengthy discourse: rather, clarity, brevity, intelligibility, and accessibility to a potentially variegated and (especially in an era of communications that can be accessed repeatedly over time) transtemporal audience is crucial.[14] Interpersonal forgiveness is addressed by one individual to another (at least in our paradigm case); but political apology is always addressed to the moral community in addition to the injured party. There is an audience behind the audience; this goes along with the aim of "setting the record straight."

Why is setting the record straight so important to the offending as well as injured party? Ultimately the reason has to be that the injury done is almost always a violation of the community's norms and that both parties wish to belong to and be recognized by the community. The urgency if repairing the breach is all the greater when the agent in question (say, an insurance company) exists at the leave of the community, because it is a socially produced abstraction.

Like forgiveness, political apology is a moral act not reducible to calculations of self-interest. The norms to which genuine political apology subscribes, implicitly or explicitly, are not "merely political" or merely of instrumental value; they are presented, rather, as ones to which reasonable people, as ones on which the community as a whole rests. The expression of the apology is negated if it comes across as motivated by self-interested business reasons alone. Some level of hypocrisy is no doubt intrinsic to the expression of political apology (for narrowly self-interested motivations are ineliminable when the agent is a political entity). But because political apology, unlike forgiveness, does not claim to articulate the sentiments and motivations of individuals, its morality does not depend on the true motives of the abstract agent in question. It does depend on the implicit or explicit reaffirmation of the moral spectator's norms, as well as the appropriate actions that demonstrate publicly the reliability of that reaffirmation. It re-establishes trust, and shows that the responsible entity or agent can be counted on to act – or at least, to intend to act – in a way that is consistent with the established norms.

Precisely because political apology is political in this sense, however, it must bring with it the risk of legal and financial liability, and therewith

---

[14] Tavuchis, *Mea Culpa*, p. 109, is very helpful on this issue. As he rightly remarks there, "the major structural requirement and ultimate task of collective apologetic speech is to put things on record, to document as a prelude to reconciliation."

the self-interested consideration of that risk. As it turns out, apology may lessen rather than increase that risk, at least in the current legal culture of the United States.[15] The moral status of apology is itself at risk in the political sphere, with respect to both the willingness to offer and accept it. This is not the kind of risk faced within the scene of forgiveness, where issues of justice and of forgiveness are kept separate.

• *Apology, Reparations, and the Wartime Internment of Japanese-Americans.* The risk may also arise when the question of reparation for past injustice comes into play. At stake here is not so much legally defined restitution for negligence or criminal actions impacting particular individuals (as when an automobile company's faulty tires cause deaths), but in some way making up "many to many" injustice committed deliberately. Thanks principally to now well-established and successful claims to reparations made as response to the Holocaust, demands for reparations are ever growing.[16] Questions analogous to those pertinent to the criteria for political apology as well as interpersonal forgiveness arise in acute form here. In particular, the question as to when a past injustice has simply to be accepted as a sad fact of history, "letting bygones be bygones," becomes pressing: for the record of historical injustice at the political level is infinitely long and universal.

It seems to me that with one possible exception, arguments for reparation should be made solely on grounds of justice, not as part of an apology. The reasons are several. First, linking reparations with apology taints the moral standing of the apology – for it may come to seem to

---

[15] See once again T. Fuchs-Burnett's "Mass Public Corporate Apology"; and Jennifer K. Robbennolt's "Apologies and Legal Settlement: An Empirical Examination," *Michigan Law Review* 102 (2003): 460–516; for the abstract of which see http://papers.ssrn.com/sol3/papers.cfm?abstract_id=708361.

[16] For discussion of the recent history of reparation claims, see J. Torpey, "'Making Whole What Has Been Smashed': Reflections on Reparations," *Journal of Modern History* 73 (2001): 333–358. Torpey remarks of efforts to justify reparations by drawing comparisons with the Holocaust: "the result is an often unseemly contest for the status of worst-victimized" (p. 342). The meaning of the term "genocide," and the applicability of the Geneva Convention as well as the legally accepted meaning of "crimes against humanity," are of course critical to justifying an analogy to the Holocaust. Difficult questions of cultural and group "identity," including the definition of "race," arise in recent proposals for reparations for injuries done by, for example, colonialism. The conceptual territory of what Torpey calls "reparations politics" has become extremely complex. Reparations obviously have a backward looking character, but may also be forward-looking instruments for social change. Debt relief, for example, has been proposed as a form of reparations (Torpey, p. 355).

be "all about money," and the level of the wrong may seem vulgarized by attaching a monetary value to it. One victim of sexual abuse by Catholic clergy, for example, is quoted as saying that "plaintiffs feel almost like 'prostitutes' now that they've been compensated financially for having been sexually violated."[17] Second, the computation of the reparations due is almost certainly going to end up as a matter of negotiation, estimation, and guesswork, always with the mediation of "expert" third parties. Third parties will bring their own interests to bear (most obviously, their own financial interests, in the form of legal fees or what have you), and to some extent will regulate the process independently of the offender and offended. Especially when the third party is not a court of law, the process easily becomes politicized.[18] The purposes, language, and procedures of reparations are considerably different from those of apology, and belong to a different moral sphere. I would argue that apology ought neither to entail reparations, nor insulate one from claims thereto (apology ought therefore not be used against the agent offering it). Because the theory of justice is not my topic here, however, I have not attempted to spell out a theory of warranted reparations.

Consider another pitfall of linking apology, or forgiveness, with restitution or reparation; namely that, as one commentator put it, "if people don't get reparation, they won't forgive. If people are not forgiven, they won't offer reparation."[19] Forgiveness and apology are held hostage to money. But as we have seen, forgiveness or the withholding thereof ought to respond to its own reasons and conditions, and not be made hostage to

---

[17] See E. Convey, "Payout Is no Relief for Abuse Victims," *Boston Sunday Herald*, December 21, 2003, p. 8. The article cites other recipients who express similar views. The Archdiocese of Boston paid eighty-five million dollars in this settlement. Notably, Elie Wiesel refused to take part in discussions of reparations with Swiss banks on the grounds that doing so would reduce the suffering of the victims to monetary value. See his Foreword to S. E. Eizenstat's *Imperfect Justice: Looted Assets, Slave Labor, and the Unfinished Business of World War II* (New York: Public Affairs, 2003), p. ix.

[18] On the "guesswork," see E. Cose's account of how the amounts to be paid by Swiss banks (as well as by the German and French governments) were arrived at: *Bone to Pick: of Forgiveness, Reconciliation, Reparation, and Revenge* (New York: Atria Books, 2004), pp. 143–144. Cose relies in part on Eizenstat's *Imperfect Justice*, who on p. 352 concedes that "the applicable lesson from our work [in the settlement cases he mediated, including with the Swiss banks] is that they will ultimately be decided in the court of public opinion more than in the court of law." He also notes that the "titanic political struggle" for which the class action lawsuits were a vehicle "caused resentment" and even, in Switzerland, anti-Semitism (p. 340). On p. 353 he characterizes the process he promoted as "rough justice" (his quotation marks). Chapter 2 of Eizenstat's book provides details about the battle with the Swiss banks for accountability and restitution.

[19] A. Krog, *Country of My Skull* (New York: Three Rivers Press, 1999), p. 170.

an issue that ought to be determined impartially and through the mediation of the equivalent of judicial process. The same is true of apology. As already noted, judgment as to what any individual or group thereof is owed by way of reparations can be extremely complicated empirically and ethically (how *does* one quantify suffering?).[20] Reparations may be made and coherently justified without obligating the party providing them to apologize (as distinguished from, say, to express regret).

Contrast an example in which the plaintiff explicitly disavows a financial interest, and insists instead on an apology and on the documenting of truth. The *New York Times* reported on March 20, 2003 (section A, p. 3) that

> Kurt Werner Schaechter, 82, is seeking just one euro as symbolic compensation from the National Railroad Service, known by its French initials of S.N.C.F. But he hopes the court will require the company to acknowledge that it played an active role in the deportation of some 76,000 Jews from France from 1942 to 1944. Of those sent to death camps, only some 2,500 survived.

Mr. Schaechter's parents were murdered by the Nazis, having been shipped out by the S.N.C.F., whose administrators were enthusiastically collaborationist. By making clear that remuneration is not at issue, Mr. Schaechter ensured that the moral exchange is clean and clear. By contrast, when remuneration and apology are linked, the moral quality of the apology is bound to be sullied and perceived as sullied. This is neither to argue that reparations are not owed – they may be, but as a consequence of a separate adjudication, and not as a consequence or precondition of apology – nor that political reconciliation is possible without them.

Now to the possible exception: it may seem that reparations should follow apology for their "symbolic" value, namely, that of showing that the apology is "not just words." This looks to be analogous to the requirement that in order to qualify for forgiveness, the offender show in deed that she is a changing or changed person. My response to this line is that the deeds appropriate to backing up political apology ought not attempt to fix monetary value to suffering or wrong done, but should instead be

---

[20] Some of the problems faced by South Africa's TRC are well summarized by D. Shea, *The South African Truth Commission*, pp. 35–37. The reparations in question come from common funds. See also L. Graybill, *Truth and Reconciliation in South Africa*, pp. 148–156. She ably recounts the moral quandaries the South Africa reparation process presented: a new government paying for the sins of its unjust predecessor (often with funds raised through taxing the victims inter alia); offenders going free (if granted amnesty) without having to make reparation to their victims; and of course the sheer lack of adequate funds. The process has, as she narrates, generated a great deal of bitterness.

such as to carry through the seriousness of the reaffirmation of public norms in question. The steps taken by the University of Alabama, for example, are precisely the sort that are appropriate given what the University apologized for doing.

And how precisely are the deeds appropriate to the demonstration on the part of the offender that the apology is "serious" to be determined? There is no a priori answer to this question; it is a matter for *judgment*. So too with the verbal formulation of the apology; what vocabulary will succeed in conveying the message clearly and accurately depends on local factors, including of course the resources available within the local language. This is another factor that political apology has in common with dyadic forgiveness: the need for practical wisdom, or judgment, in determining the specifics. Notice that in the public sphere, appropriate actions might include the elaboration of the public record (typically, through the establishment of a truth commission or its equivalent), the erection of memorials, and the appropriate naming of public spaces. Such measures were even requested of the South African Truth and Reconciliation Commission, though by and large the requests have been financial.[21]

I conclude this section of my discussion of many to many apologies with a brief consideration of an example of a genuine apology accompanied by reparations. I refer to the U.S. Government's apology to Japanese-Americans for their internment during World War II. The Civil Liberties Act of 1988 explicitly apologizes for the government's wrong-doing, specifies exactly what the wrongs were and to whom they were done, citing the documentary work of the Commission on Wartime Relocation and Internment of Civilians – in effect, a sort of truth commission (its 1983 report is entitled *Personal Justice Denied*). The Act explains that "for these fundamental violations of the basic civil liberties and constitutional rights of these individuals of Japanese ancestry, the Congress apologizes on behalf of the Nation," and details further steps to be taken including restitution (the amounts to be determined subsequently) and the

---

[21] See L. Graybill, *Truth and Reconciliation in South Africa*, pp. 148–156. This raises the important thought that reparations, even when seen as demanded by corrective justice (as I am suggesting) rather than other moral considerations, might be understood in much broader terms than cash transactions. Consider D. Lyons' intriguing proposal for a "National Rectification Project" that offers creative suggestions for improving the life of economically poor children with respect to such matters as health, family life, and education, whether through the agency of the government or not. "Corrective Justice, Equal Opportunity, and the Legacy of Slavery and Jim Crow," *Boston University Law Review* 84 (2004): 1375–1404.

funding of a public education program. Interestingly, it also declares as one of its purposes "to make more credible and sincere any declaration of concern by the United States over violations of human rights committed by other nations." In signing the bill into law, President Reagan is quoted as saying "'No payment can make up for those lost years. What is most important in this bill has less to do with property than with honor. For here we admit wrong.'" President Clinton's letter of some five years accompanying reparation payments, also was explicit, succinct, and unambiguous in its apology (interestingly, it does not refer explicitly to the enclosed check).[22] The apology meets the criteria for which I have argued.

Is it compromised by the promise and eventual delivery of restitution? It seems to me that the answer is mixed. On the one hand, the "many" to whom the apology and payments were offered could still be identified with precision. The reparations seem to have gone to the proper recipients, and a sound argument on grounds of justice could probably be mounted that they deserved, in amounts proportionate to the injury done, restitution. On the other hand, the amount of the payment in fact offered is arbitrary – or rather, it is the result of political negotiation and not an accurate calculation of the damage done to each individual. In many cases, the damage was surely very much more substantial than $20,000; we shall never know, for any such investigation was foreclosed by the deal reached, and recipients of the check had to agree to drop all legal claims pending against the Government.

The checks must therefore be considered "symbolic," but symbolic of what? It would be absurd to answer "of what the victims are justly entitled to," let alone "the negotiating skill and political power of the

---

[22] The text of the 1988 Act may be found at: www.children-of-the-camps.org/history/civilact.html. For the quotation from President Reagan, see the *NYT* report by J. Johnson ("President Signs Law to Redress Wartime Wrong") of August 11, 1988, p. A16. He also said "Yes, the Nation was then at war, struggling for its survival and it's not for us today to pass judgment upon those who may have made mistakes while engaged in that great struggle." The statement is, unfortunately, incoherent, as his next sentence underlines: "yet we must recognize that the internment of Japanese-Americans was just that: a mistake." To declare it a mistake *is* to pass judgment, all the more so when, as is also explicit, the "mistake" was a grave injustice. For the full text of his remarks on the occasion of the signing, see http://facstaff.uww.edu/mohanp/ethnic7b.html. For the text of President Clinton's October 1, 1993 letter that accompanied the reparation checks of $20,000, see www.children-of-the-camps.org/history/clinton.html. The checks were paid from a 1.25 billion dollar trust fund. The process of sending out the payments began during President George Bush Sr.'s term; his letter may be found at http://reserve.mg2.org/apology%20events/Civil%20Liberty%20Act%201998.htm.

individuals involved." If the answer is ultimately "of the nation's contrition," then I reiterate the argument already offered to the effect that the appropriate deeds backing up an apology ought not to sully the apology by making it look like a "buy-off," and should instead support the case that the injustice has been recognized and will not be repeated. The fund for education mentioned in the 1988 Act is an excellent example of an appropriate accompaniment to the apology.[23]

• *Desmond Tutu and South African Churches.* I turn now to a rather different test case of "many to many" apology. It was presented in the language of forgiveness; sorting through it helps further to explain the difference between these notions, as well as why the language of forgiveness is misleading in this context.

Desmond Tutu's argument for political forgiveness (forgiveness functioning in a political context) was presented in the course of the transition from apartheid to a democratic state in South Africa. The argument was made through his many public speeches, his writings, as well as his position as Chair of the Truth and Reconciliation Commission, and in that broad sense was a political act. As already noted, the TRC also included a committee that granted amnesty, but I am not here concerned with that part of the process.

It is important for purposes of conceptual clarity to distinguish various levels at which "forgiveness" was supposed to do its work in Tutu's view. Some of them fit perfectly with interpersonal forgiveness as I have analyzed the notion, others would better be seen as bearing a family resemblance to it (in particular, as instances of political apology rather than forgiveness). Let us consider a less well-known example than the instances of interpersonal forgiveness that came before the TRC, as it is a compelling illustration of the process in which groups or institutions attempt to mend moral ties with other similar entities.

---

[23] This would be my response to J. Waldron's point (made with reference to the reparations to Japanese-Americans) that "like the gift I buy for someone I have stood up, the payment is a method of putting oneself out of one's way, to apologize. It is no objection to this that the payments are purely symbolic. Since identity is bound up with symbolism, the symbolic gesture may be as important to people as any material compensation." "Superseding Historical Injustice," *Ethics* 103 (1992), p. 7. Even granting the point about identity, and its ethical relevance, the gesture comes at a price. At the same time, Waldron's nuanced account of the problem of reparations and of what he calls the "supersession of historic injustice" is excellent. I reiterate that I am not taking a position on the matters he addresses, but instead disagreeing that political apology and reparations fall into the same sphere of moral consideration.

Tutu recounts that at the ecumenical Rustenberg Conference (1990), the churches that had opposed apartheid "through their membership in the South African Council of Churches" and the "major white Dutch Reformed Church [DRC] ... which had supported apartheid," as well as yet other churches that "had tried to be apolitical," met face to face.[24] The DRC "had introduced apartheid into church structures" (p. 277). A representative of the DRC "made an eloquent plea for forgiveness to his black fellow Christians" (p. 276). Of course Tutu was a leading representative of the black Church. In light of that, as well as the need for the churches to be "agents of reconciliation" at that crucial stage of regime change (p. 277) – note the political rationale here – Tutu consulted with a senior member of his denomination, and then accepted the plea for forgiveness on its behalf. Quite obviously, this was a controversial step, as he acknowledges. The points of controversy include his standing to forgive on behalf, as he puts it, of "millions of contemporary victims of apartheid and, even more seriously, for those many millions who were no longer alive" (p. 277). This is a variation of our issue of third-party forgiveness, though as a victim of the white Church's actions, Tutu could also speak on his own behalf as well. It was also not clear whether the DRC had met the conditions for being forgiven, or indeed, what those conditions are exactly. Tutu notes that the DRC had not signed a document condemning apartheid as a heresy, and was "dragging its feet on the question of uniting with the black churches" (p. 277).

Tutu makes it quite clear that he views forgiveness in both a one to many and a one to one context, as morally appropriate as well as politically salubrious (the "future" referred to by the title of his book is political, not just interpersonal; see inter alia p. 120, "forgiveness will follow confession and healing will happen, and so contribute to national unity and reconciliation").[25] He uses the term "restorative justice" as synonymous

---

[24] D. Tutu, *No Future without Forgiveness*, p. 275. All further references to this text advert to this edition, and the page numbers are incorporated directly into my text. For a list of Pope John Paul II's pleas for forgiveness on behalf of the Catholic Church, see L. Accottoli's *When a Pope Asks Forgiveness*, trans. J. Aumann (Boston: Pauline Books, 1998). Accattoli notes on p. 123 that the Church still has not offered anything resembling an appropriate apology for its wrong-doing toward Jews. For a detailed and instructive study of the efforts by four Canadian churches to apologize to Canada's indigenous peoples, see J. Bavelas's "An Analysis of Formal Apologies by Canadian Churches to First Nations," Occasional Paper #1, Centre for Studies in Religion and Society, University of Victoria, 2004; available online at http://web.uvic.ca/csrs/publications/occasional/apologies.php.

[25] Tutu also makes such remarks as: "It is ultimately in our best interest that we become forgiving, repentant, reconciling, and reconciled people because without forgiveness, without reconciliation, we have no future" (the context is his discussion of the purposes

with the forgiveness that is offered in times of great social and political conflict and wrong-doing, and in contrast with retributive justice (p. 260; also pp. 54–55, "thus we would claim that justice, restorative justice, is being served when efforts are being made to work for healing, for forgiving, and for reconciliation," this being distinguished from "retribution or punishment"). Especially where systematic wrongdoing has privileged one class above another economically, forgiveness requires reparations "wherever feasible" (p. 273). At least in this book, Tutu does not explain clearly how the demand for reparations figures into restorative justice, except to say that without an improvement of the situation of the victimized non-whites, reconciliation will ultimately be impossible (p. 274).

I have no objection in principle to the notion of one to one forgiveness, of course, though when it is sponsored for political purposes, however noble they may be, difficult questions arise (I confront them later). But I want to suggest that in the first instance, the many to many, and many to one scenes of reconciliation Tutu narrates are more accurately characterized as pertaining to apology and the acceptance thereof, rather than forgiveness. "In the first instance," because genuine interpersonal instances of forgiveness may result from or accompany them. I have already offered reasons in this chapter for reserving "political apology" rather than "forgiveness" for cases other than the relevant one to one moral exchange. There is a deep assumption underlying Tutu's contrary view that they may all be termed "forgiveness," for which his paradigmatic instance is indeed interpersonal forgiveness. That assumption is that civic peace will not be possible unless the souls of the citizens are freed from resentment, or differently stated, unless what we might call a "culture of forgiveness" takes root. I will examine this crucial assumption in a moment.

• *King Hussein in Israel.* We have accepted the principle of apology by proxy. The apology is on rare occasions offered by a many (through its representative) to a few identified individuals. Where the recipients are more than one in number, the apology is technically a many to many apology. But what distinguishes the sort of case I want to examine very briefly here is that the number of recipients is small, they are identified by name, and the apology is "personal" in the sense that it is delivered in a manner that gives it the appearance of a personal plea for forgiveness.

---

and achievements of the TRC; p. 165). Or again: "thus to forgive is indeed the best form of self-interest since anger, resentment, and revenge are corrosive of that *summum bonum*, that greatest good, communal harmony that enhances the humanity and personhood of all in the community" (p. 35).

Consider the apology delivered in Israel by Jordan's late King Hussein to the parents of several Israeli school girls murdered by a Jordanian soldier. Hussein visited each of the seven parents individually, and on each occasion begged forgiveness (the term used here by the *Washington Post*), often on his knees. The scene was of course photographed and very widely disseminated.[26] Some families accepted his statement that "your daughter is like my daughter, your loss is my loss. May God help you to bear your pain." Other parents did not accept this gesture, and wanted answers. None are reported as actually forgiving him. And that would be entirely appropriate. First, Hussein is not himself the wrong-doer; he personally bears no responsibility for the wrong-doer's action, and because the Jordanian soldier in question was not acting on orders implied or expressed, but appears to have gone berserk, the Jordanian state seems not responsible for his actions (let us assume that there was no history of mental illness or hate-filled diatribes that the Jordanian military had negligently overlooked). Hussein represents the sympathy of relevant strangers; apologizes on behalf of his people; and has standing to undertake this solely because he is head of the state to which the soldier belonged. It is a tenuous thread of authority and responsibility by proxy. It does not bear the label "forgiveness," and granting forgiveness to Hussein would make little sense. I add that because none of the victims survived, their loss could only be addressed by means of their parents, and thus in third-party mode (of course, the parents also had their own loss, and that is what Hussein addresses in the statement quoted).

And yet by appearing in person and expressing regret in so dramatic a fashion, the act takes on the *appearance* of an appeal for forgiveness. Or to be more precise, it is *symbolic contrition*. There is no attempt to deny the facts – on the contrary, it helped to put them indelibly on the record – or to excuse, justify, or otherwise explain the wrong-doing away. I want to credit the genuineness of any sentiments experienced on either side, but also add that – unlike interpersonal forgiveness – the scene here is intensely political. As the *Washington Post* article also details, the immediate context of Hussein's visit included the bitterly divisive question of Jewish settlements on historically Arab land (the *Post* notes that "just a week ago, Hussein sent a letter to Israeli Prime Minister Binyamin

---

[26] My information about this event comes entirely from the *Washington Post*, "Hussein, on His Knees, Begs Forgiveness for Massacre," by B. Gellman, March 17, 1997, p. A1. The events took place the preceding day.

Netanyahu so drenched in rage and pain that their relationship seemed to be irreparably breached"). Hussein was attempting, in his moving gestures to the Israeli parents, to restore working relations with Israel and to solve the settlement issue. His act was profoundly symbolic: in particular, of the theses that Jordanians are still "our" friends, are not to be classified as moral monsters, are capable of sympathy in just the way "we" are, and that they repudiate the wrongs committed by one of their own (humanity, not the nation state, is therefore their primary claim for identification). The multivalence of his gesture, its simultaneous occupying of private and public places, and its thoroughly third-party character, makes it impossible to see it as the enactment of forgiveness. It enacts apology to individuals, to a nation, and a plea for the reconciliation of nations on that as well as other counts. And it is not the less noble because it is an instance of political apology rather than forgiveness.

• *The United States Senate and the Victims of Lynching.* A collectivity, especially a government, rarely apologizes to a specifiable person or persons. Yet we have seen one case (the apology offered to Japanese-Americans) in which that took place; let us examine another.[27] In both its success and its failures it illustrates how such an apology should be discharged. The United States Senate has a history, thanks to Southern conservative senators, of failing to act on legislation proposed by the House or the president that would have made lynching a federal crime. Yet nearly five thousand recorded cases of lynching have been recorded, some into the 1930s; almost none of the perpetrators were prosecuted by local officials. There is reason to think that federal legislation would have had the intended effect. In 2005, the Senate passed a resolution by voice vote that reads, in part:

Whereas an apology offered in the spirit of true repentance moves the United States toward reconciliation and may become central to a new understanding, on which improved racial relations can be forged: Now, therefore, be it Resolved, That the Senate (1) apologizes to the victims of lynching for the failure of the Senate to enact anti-lynching legislation; (2) expresses the deepest sympathies and most solemn regrets of the Senate to the descendants of victims of lynching, the ancestors of whom were deprived of life, human dignity, and the Constitutional

---

[27] One of the most impressive and eloquent recent pleas for truth telling, acknowledgment of wrong-doing, memory, and reconciliation is that offered by German President G. von Weizsäcker on May 8, 1985, shortly after Ronald Reagan's controversial visit to the Bitburg cemetery in Germany. For the text and discussion, see *Bitburg in Moral and Political Perspective*, ed. G. Hartman, pp. 262–273.

protections accorded all citizens of the United States; and (3) remembers the history of lynching, to ensure that these tragedies will be neither forgotten nor repeated.

Some two hundred persons attended the event (including the last known living survivor of an attempted lynching), about one hundred of whom are descendants of an African-American farmer whose murder is described by the *New York Times* as follows:

The memories were especially painful for the relatives of Anthony Crawford, whose family was torn apart by the lynching. Mr. Crawford had been a wealthy black landowner in Abbeville, S.C., a cotton farmer, registered voter and community leader who founded a school for black children and a union for black families. In 1916, after a dispute with a white man over the price of cotton seed, he was hanged from a pine tree and shot more than 200 times. His family lost his land, and the relatives scattered.

It appears that Mr. Crawford's descendants were prime movers in getting the Resolution passed, although a book of photographs of lynchings is also cited as providing significant motivation.[28]

The text of the apology meets the criteria for political apology I have suggested. It gives the essentials of the history of lynching, the number of documented lynchings and their time frame, and the number of times the Senate failed to act. It takes responsibility for specific failures, identifies those to whom the apology is directed, and the ideals in the name of which it is offered. The formulation of the apology is a success, and that its passing was celebrated with several hundred of the descendants further helps to direct the apology to the specific individuals harmed. Of course the exchange is accomplished in part by proxy: the senators as representatives of the institution they serve, the descendants as (in part) representatives of the victims. Because the descendants too were victimized by the murders, they are appropriately recognized.

But as is also noted in reports of the occasion, the vote was not unanimous, and the individual names of those in favor and against were not recorded. The collectivity did not quite speak unambiguously and fully. The Senate's history mentioned by the text of the Resolution, the anonymity of those supporting it as well as of those who failed to do so, and that only 80% of Senators voted, are disturbing and invite a subverting

---

[28] The text of the Senate Resolution 39 IS of Feb. 7, 2005, may be found at through the Library of Congress website, at http://thomas.loc.gov/home/c109query.html. The *NYT* report, "Senate Issues Apology Over Failure on Antilynching Law" by S. G. Stolberg, is dated June 14, 2005, p. A1.

question: are there still Senators, and citizens they represent, who do *not* apologize for the Senate's inaction on anti-lynching legislation? And why would that be? In other words, the Resolution goes a long way to establishing the public record, which as we saw is essential to political apology. But it did so in a way that continued to raise the very questions it meant to put to rest.

Of course the ambiguity in question is an extension of the structure of democratic political organization. At one level, the majority vote does represent the sovereign view; yet in this context, the procedure also raises doubts. By contrast, King Hussein spoke as sovereign of his nation; thus his apology could not be faulted on the sorts of grounds the less than unanimous Senate vote can be. And this point allows me to underline once more the importance of *judgment* in assessing whether an apology has met the requisite criteria. Something will depend on how the apology was arrived at, and only an inspection of the particulars will provide the answer. It is the burden of judgment to assess them in relation to the moral issues at stake.

[ii.b] One to Many Apology: Two Failures

The two cases of one to many political apology I shall examine illustrate a failure in apology, in different ways: the first is a refusal to apologize, when apology is due, even though responsibility is taken; the second is a misunderstanding as to what apology requires, one that comes to an avoidance of apology.

• *Robert McNamara's War and Mea Culpa.* I begin with Robert McNamara, who as Secretary of Defense was one of the chief architects of America's involvement in Vietnam War. About three decades after the conclusion of that conflict – one that cost over 59,000 American and approximately three million Vietnamese lives – McNamara published *In Retrospect: The Tragedy and Lessons of Vietnam.* (In 2003, a documentary reflecting the themes of the book, as well as covering other parts of McNamara's life, was also made.)[29] With reference to his May 19, 1967 memorandum to

---

[29] *In Retrospect: The Tragedy and Lessons of Vietnam* (New York: Vintage Books, 1995). My paginal references advert to this edition. The documentary movie is *The Fog of War: Eleven Lessons from the Life of Robert S. McNamara*. At its end he is asked whether he feels guilty about his role in the Vietnam War, or feels responsible for the war, or thinks that he ought to have spoken out against the war upon leaving his office as Secretary of Defense. He refuses to answer, on the grounds that he would be misunderstood and

President Johnson, McNamara makes clear that by 1967 – years and many deaths before the end of the war – he knew the war could not be won (pp. 266–271). Indeed, by 1965 he already had reason to entertain grave doubts about the war (pp. 191–195, 321). He left office in 1967, and did not speak publicly on the matter until the publication of his book. To be sure, his views became publicly known when the *New York Times* began to publish the "Pentagon Papers" in June of 1971. But that is hardly the same as actively seeking, upon his departure from office, to end the war. And there is no reason to believe that when in office he did what the evidence and his assessments dictated, viz., push uncompromisingly for United States withdrawal from Vietnam (he instead sought de-escalation, and a negotiated settlement – and failed on both counts).

McNamara would seem to have three wrongs for which to apologize: furthering so destructive and unjust a war; not using his authority and power to end it when he understood it was doomed, thereby saving many lives; and not speaking out against the war once he had left office, when it might have made a difference. Although his book is presented as a *mea culpa*, and no doubt was understood by many as attempting to offer an apology, the author himself denies that it is an apology.[30] He therefore has a fourth reason to apologize *after* the publication of the book, namely his passing up a chance to say clearly, publicly, and for the record that he apologizes.

The book does specify the "mistakes" made by the United States in both the rationale for going to war and in its conduct of the war. McNamara

would generate yet more controversy about the war as well as ill will against himself. At one point he volunteers that he is "sorry" for any mistakes he made (he does not specify them). As with the book, his aim is to explain, justify, and critique; but he refuses to draw the consequences of his own account and to apologize.

[30] See P. xx: "I truly believe that we made an error not of values and intentions but of judgment and capabilities"; he admits this will "appear to justify or rationalize what I and others did." Cf. the list of eleven errors he provides on pp. 321–323; numbers 2, 3, and 4 amount to the view that the rationale given for the war was false, and number 8 seems to indicate that the United States had no "God-given right to shape every nation in our own image or as we choose." Yet he refuses to state explicitly that the war was unjust, and to apologize for his enormous role in its prosecution. Instead, we are told by way of conclusion "Although we sought to do the right thing – and believed we were doing the right thing – in my judgment, hindsight proves us wrong. We both overestimated the effect of South Vietnam's loss on the security of the West and failed to adhere to the fundamental principle that, in the final analysis, if the South Vietnamese were to be saved, they had to win the war themselves" (p. 333). He adds: "that our effort in Vietnam proved unwise does to make their [the soldiers'] sacrifice less noble." The "eleven errors" structure the 2003 film documentary.

is clear that they are mistakes, details their character in an illuminating way, and states that he made them. He admits that the "domino theory" was false, and that the explicit assumption for American involvement (namely that the struggle between North and South Vietnam was not a civil war, but a proxy war waged by Communism against the innocent South) was false. That would entail that the war was at a minimum not just for the reasons given by the government, and that the government misled its own citizens about the rationale for the war, which is a clear wrong. Yet his admission does not elicit an apology, so much as an excuse, for McNamara seeks to justify it in terms of the thinking of the times.[31]

At the moral level, McNamara's *mea culpa* is a masterpiece of equivocation that manages to present itself as a regretful, almost-apologetic gesture. Yet it fails actually to apologize. Given the multiple reasons for which he owed the nation (the relevant "many" in our terminology) a straightforward apology – reasons he himself in effect provides – his is an example of a culpable failure to apologize. As he quite accurately says in a statement already quoted, his presentation will "appear to justify or rationalize what I and others did" (p. xx). To be fair, his failure is consistent with the refusal of America's leaders and of the general public to draw the appropriate conclusions from the excruciating truths about the Vietnam War that McNamara sets out, conclusions such as that Americans died or suffered in vain (for the war was not only unjust, it did not succeed even in its own aims), and that millions of Vietnamese were killed unjustly. The reasons for engaging in the war were unsound. American involvement in Vietnam was a calamitous mistake, and not simply because it did not win. The nation's leaders should be the first to apologize.

In Chapter 5, I shall return to the question of the consequences of national avoidance of truth telling and of the refusal to draw the appropriate moral inference, and my chief example will be the way in which the Vietnam War is remembered by the United States. The context will concern the requirements of political memory and reconciliation.

• *Richard Nixon's Resignation and Pardon.* My second example of a one to many apology – also an instructive failure – is drawn from Richard

---

[31] As is rightly noted by A. Lazare, *On Apology* (Oxford: Oxford University Press, 2004), p. 104.

Nixon's statements when resigning the Presidency of the United States (August 8, 1974) and accepting President Ford's executive pardon (September 8, 1974).[32] In neither speech did Nixon use the word "apologize" or cognates. He does say, in the first of these speeches:

I regret deeply any injuries that may have been done in the course of events that led to this decision [to resign]. I would say only that if some of my judgments were wrong, and some were wrong, they were made in what I believed at the time to be in the best interest of the Nation.

I am hardly the first commentator to note just how far this statement is from what is needed, viz., a true apology.[33] Nixon does not actually apologize; his expression of regret is linked both to conditional wrongs ("if some of my judgments were wrong") and the unspecified wrongs ("some were wrong"). Neither meets the requirement of apology, and taken together they are probably inconsistent. The statement as a whole is an effort to justify and thereby excuse his deeds.

In accepting Ford's pardon, he said that "no words can describe the depths of regret and pain at the anguish my mistakes over Watergate have caused the nation and the Presidency," and that "the way I tried to deal with Watergate was the wrong way." The first statement comes across as a combination of a personal psychobiography and legalistic evasion: psychobiography, because he does not straightforwardly express regret for wrongs done, but instead records a feeling he has had; evasion, because the "mistakes" sound like strategic or managerial errors rather than moral faults worthy of impeachment. Nixon's statements sound a bit like apologies, but fail in ways that illustrate what an apology would have to be in order to succeed.

Nixon nonetheless claimed that he had apologized – but through his deeds rather than words. On national television on June 10, 1983, Nixon

---

[32] Although it is not my purpose to analyze political *pardon* in this book, it is worth noting K. Moore's objections in her *Pardons* to Ford's pardoning of Nixon. She notes that the pardon was for *unspecified* crimes, which therefore "gives the appearance of injustice, looking more like an effort to cover up wrongdoing than an effort to match punishment with desert" (p. 220); and that it was granted before rather than after a trial. A pardon should "protect people from punishment they do not deserve . . . it follows that a pardon should not be granted until the courts have *tried* to achieve justice and have failed" (pp. 217–218).

[33] For similar assessments by other commentators, see Tavuchis, *Mea Culpa*, pp. 55–56; and Lazare, *On Apology*, pp. 91–92. My quotations from Nixon are taken from Tavuchis' transcription in the pages just cited.

responded to interviewer Frank Gannon's question as to whether he is "sorry":

My answer to that question and to those who say, 'Will you apologize? Are you sorry?' is simply a fact. There's no way that you could apologize that is more eloquent, more decisive, more finite, or to say that you were sorry which would exceed resigning the presidency of the United States. That said it all, and I don't intend to say any more.[34]

Nixon is mistaken in an instructive way. The deed does *not* say it, it accompanies what ought to be expressly and verbally said. The meaning of the deed as such is underdetermined; there are many reasons Nixon might have resigned when he did (indeed, in the interviews with Gannon he discusses his ruminations about several about them). The apology must be discursively and explicitly communicated. In truth, Nixon never did apologize. It does not surprise that neither his deed of resignation nor the remarks we have examined produced civil reconciliation so desperately needed at the time.

[iii] TRADITIONAL RITUALS OF RECONCILIATION: APOLOGY, FORGIVENESS, OR PARDON?

I turn now to the acknowledgment of and contrition for wrong-doing that is performed ritually, according to custom, by an individual for injury done by an individual to one or more individuals. This is a species of one to many apology.

The critical word here is "ritual." The so-called "forgiveness rituals," traditionally practiced in many societies as methods of conflict resolution, reconciliation, and restoration of community, complicate the contrast between interpersonal forgiveness and political apology. They do not form part of the administration of justice in a familiar modern sense, and indeed are sometimes offered as alternatives to that. At the same time, these rituals serve an explicitly political or civic function of restoring wrong-doers to the community, i.e., of reconciliation, on terms that are defined as morally appropriate and (in some sense) just. "Forgiveness rituals" do not map perfectly either onto our paradigm or non-paradigm cases of interpersonal forgiveness or onto familiar models of pardon. Let

---

[34] Quoted from the transcript of tape 4 (close to the end), day 7 of the interviews, available at www.libs.uga.edu/media/collections/nixon/nixonday7.html (copyright held by the University of Georgia); the lines are quoted in a slightly different form by Tavuchis, *Mea Culpa*, p. 57, though he identifies the interview as occurring in April of 1984.

me reiterate that my purpose here is not to consider them in light of the possibly competing claims of rectificatory justice. What concerns me here is their place within the family of concepts of which forgiveness and political apology are members.

Consider a recent example from Northern Uganda, where a violent guerrilla war raged for decades. On the one side, the "Lord's Resistance Army" (LRA), abducting children to fight their own people for its nebulous and cruel cause; on the other side, the Acholi people, from whose ranks many of the LRA's fighters are drawn; and in the background, the government of Uganda.[35] A recent front page *New York Times* report (April 18, 2005; p. A1) states that at the request of the President of Uganda, the International Criminal Court was on the verge of issuing arrest warrants for the leaders of the LRA. Some of the war victims, as well as representatives of the Acholi, asked that the wheels of justice be stopped, and that an ancient "tradition of forgiveness" (as the *Times* calls it; as just noted, there exists a serious question as to whether the word being used in the original language ought to be translated "forgiveness") be given a chance. One part of the argument is that the promise of reconciliation and amnesty would better disarm and defeat the LRA than would any attempt to serve the International Court's arrest warrants. And another part is that "the line between victim and killer is too blurred"

---

[35] For discussion of the war and the LRA, see H. Berhend, *Alice Lakwena and the Holy Spirits: War in Northern Uganda 1985–1997*, trans. M. Cohen (Athens: Ohio University Press, 1999). T. Allen's *Trial Justice: The International Criminal Court and the Lord's Resistance Army* (London and New York: Zed Books, 2006) is especially helpful and relevant to the present discussion. On pp. 130–131, Allen refers to the *New York Times* article I am about to cite, and voices skepticism that "forgiveness" is the correct translation of the term being use in the Two language (apparently the term can mean amnesty, forgiveness, or reconciliation). I am grateful to Sandy Barnes, Heike Berhend, and Steve Feierman for discussion of the Ugandan ritual. Berhend informs me that the *NYT* report of the ritual is severely attenuated; the ritual is in fact much more elaborate. She also points out that in the pre-colonial era (and thus before the Christian Missionaries arrived), and to some extent still today, the ritual was understood not so much as responding to "wrong-doing" but to "uncleanliness"; it was a purification ritual. Impurity resulted from spilling blood or violating prohibitions. In the Acholi's self-understanding, "wrongdoing and misfortune are not clearly differentiated" (private correspondence, June 15, 2005, quoted with permission). Further, she notes, one of the main purposes of purification rituals was to obviate revenge taken by the spirits of the dead. Finally, any requirement that the candidate for moral cleansing confess is, Berhend suggests, probably the result of Christian influence, as it introduces notions of guilt that are not at home in the earlier Acholi outlook. For an interesting philosophical discussion of these ancient but increasingly unfamiliar notions of impurity, stain, and defilement, see P. Ricoeur's *The Symbolism of Evil*, trans. E. Buchanan (New York: Harper and Row, 1967), Part I. A follow-up report on the process in Uganda will be found in the *New York Times* of September 15, 2006, p. A1.

for retributive justice to work effectively, as the kidnapping of children shows. The *New York Times* article indicates that similar rites are known in Kenya, Rwanda, Sudan, and Somalia.

How does the ritual work? Before an assembly of Acholi chiefs, several dozen former guerrillas line up and

one after the other, they stuck their bare right feet in a freshly cracked egg, with the lieutenant colonel, who lost his right leg to a bomb, inserting his right crutch in the egg instead. The egg symbolizes innocent life, according to local custom, and by dabbing themselves in it the killers are restoring themselves to the way they used to be. Next, the former fighters brushed against the branch of a pobo tree, which symbolically cleansed them. By stepping over a pole, they were welcomed back into the community by Mr. Acana [the 'paramount chief'] and the other chiefs.

That is not all. The penitent asks for "forgiveness," and then "must sit down together with group leaders and make amends. After confessing to his misdeeds, the wayward person is required to pay the victim's kin compensation in the form of cows, goats and sheep." So the ritual apparently includes truth telling, apology, and restitution negotiated with third parties (the tribal elders). The candidate for readmission does not seem to address his or her apology to the individuals for whose injuries he or she was responsible. Rather, the address seems directed to the representatives of the community. At the same time, by forming a line and undergoing the ritual one by one, the process is individualized: not groups but identifiable individuals are "forgiven." In return, the penitent receives what amounts to amnesty; the slate is wiped clean; and he or she is supposed to be allowed back into the community.

Is this a case of *pardon*? Certainly not if we have in mind something like a judicial pardon, for there has been no trial, and no determination that the offender's just punishment ought be mitigated given the particulars of the case. It is not like an executive pardon granted after a judicial procedure, or to obviate one before the facts of the wrong-doing are established (as in President Ford's pardon of Nixon). And yet there is an element of pardon involved, viz., that the wrong-doer is not punished. Because political apology normally does not bring with it immunity from punishment for the wrongs at issue, this sort of ritual of reconciliation is not an instance of apology pure and simple.

Is this a ritual of *forgiveness*? Some of the markers are there, but several crucial ones are not. In particular, the offender is not required to show any sympathetic understanding of how his or her deeds affected the victim, to engage in the victim's point of view. As noted, it seems that the offender does not have to apologize to his victim(s) even when that is possible. And readmission to the community is not granted unless proper restitution is made. The offender is not required to provide a narrative explaining how he came to do wrong, and while there is an assumption that he will change his ways, no narrative seems required that substantiates that commitment. The injured party is not required to let go of resentment; indeed, her resentment seems irrelevant. What matters is that she forswears revenge – plainly a central point of the exercise. In these respects it is a markedly impersonal process.

The ambivalent response on the part of the victim is therefore entirely understandable. The *Times* report contains a picture of a horribly muti-lated woman who must now reconcile – in the minimal sense of not inter-fere – with the rebels who have gone through the ritual. We are told that

Conacy Laker, 25, finds it hard to look anyone in the eye after losing her nose, ears and upper lip to rebels more than a decade ago. Her physical wounds have healed, but her suffering goes on. 'I have nothing to say to the person who cut me,' she said sternly, staring at the dirt. 'But the person needs to be punished like I was punished.' A moment later, though, forgiveness seemed at the fore. 'What I'm after is peace,' she said. 'If the people who did this to me and so many others are sorry for what they did, then we can take them back.'[36]

By "peace" she presumably means the cessation of warfare; and by "take them back" she presumably means something like readmit them as members of the community, without holding them to further account for their deeds. In effect, the ritual serves the end of political or civic reconciliation. It is not a ritual of *forgiveness*, properly speaking; there is no indication that Ms. Laker has forgiven her attacker, and no reason to think that she ought to. It is a kind of social or political procedure in which the individual is released from threat of punishment in return for abjuring further violence. As mentioned above, it has been explicitly offered as an alternative to arrest and trial.

The ritual is a public affair, reasserting the community's norms, and obligating all involved to cease hostile action. It simultaneously absolves the offender from further account giving, records publicly that specific wrongs were done (by whom and to whom), and establishes that they no longer warrant excluding the offender. Notice that precisely because this

---

[36] I cannot help but note how misleading it is to say that her "physical wounds have healed"; as the picture and description of Ms. Laker makes clear, the mutilation she has suffered is horrific and permanent, absent massive plastic surgery. It is astonishing that she is able even to consider forswearing revenge, and her doing so presumably reflects the very high value her culture places on repairing the social fabric.

transformation is achieved through ritual, its steps are set, uniform, and administered by the relevant representatives of "the moral community" who act by proxy on behalf of the whole. As befits a public procedure, there is little room for judgment as to how the ritual is to be carried out. Presumably, there is some space for judgment when it comes to restitution; but notice too that the representative "impartial spectators" decide the matter, not the injured party, and presumably there are well-understood customs guiding any such decision. This constitutes another difference from interpersonal forgiveness where, as we saw, judgment is unavoidable at every step (for example, with respect to the precise choice of words in which contrition and forgiveness are stated, the precise choice of deeds to be enacted, the assessment of shades of sentiments and inflections of narrative, and so forth). The traditional ritual of apology and reconciliation in one respect resembles the "forgiveness of debts": once the debt is repaid, the matter is concluded, and the sentiments of the debtor or lender are irrelevant.

The ritual of reconciliation is a species of one to many exchange, and is supposed to achieve restoration of civic collaboration but not necessarily a change of sentiment. The emphasis is on behavior rather than on the heart (indeed, the *Times* quotes some absolved rebels as complaining "that they are sometimes shunned and subjected to taunts," which by implication violates the rules). It may be objected that this takes too simple a view of ritual. Common life teaches us that ritual can be productive of a change of sentiments over time. It was for such a reason that I suggested, in discussing interpersonal forgiveness, that interpersonal "rituals" (such as the commitment to break bread together once a day) may help a victim committed to forgiveness to let go of lingering resentment. But my claim here is not that the collaboration made possible by a ritual of reconciliation precludes a change of sentiments, but that neither the ritual nor the ensuing modus vivendi requires any such change. Or to be more precise: it requires moderating the anger that would demand revenge or would make the co-existence possible – whatever "moderating" might mean – but no more.

For the sake of clarity, let us note that the sort of ritual of reconciliation just examined is not the performance of clemency or mercy. The Ugandan rebels were not captured and then spared. Rather, they returned to the community when told that they could rejoin if "cleansed" by this ritual.

We must conclude that the ritual is a mixed case: part political apology, part amnesty, part pardon.

[iv] APOLOGY AND THE UNFORGIVABLE

I argued in Chapter 2 against the thesis that wrong-doers should be categorized as "moral monsters." I also argued against the view that because one cannot preclude the possibility that an offender will undergo the moral changes requisite to forgiveness, she is forgivable. No matter what steps she takes, the injury she inflicted may be of such a scale as to make it impossible for her victim(s) to forswear resentment. My conclusion was not that some wrongs are unforgivable, but that when it is humanly impossible to forgive – as determined by the suitably engaged and informed sympathetic representative of the moral community – then the wrongdoer is unforgiven.

When we move to the political level, the appropriate vocabulary is not that of forgiveness but of apology and the acceptance thereof, or so I have been arguing. Are there wrongs of so great a magnitude that acceptance of apology is unwarranted? Crimes against humanity have, unfortunately, been common throughout human history. Both they and myriad other large scale wrongs are obviously candidates for the political equivalent of the unforgivable. If the magnitude, pervasiveness, and regularity of the crimes and injuries to which history testifies were decisive, political apology and its acceptance would be obviated from the outset. Yet it is precisely such wrongs that political apology is often meant to address.

I want to suggest that, first, the conceptual differences between apology and forgiveness actually provide the former with latitude to do its moral work at the communal or political level. Because the forswearing of resentment is not a requirement for political apology, and because of its proxy structure and symbolic medium, apology may accomplish its ends even when the wrongs in question are *unforgiven* in the sense defined in Chapter 2. At first sight, this seems counter-intuitive: accepting an apology for a wrong that a reasonable person cannot forgive? And yet that is what often occurs at the political level, whether in the context of a "forgiveness ritual" or of a many to many apology. Individual resentment is unaddressed, and forgiveness is neither requested nor granted. But what can be gained is the forswearing of revenge, the sense that cooperation is possible, and in that minimal but crucial sense that reconciliation has taken place. The moral sphere of apology is wider in that sense than that of forgiveness, as is entirely appropriate to the political sphere where the ideals of the morally achievable ought to be lower than in the private sphere. The redemption of the soul ought not be the aim of politics.

If that is granted, we are still left with the question of the limits of apology, or to be precise, the limits of the acceptance of apology. Suppose an apology has been offered in a way that meets the conditions I have specified: might there be conditions under which it is inappropriate to accept it?

One cannot declare a priori that there are duly offered apologies that are *unacceptable* "in principle," no matter what. For what would the principle be? The phenomenology of the subject amply shows that apologies are demanded, and sometimes genuinely offered, even when the wrongs in question are unimaginably large. Consider for example recent demands that the Japanese government apologize for the sexual enslavement by the Japanese military in World War II of many Korean and Chinese women. It would be pointless to demand an apology one could never accept (unless what is sought is to humiliate, but then subjection and not apology is in fact being demanded). But it may be the case, in a way that is analogous to the "unforgiven," that an apology is rightly *unaccepted*, even though it is offered in a way that meets all of the relevant criteria. What would make such an apology *rightly* unaccepted?

Stipulate that issues of reparation are delegated, as I have suggested, to the sphere of justice; that the timing of the apology is appropriate; and that it is understood that the apology is not a request for forgiveness. It may be that the injured party is too angry to listen to the apology; but this does not answer the question just put, unless it is also shown that the anger is rightly held *and* that accepting the apology requires forswearing anger. Suppose that the anger *is* rightly held or warranted. Because it is not a condition for accepting a political apology is that anger be forsworn, I am led to the conclusion that under the stipulated conditions, and only under them, an apology cannot be rightly refused. Of course, if any of the stipulated conditions is not in place, then there may be good reasons for not accepting the apology.

With respect to forgiveness my argument was that if the moral community (the impartial or moral spectator) found, upon informed and sympathetic examination, that in light of the injury suffered it is humanly impossible for the injured person to give up resentment, then the wrongdoer is unforgiven even when the offender has met all of the qualifying conditions for forgiveness. My argument here is that if the offender has fulfilled all of the qualifying conditions for apology, then the moral spectator should find the apology acceptable. The bar for accepting a political apology is, to put it differently, significantly lower than for forgiveness.

And that accurately reflects the different standards for demandingness appropriate to the political and interpersonal spheres.

In discussing forgiveness, I argued that the person who forgives must meet several criteria, if she is make a warranted claim to have forgiven. These were:

1. forswear revenge
2. moderate resentment
3. commit to let go of any lingering resentment
4. re-envision the wrong-doer ("re-framing")
5. re-frame one's view of self
6. address the offender and communicate that forgiveness is granted

The person claiming to have accepted a duly offered *apology* must certainly meet the first criterion. She meets a version of the fourth, in that she agrees to trust that the person or entity apologizing adheres to shared norms of behavior. I have argued that she does not have to subscribe to the second or third criteria, though the *effect* of accepting an apology may be the moderation of resentment. The fifth criterion is accepted insofar as self-definition is affected by one's oppositional relation to one's enemies or oppressors. And the sixth criterion has its analogue here: the apology and its acceptance must be extended and understood to have been extended by both sides if it is to be fulfilled.

[v] APOLOGY, FORGIVENESS, AND CIVIC RECONCILIATION

What each side, in the aftermath of a civil war, essentially demands is that 'the other side' face up to the deaths it caused. To deny the reality of these deaths is to treat them as a dream, as a nightmare. Without an apology, without recognition of what happened, the past cannot return to its place as the past. The ghosts will continue to stalk the battlements. Of course, an apology must reflect acceptance of the other side's grief, something deeper than the Englishman Haynes' well-meaning but offhand remarks in *Ulysses*: 'An Irishman must think like that, I daresay. We feel in England that we have treated you rather unfairly. It seems history is to blame.'   Michael Ignatieff [37]

The case for the expression of political apology as a political virtue rests on its moral appropriateness, as defined by its norms and the relevant political ideals. I have argued that the forswearing of sentiments, in particular resentment, is not a necessary condition of political apology. But

---

[37] M. Ignatieff, *The Warriors' Honor: Ethnic War and the Modern Conscience* (London: Chatto and Windus, 1998), pp. 189–190.

were political apology an admirable but utterly ineffectual virtue, its place would be in a perfectionist or utopian community, not in the deeply marred and imperfect context that constitutes the framework assumed by the present investigation. Fortunately, political apology can and often does have an eventual effect on attitudes and sentiments, and through them on action. This is a defeasible empirical hypothesis, but common life as well as some empirical research lends it support. How is the connection between apology and sentiment and action supposed to work? This is a very large question, and I do not believe that the answer to it is as yet fully understood. I shall nonetheless offer some suggestions.

First, accepting an apology defeats principal reasons one may have for not forswearing revenge (one could not simultaneously accept it and continue taking revenge!). One such reason would be that of honor or "face"; an apology expresses a respectful regard for the offended person, in that sense honoring her. The apology acknowledges allegiance to common norms, and thus offers the hope that cooperation is possible. It thereby defeats another reason for revenge, viz., that a modus vivendi is impossible because the norms governing it are not shared. Apology brings the offender to a level of moral parity with the offended by recognizing the capacity and fact of moral error on the former's part, and that the offended is due a public expression of that recognition. As we have seen, political apology is a public act: the offended person's comparative status is reaffirmed by it. It is reasonably clear why an indication of the trustworthiness of an offender might matter. As to why one's own social standing and sense of moral parity should matter, the end of the day answer can only be that one regards oneself as a social being, and sees oneself through the eyes of others. I sought to explain this phenomenon by appeal to a concept of "sympathy."

Second, empirical research supports the idea that while in a domestic or civic context apology contributes to reconciliation, efforts at reconciliation in the international sphere can "signal" in a way that lessens conflict even though apology is *not* involved. Political apology plays a different role in civic and international contexts, and the reasons why are consistent with the point just made about sympathy. Signaling in the international context seems effective if it has five characteristics: costliness (for the initiator, and for the party that reciprocates; this helps the offer and its acceptance to "stick," because an investment in the process has been made); vulnerability for the initiator (to exploitation, and risk); voluntariness (the signals "are best when made unilaterally"); novelty (as when they are "dramatic . . . unexpected, and thought provoking"); and

irrevocability or noncontingency.[38] The idea is that a signal characterized in these five ways is interpreted as trustworthy by its recipient, and
when reciprocated involves both parties in a process that is difficult to
break off without penalty (it takes on a life of its own, as it were). Signals
are given by means of a "reconciliation event," which Long and Brecke
define as including "senior representatives of respective factions; a public
ceremony accompanied by substantial publicity or media attention that
relays the event to the wider national society; and ritualistic or symbolic
behavior that indicates the parties consider the dispute resolved and that
more amicable relations are expected to follow" (p. 6). In other words, in
this context reconciliation is arrived at through bargaining, compromise,
and deal making, the essentials of which can (they claim) be explained
game theoretically.

They also analyze an alternative to the "signaling model," viz., the
"forgiveness model," which they find useful in civil rather than international disputes. Forgiveness is not effective in the latter arena because
"international society lacks the will and the ways necessary to pursue a
forgiveness process"; because forgiveness engages the sentiments in a
way that signaling does not; because it requires "truth telling, redefinition of the identity of the former belligerents, partial justice, and a call
for a new relationship" (p. 3); and because it is a time-consuming process
(as the work of the many Truth Commissions shows), much more likely
to unfold in the context of intra-national than international conflict.
What sentiments are engaged by "forgiveness" and not by bargaining?
Their answer is attenuated, and seems to come to this: "reconciliation
occurs when shame and anger that often lead to aggression or a desire
for revenge are superceded by a different emotive and cognitive path –
empathy and desire for affiliation. . . . Empathy implies a realistic understanding resulting from feeling with (not for) another, and affiliation is
a basic human motivation, a desire for belonging with another" (p. 28).
While the vocabulary differs from mine, the thoughts here are consistent
with my discussion of sympathy. Long and Brecke do leave the door open
to the possibility that long-term resolution of some international conflicts
may be furthered by a process that closely resembles what I have been

---

[38] The phrases quoted and the distinctions just drawn are from W. Long and P. Brecke,
War and Reconciliation: Reason and Emotion in Conflict Resolution (Cambridge: MIT Press,
2003), p. 20. Their ultimate quarry is the "rational choice" model, and they attempt to
broaden "what we mean by rationality in human problem solving and decision making"
(p. 4). Further paginal references to this book are included directly in my text.

calling apology (p. 154; they mention the relations between Germany and Israel).

Long and Brecke analyze ten relatively recent examples of attempts at reconciliation after civil (intra-national) conflict and ten examples of international attempts at reconciliation. They conclude their discussion of the former as follows:

> those countries that reconciled successfully, that is, restored lasting social order, did so through a protracted process of recognition of harm and public truth telling, re-definition of identities and social roles and antagonists, and partial justice short of revenge, not merely through signal sending in a negotiated bargain. An untidy, seemingly idiosyncratic, but undeniably pattered process of national forgiveness was the foundation of successful national reconciliations. (p. 65)

For reasons I have given, what they are here calling "forgiveness" I am calling "apology." The distinction reflects the relevant differences between collectivities and individuals. With that crucial definitional point in mind, their empirical research helps to explain why apology, when rightly performed in conjunction with apposite institutional arrangements (such as Truth Commissions, if appropriate), has an effect on the sentiments of individuals who are members of the same society, even though the medium through which the apology is offered tends to be heavily symbolic, impersonal, and at times ceremonial.[39] Let me reiterate that I am not arguing that political apology alone will lead to reconciliation either within a society or between societies. Nor am I arguing that political apology cannot be accompanied by or even give occasion to dyadic (interpersonal) forgiveness. I take it for granted that in many "reconciliation events," especially on the international front, neither apology nor regret will be expressed. However, Long and Brecke are focusing on reconciliation after violent conflict. There are many instances where apology has helped to reconcile nations that are not engaged in war, but whose relations are to one degree or another jeopardized (for further examples, see B. O'Neill's *Honor, Symbols, and War*).

It is important to recognize that the distinction between the national and international spheres is not a fixed one so far as the forgiveness and signaling models are concerned. For with an expansion of the sphere

---

[39] Cf. a finding by Ferh and Rockenbach to the effect that cooperation that can be motivated by reciprocity that is seen as just can be undermined by purely strategic and self-interested behavior. E. Fehr and B. Rockenbach, "Detrimental Effects of Sanctions on Human Altruism," *Nature* 422 (2003): 137–140. (I am indebted to S. Darwall for this reference.)

of sympathy, and the implementation of various procedures and institutions, what is by and large true of civil reconciliation may become true of international reconciliation. The main point is that there is a difference – at this historical moment aligned with the national/international distinction – between two avenues to reconciliation. In another formulation of the reason for the difference: the "exploration of truth; expeditious redefinition of the actors' identities through legal, constitutional, or institutional means; or application of limited justice" needed at the national level do not tend to take place at the international level (Long and Brecke, pp. 110–111; the hedging of the claim reflects their formulation on p. 111). Truth telling *is* required for success at the international level, but an "extensive truth-telling process" is very unlikely to take place (p. 113). International instances of reconciliation that involve apology may increase if people come to view themselves in a more cosmopolitan way. It is a matter of spheres of sympathy backed up by appropriate institutional mechanisms.

My argument about political apology – and all of my examples excepting that concerning King Hussein – concern civic rather than international conflict, that is, a context within which the parties concerned in some way identify themselves as part of the same community, and practically speaking find it advantageous to cooperate. I have argued for a distinction between political apology and forgiveness, and take what Long and Brecke say about the latter as holding of the former (it should be clear by now that this is not merely a semantic quibble). Apology, then, is part of a successful effort at reconciliation at the civic level, and may or may not be part of such efforts at the international level. Long and Brecke's findings support the proposition that political apology may help to effect a change in sentiments and attitudes that over time encourage reconciliation. As I would put it, when apology signals not just a bargaining position, but conveys moral content as well, then moral sentiments respond. At the same time, the distinction between spheres of sympathy helps to underline the fact that efforts at reconciliation on the international scene tend be even more impersonal – though not necessarily less successful for that reason – than efforts at the national level.[40] Apology, unlike forgiveness, is conceptually suited to the impersonality in question.

[40] Long and Brecke point out that the *lack* of intimacy between the negotiating parties in international conflict may reduce their vulnerability and make it easier to secure an agreement. At the end of the negotiations, each re-enters his or her own borders. *War and Reconciliation*, p. 118.

I would contend that a successful international effort to reconcile that results from Long and Brecke's criteria also entails – just as in the national case – a change in the way in which citizens understand their identities (contrary to Long and Brecke, p. 153; though see their comment on Poland, p. 100). "We" are no longer defined in part by our enmity to "them," and the damage "they" did to "us" now receives a different interpretation in our collective narrative. Granted, the change in definition of identity will not cut as deep as that accompanying political apology.

It is an observable fact that passions such as resentment can multiply their intensity and duration in the echo chamber of public opinion (the infamous "mob mentality"). Passions enflamed in this way interact with economic and political interests in a complex manner that easily leads to political faction and violence. As winners and losers in the struggle emerge, the line between resentment and *ressentiment* in Nietzsche's sense blurs. Resentment works in tandem with envy and greed, producing a potentially toxic brew even in a democratic regime, as Tocqueville saw.[41] The solution to such problems is enormously complex, and is not my topic here. I have been concerned to analyze the norms that govern political apology, to draw distinctions between it and forgiveness, and to consider empirical hypotheses about the social effects of political apology. I have not suggested that political apology alone is the magic wand that reconciles members of the community. I do suggest that in and of itself, and especially when it is offered to a many by either a many or one, political apology can contribute significantly to reconciliation, but in a relatively restricted, if crucial sense: the reconciliation it promotes is primarily that of non-aggression, combined with a resumed willingness to cooperate and collaborate. This may mean anything from the cessation of violent conflict, to a willingness to do business with a corporation, to participate in the activities of a church, or to attend and support a university.

The exact character of political apology will modulate in light of the differences between kinds of political bodies in question. Truth telling, for example, is a necessary condition of all political apology; but the way and the extent to which it is told will vary. As Long and Brecke show, successful efforts at civic reconciliation following violent conflict typically require a statement of truth that results from the work of some sort of official truth commission (such as was the case in Chile, Argentina, El Salvador,

---

[41] For a helpful study of Tocqueville's views, see P. Zawadski, "Le Ressentiment et l'Égalité: Contribution à Une Anthropologie Philosophique de la Démocratie," in *Le Ressentiment*, ed. P. Ansart, pp. 31–56.

South Africa, and Honduras; though in Uruguay and Mozambique the inquiry into the facts was conducted by private organizations; pp. 48, 56). By contrast, corporate apologies rarely result from the work of any such truth commission. And yet the effectiveness of truth telling in both cases would seem to rely on the same sort of mechanisms. As Long and Brecke note in their summary discussion of reconciliation after civil conflict, truth telling recognizes

the right of the other to the truth, it begins a process of redefinition of identity of the other from enemy to potential partner in a negotiated settlement and a new common future. Truth telling also strips away the impunity of some individuals or groups and begins a reorientation of their role in a reconciled society. . . . It [truth telling] allows the injured to transcend the role of victim and assume a more complete identity as citizen, and it punctures the aura of impunity of aggressors, thus beginning a process of redefining their role. (p. 149)

This is well put, and goes some way to explaining why the steps intrinsic to political apology affect the sentiments. Of course, a full account would still have to explain how "identification" works, and why it matters to the self-understanding of individuals. "Sympathy" in something like Adam Smith's sense is, I have argued, key to any such explanation.

My discussion suggests that as the bonds of affinity weaken along with the thinning out of a sense of affinity – itself the product of cultural difference and perhaps geographical distance – the efficacy of apology lessens; and that the converse holds too (the bonds of affinity strengthen along with thicker ties). Thus in a relatively intimate political setting, such as that of a university located in the American deep South, where the contested issue is profoundly embedded in the life of the university and its community, political apology may have quite a deep impact. In the international context it may play little role in settling a high stakes matter such as violent conflict, though it may be more effective in the overcoming of lower stake issues.

Given the salutary potential of apology in the public sphere, and of interpersonal forgiveness in the private, it would seem to follow that the more they are woven into the civic life of a community, the better off it will be. Is this inference sound?

[vi] A CULTURE OF APOLOGY AND FORGIVENESS: RISKS AND ABUSES

Desmond Tutu and Pumla Gobodo-Madikizela have argued for what amounts to a civic culture of forgiveness. The argument is in part that when a democratic regime attempts to replace an unjust regime, it is essential that ordinary citizens forgive each other many injuries. And in part the argument is that because wrong-doing is pervasive in human life, things will go on better if we accept forgiveness as a virtue central to our individual as well as political lives. Tutu and his supporters made forgiveness a central theme of the TRC proceedings, even though the legal charter for the TRC spoke of reconciliation but not forgiveness, and though some objected that doing so amounted to the inappropriate imposition of a Christian value.[42] And as I have already noted, we have entered an era in which public apology has become a commonplace.

Should a culture of forgiveness and apology be encouraged by political bodies, including governmental? Such a culture would weave the disposition to request and offer forgiveness, or to apologize and accept political apology, into the characters of citizens in private as well as collective life. At first blush such a prospect seems undeniably desirable. And yet the matter is more complicated.

I have argued that interpersonal forgiveness is a virtue, and that it is appropriate to an irremediably non-ideal world. I have also argued that apology has an important place at the political level. Because I have also given reasons why political bodies should not engage in forgiveness (as distinguished from apology), one danger in their actively encouraging a culture of apology and forgiveness is that the two notions will be confused with each other, to the detriment of each. An officially encouraged culture of forgiveness and apology also risks politicizing them: think of the ways in which the demand for expression of apology, or for a request for forgiveness, could subject an individual to coercion or control by a group. The "re-education" camps in China and Cambodia, and more broadly the history of forced religious conversion, undoubtedly offer cautionary tales. One of the characteristics that makes apology effective – namely that it is public – could easily turn it into something that is manipulated, and reduced to a theatrical gesture on the political stage. This would a fortiori be true were forgiveness (both the asking for and granting thereof) "pushed" by political entities, or brokered by third parties

---

[42] On Gobodo-Madikizela's view of the role of forgiveness during the transition to democracy, see her *A Human Being Died that Night*, pp. 132–133. In these pages she argues that the vocabulary of forgiveness "needs to be reinforced at the level of political leadership," and that "through the vicarious experience of stories of forgiveness, a society can begin to heal itself, and a more authentic and lasting sense of self-esteem and of collective worth can come to permeate public discourse about the past." On Tutu's encouragement of forgiveness in the TRC proceedings, see Graybill, *Truth and Reconciliation in South Africa*, pp. 49–50.

such as judges, commentators, or professional mediators. Political apology and forgiveness would easily become expected, then demanded, and sanctions imposed on those who fail to participate correctly in what in effect are public rituals.[43]

The social demand for an apology could also be used to humiliate, even if there is much to apologize for. Imagine that the demand comes from a now-powerful, formerly subject power that is prepared to apply pressure to elicit the apology. Issues of payback, social hierarchy, power, public perception, and honor come into play, obscuring both the moral content and the question of the timing of the apology.

When forgiveness becomes the public rallying cry, played out on daytime television soap operas, encouraged by civic and religious leaders, and praised far and wide for its power to heal, its slide into confusion and vulgarity is almost inevitable. It becomes identified with "closure," it is sentimentalized and transformed into therapy, and the criteria for its practice are obscured. It melds into forgetfulness of wrong, and is granted all too easily, once the expected public theatrics are performed. So too with apology; under such conditions it can easily degenerate into lip service and a morally meaningless formality that may nonetheless pay dividends in the marketplace of goods and public opinion. In short, there is a real danger – one that has to some extent come true – of forgiveness and apology degenerating into what one commentator has called "contrition chic," that is, "a bargain-basement way to gain publicity, sympathy, and even absolution by trafficking in one's status as victim or victimizer."[44]

Religious organizations seek to mold the characters of their adherents, and I have no a priori objection to their including forgiveness on their agenda, although my analysis of the virtue is entirely secular. But when it comes to efforts to enlist the government or any of its many branches (such as the public education system or the courts) in promulgating their views, a distinct set of dangers arise in addition to those already adumbrated. A church will by definition promote a conception of forgiveness (or indeed political apology) that is based on its religious tenets. In addition to worries about staged and coerced confessionals and sentimental

[43] For discussion of some of these dangers, see Tavuchis, *Mea Culpa*, pp. 50–53. On pp. 37–44 he discusses the important role of apology in Japanese culture.
[44] J. B. Elshtain, "Politics and Forgiveness," in *Burying the Past*, ed. N. Biggar, p. 40. She goes on to say: "This confessional mode now extends to entire nations, where separating powerful and authentic acts and expressions of regret from empty gestures become even more difficult than it is on the level of individuals, one to another."

dramas of forgiveness – especially self-forgiveness – there is the issue of coercively introducing religious notions into public life.

Forgiveness and political apology are valuable private and civic virtues. In the ways I have indicated, they are also easily corrupted when put to social or political use. It belongs to considerations of moral and civic education to decide how best they should be fostered. As with virtues such as gratitude, their genesis seems a paradox: they are to be fostered and encouraged, but not demanded or coerced. They are the "right thing to do" under appropriate circumstances, and thus something one should do, something one can be blamed for failing to do. Insofar as blame exerts pressure, one can be actively discouraged from failing to exercise the virtue. And yet the virtue is corrupted if it is fostered in the wrong way, or its absence penalized in the wrong way. The hand of political bodies such as government, corporations, churches, and educational institutions is generally too heavy to perform so delicate an operation as fostering public virtue. They may safely remove impediments to virtue, however, and erect barriers to vice. Perhaps they will most ably promote these virtues by setting a good example: practice what you preach, preach the right ideals, and apologize when you fail to live them out. Simple though the advice is, public life does not provide many illustrations of its being taken.

[vii] POLITICAL APOLOGY, NARRATIVE, AND IDEALS

We are not enemies, but friends. We must not be enemies. Though passion may have strained, it must not break our bonds of affection. The mystic chords of memory, stretching from every battle-field, and patriot grave, to every living heart and hearthstone, all over this broad land, will yet swell the chorus of the Union, when again touched, as surely they will be, by the better angels of our nature.

Abraham Lincoln[45]

In Chapter 2 (section viii) I developed the thesis that forgiveness is intertwined with narrative. I argued that in order to qualify for forgiveness, the offender would have to show that she has sympathetically entered into the situation of her victim, and understands the victim's narrative from that point of view. The offender would also have to offer a narrative accounting for how she came to do wrong, how that wrong-doing does

---

[45] A. Lincoln, First Inaugural Address, March 4, 1861; in *Abraham Lincoln: Speeches and Writings 1859–1865*, ed. D. E. Fehrenbacher (New York: Library of America, 1989), p. 224.

not express the totality of her person, and how she expects to become worthy of approbation. The offender who addresses a request for forgiveness presents a narrative of guilt, regret, and remorse, explains how she came to do the injury, describes the moral sentiments that ensued, and convincingly depicts a change of ways that will unfold over time.

For her part, the victim must re-frame both her view of the offender, and her view of herself. The irrepressible need to narrate is most obvious when one is injured; people typically tell their story vividly and repeatedly, in some cases compulsively. Re-framing your perspective on the offender, and eventually yourself, means that your resentful "stories," which have perhaps expanded to the point of characterizing the offender as a "monster" or "animal," must be revised. Furthermore, you must re-frame your view of yourself, in part insofar as your self-definition is affected by your oppositional relation to enemies or oppressors. Your narrative too projects forward a story of who you want to be in relation to self-past, given the wrong(s) you have suffered. For both oppressor and oppressed, the narratives are a crucial part of forging a future that is not trapped in a closed loop determined by the past. In the paradigm case of forgiveness, the offender's and the injured person's narratives are intertwined in the dyadic relationship that is interpersonal forgiveness. Their relationship is, as I put it, dialogical. The giving and receiving of accounts, and the demand for as well as offering of explanations that make intelligible one's past deeds and warrant trust in promises about the future, weave a narrative of forgiveness.

At stake is not simply the "story" (the bare chronicle of facts), but a meaning-making unification thereof, and especially the interplay of *perspectives* over time. I suggested that notionally, story is content abstracted from viewpoint, and that there will be different ways of trying to convey the content. Narration does the conveying or the telling; it organizes events into some sort of pattern – say, a temporal pattern, a causal one, or one that supplies insight into motivations (this is not a complete list, and these could be made to overlap) – *and* implies one or more perspectives. The basic ideas of narrative include (i) the organization of events into a pattern or whole with beginning, middle, and end – plot, in short; and (ii) the perspective of the narrator on events and perspectives of the agents or actors – a point of view implicit or explicit in the telling. That the telling is perspectival does not mean that it is false.

The narratives of both parties in our paradigmatic scene of forgiveness are both backward looking and forward looking – they involve a commitment to make certain changes such that one's life story will unfold in the ways desired. A narrative of forgiveness will be projective as well as recollective, both remembering and reinterpreting so as to go forward meaningfully. Its discourse is typically quite elaborate, with a marked tendency to expand. Forgiveness understood as a process, rather than simply as the end result, is much concerned with the temporalization of relations (to action, to other agents, to the actual and ideal self, to ideals as such), and narrative is a form of explanation ideally suited – and universally deployed – to articulate and convey a unity-making perspective through time in a way that attempts to make it meaningful. That attempt requires the engagement of the appropriate emotions; but it is also rhetorical in that it seeks to persuade both its owner and auditor of its truth.[46] As I put it, the narrative is a telling *to* someone (including, to oneself!); it seeks to convey how things really stood, how they developed, how they stand now, and why one's responses and perspective were and are intelligible and appropriate. At several levels, narratives of resentment and forgiveness typically seek a public.

I also argued that certain ideals guide the narrative; in particular, ideals of trust, renewal, growth, respect, harmony of self and reconciliation with others, affection, and love. These help define the sort of person one would wish to be, the principles one would wish to live out. Forgiveness stands on the principle that these ideals may be realized over time, and are not "mere ideals" in spite of the fractured state of the world. Forgiveness assumes a background narrative of human life as temporal, embodied, emotive, and interdependent or social.

Is there an analogy, at the level of political apology, to the role that narrative plays in forgiveness? And is there a political analogy to the ideals that undergird forgiveness?

It would be surprising if there were no similarity between the making-intelligible discourse of political apology and that of interpersonal forgiveness if it is true, as I have claimed, that they belong to the same family of concepts. Ordinary life teems with story telling; and every community has a narrative – or possibly several – about its origins, virtues, suffering, and ideals. The construction of social identity within a group presents itself narratively as well.[47] Large scale social or political narratives of

---

[46] On the connection between a successful narrative and the engagement of the emotions, see once again P. Goldie's "One's Remembered Past: Narrative Thinking, Emotion, and the External Perspective," p. 305.

[47] For an interesting analysis, see C. Tilly's *Stories, Identities, and Political Change* (New York: Rowman and Littlefield, 2002). Tilly's main focus is on the place of narratives "in political mobilization, conflict, and change," and particularly on "political identity stories in

collective resentment or endurance or overcoming (those three may form stages of a single narrative) are legion. Sometimes they are cast in religious or quasi-religious forms, sometimes not. We may term this "political mythology," if we keep firmly in mind that contrary to contemporary usage, a "myth" simply means "story" or "account," and is not necessarily a falsehood or fiction. We would also have to keep in mind that "political" is being used in the broad sense specified at the start of this chapter. A political myth may represent truth, or a blend of truth and falsehood, or falsehood, or fantasy, as the case may be, but will be taken by those who believe in it to be true. It can be *expressed* discursively or non-discursively (through images, for example).[48] If conceived as "a nation's" or "a community's" account of itself, its character is that of political autobiography – a narrative of collective self. This collective autobiography may take any of several forms, and indeed interweave several forms, from the genealogical (tracing "us" back to the Founders, the origin, divine intervention, etc.), to the exemplary deeds of the greats (the *Aeneid* as political mythology), to a detailed history told "from below" (as from the perspective of the ordinary worker, say) – to name just a few of the many possibilities.

nationalism, citizenship, social movements, democratization, and state transformation." He sees them as "outcomes of contentious conversation" (p. 6), and notes that "stories emerge from active social interchange, modify as a result of social interchange, but in their turn constrain social interchange as well. They embody ideas concerning what forms of action and interaction are possible, feasible, desirable, and efficacious . . . Even if the individuals involved harbor other ideas, the embedding of stories in social networks seriously constrains interactions, hence collective actions, of which people in those networks are capable" (pp. 8–9). My discussion of "sympathy" chimes with his thesis that "social identities at all scales, from individual to international, combine three elements: relations, boundaries, and stories. Let us think of an individual as one kind of *social site* – a locus of coordinated social action" (p. 11). One of Tilly's claims is that the construction of social identity through narrative can have important political consequences, and he argues for the view that "transactions among social sites (including persons)" are "real" (p. 208), a view he calls "relational realism." Although my concern here is neither with the ontology of social entities or relations, nor with the creation or structure of "identity," Tilly's point about the reality of transactions also meshes well with my discussion of the role of apology in political life.

[48] As Flood puts it in *Political Myth*: "a political myth can be said to exist when accounts of a more or less common sequence of events, involving more or less the same principal actors, subject to more or less the same overall interpretation and implied meaning, circulate within a group . . . political myths can be represented in iconic forms such as paintings, posters, and sculptured monuments" (p. 42). In the next chapter, I discuss one such monument, or more precisely, memorial. Or again, political myth "would be an ideologically marked narrative which purports to give a true account of a set of past, present, or predicted political events and which is accepted as valid in its essentials by a social group" (p. 44).

Just as we distinguished between a story and a narrative, so on the political level let us distinguish between the historical story – the bare chronological chronicle or listing of events – and the unifying perspective on the story that is a historical narrative. Williams notes that "a chronicle does not try to make sense of anything," unlike a (historical) narrative.[49] The point is a bit overstated – even a chronicle makes *some* sense of events – but the contrast between chronicle and narrative is nonetheless useful. Obviously that history can be told with respect to the community as a whole, with an eye to this or that relation (say, in its international affairs, or economic development, or what have you), or at the micro-level (the history of this organization, for example). A leader with great rhetorical gifts will often, when faced with crisis, seek to invoke a unifying narrative or political myth. An excellent example may be found in Lincoln's words, quoted at the start of this section, uttered on the eve of the American Civil War.

And yet the relevant differences between the two contexts – the political and the personal – immediately suggest significant disanalogies between the narratives of political apology and forgiveness. As already noted, the historical narrative of a society is the upshot of extraordinarily complex interactions over time, and because the perspective of the narrator(s) itself forms part of those interactions, it will invariably be liable to emendation and controversy. The debate as to whose narrative it is, and under whose control it lies, may in principle always be raised at the socio-political level; and every example of apology we have discussed did in fact raise it. In a complex society containing divergent and rival viewpoints, passions, interests, commitments, histories, more and less powerful players, the chances of there being a single "national narrative" to which everyone sincerely subscribes are not great. And even were they to do so, the chances that they would understand the narrative in the same way are small.[50] In the paradigm case of forgiveness, the narrative was "dialogical"; it is unlikely that something analogous will occur

---

[49] B. Williams, *Truth and Truthfulness: An Essay in Genealogy* (Princeton, NJ: Princeton University Press, 2002), p. 238.

[50] Consider Williams, *Truth and Truthfulness*, p. 256, with reference to various historical stories seeking to make sense of periods and institutions: "there is no one thing that these various stories are 'for,' other than trying to make sense of the past. There is no one kind of thing that different audiences are seeking when they seek something that makes sense to them. . . . Many interpretations and styles of interpretation, then, can be found between false teleological history, on the one hand, and minimalist history on the other." A key contention here is that each "style can, in its best examples, sustain a decent respect for the truth," without requiring that there be such a thing as *the* truth.

in the context of political apology in a complex and pluralistic society, even under ideal conditions. At the same time, the narratives of apology are not simply "monological" in the sense that was appropriate – or so I argued – to non-paradigmatic cases of forgiveness (such as third-party forgiveness).

I argued that political apology must meet several criteria or norms, namely (a) recognize the truth; (b) state expressly and clearly that wrong-doing occurred, identify the party that did wrong and to whom, and assume responsibility; and (c) state expressly and clearly that an apology is hereby offered. Political apology is neither forgetting nor excusing. I also argued that political apology does not necessarily record or express sentiments, on the part either of the party that offers it or receives it, and that a successful apology is "accepted" or "noted." The appropriate response to it is not forgiveness. Unlike forgiveness, political apology seeks to put the matter on the public record – and therefore cannot be offered in secret or in private – and its discourse is typically brief, impersonal, to the point. Its goal is not an explanation of how the injury came about – the details of the causality moral or otherwise that led to the wrong-doing – but rather the assurance that it will not happen again, the affirmation of a shared moral perspective. Political apology is rhetorical in the sense that it seeks to persuade its audience that the wrong for which the offender has apologized ought no longer be "held against" the offender. Political apology is a form of *address*, seeking to convince that conflict, or the threat of retaliation, should cease, and cooperation based at least on minimal trust in the reliability of the offending party should be unimpeded by the wrong in question. The rhetorical character and quality of address evident in the Resolutions of the University of Alabama and the United States government discussed above are particularly striking.

The person requesting forgiveness should enter sympathetically into the narrative of her victim, as well as offer a narrative of her own that accounts for her having done wrong, and that makes credible her commitment to change. Neither of these expectations obtains for one offering political apology. The offender need not and typically does not sympathetically grasp the situation of the offended from the latter's point of view, as that point of view is made accessible through a narrative. No such narrative need be offered. Further, the person offering forgiveness must change her narrative both of herself, and of the offender. Except in a relatively "thin" way, this is not a requirement for acceptance of apology. And so in political apology, the perspective of both parties is "external" in that it is held from outside the story world temporally, and also detached from that world in that it need not attempt to change places in imagination with the other, to "simulate" the other's perspective, or to see the matter through the other's eyes. The context of political apology is impersonal, as I have said, not only in that the relevant members may be "manys" and not individuals, but in that social relation rather than one's affective state is primary.

What room then is left for narrative, in the context of apology? I shall seek to answer this question by focusing on civic rather than international contexts. Within the former there will be at least some minimal acceptance of a common narrative, whereas in the latter common or national narratives may themselves compete. Of course the question here is not whether the request for forgiveness *is* a narrative; its verbal declaration may consume all of three words. So too with apology. Our question is whether the background story telling, so important to forgiveness, has its parallel in the sphere of political apology. In spite of the disanalogies just mentioned, I shall argue that there are several ways in which narrative does continue to function in connection with political apology.

First, the basic shift from an "internal" perspective on one's wrong-doing or injury to an increasingly external perspective – one as from the standpoint of the moral community – is as fundamental to political apology as to forgiveness. This "formal" dimension of narrative is worked out on the political plane; the touchstone of the matter is one's place in the community. The party offering apology wishes to be viewed as a cooperative member of the group; the apology is addressed to the injured party as well as the community. Where the offender is the government, the effort is also to draw the injured party back into the community fully (note the reference to "reconciliation" in the United States Senate's apology for its failures with respect to the lynching issue, for example). In accepting the apology, the injured party agrees to mend this part of the social fabric; its perspective on its injury is decidedly social. An apology put on the record is in part a performative act that by its nature as public documents a perspective larger than that of the dominant group, and implies accountability to ideals. Hence it also reaffirms that there is a larger moral community to which the offender too wishes to belong. Apology defines a greater "we," and activates a perspective that expresses as well as seeks to preserve a common story. This will convey unity through time, shared outlook, and responsibility.

In the background of political apology lies a narrative about the desirability of belonging to the moral community, and of one's role in it. I will return in a moment to the question of the relevant ideals that make the community desirable in this respect. It is clear that communities within which political apology can take place are distinctive on several counts. Most obviously, the notion of public accountability is recognized, along with the notion that power is answerable to the injustices it does or even tolerates. A society hospitable to political apology not only values speaking truth to power; but also power speaking truth to the less powerful. The conditions under which political bodies or individuals may demand and receive an apology necessarily share some "family resemblances." In spite of their many structural and cultural differences, they will possess a "common narrative" in the sense that they will share certain ideals.

Second, at least one "many" is party to every political apology. Now, the given collectivity or political body does not imagine, via mediation of the impartial spectator, what the other would feel were they willing or able. Groups qua collectivities do not exercise "sympathy" with each other, or adopt each other's perspective on themselves, by means of sympathy understood in that way. Rather, they personify themselves and other collectivities. The proxy structure discussed above requires that the many be treated as though it were one; the collectivity is in effect anthropomorphized, viewed as a person capable of offering meaningful statements in its own name. In this sense, political apology moves in a medium of metaphor, and metaphor is an element of any political or personal narrative.

Third, both parties to the exchange signal that the disposition to retaliate shall cease; they project forward a picture of self in relation to their self-past. As in the case of forgiveness, the overarching tenet is that the future need not be a repetition of the traumas of the past. The common narrative will not, therefore, be *fatalistic* (whether "fate" is understood in secular or religious terms does not matter for present purposes). Crucially, it is open to revision, and thus open to constructive criticism.

Fourth, political apology puts the relevant truth on the public record, and formally speaking that record is a narrative; it is not just a bare chronicle or story. Political apology is a form of public *memory*, and hence is opposed to burying wrongs in the depths of forgetfulness. The narratives to which the parties to political apology are committed necessarily place value on remembering injury – though in a way that does not make the injury *defining*. To be sure, each party is defined by the history of wrongdoing – and of apologizing as well as accepting apology – in the sense that the history shaped a phase of their existence. But thanks to political apology, their self-now does not identify itself or the other simply as the victim or wrong-doer. Remembering is supposed to be compatible with the possibility of redefining identity in such a way that peaceful cooperation between the parties – call it "reconciliation" – is possible. Political apology is a temporalized process that holds open the possibility of a future relevantly different and better. This entails that a group's sense of identity will not express itself through a narrative immune to revision, and therefore that its identity is not immune to emendation.[51]

It tells its story on a time-line that is pedagogic not only in the sense that it is committed to learning from the past (as the U.S. government apologies we have examined explicitly declare), but to setting an example for the future. It values honesty, truth telling, accountability, trustworthiness, and subscription to the community's norms, on the part of the offender; and on the part of the offended, the forswearing revenge, willingness to re-envision the offender as well as self, and the insistence that the relevant norms be met. All this is publicly performed, as it were, and shapes the communal future. The narratives of apology preserve memory in order to encourage the appropriate kind of growth. In this political context, the relevant growth is more appropriately termed *progress*.

The narrative of political apology is shaped by a number of ideals, and I have referred to them at various junctures already. These include the ideals of accountability and responsibility; of self-governance according to justified shared norms; trustworthiness; cooperation; forswearing of violence, of revenge, and of hostile behavior that threatens peaceable cooperation; the obligations of power to those over whom it is exercised; and the indispensability of both truth and of publicly stating the truth. These are substantive ideals, and many societies either reject them or pay them only lip service. A society hospitable to political apology is a significant achievement.

Another ideal is that of a future not captive to the morally objectionable aspects of the past. I referred to this as the idea of "progress," but one might also speak of "hope." Historical time is here viewed as non-reiterative or non-cyclical. It is difficult today to affirm the possibility of progress with any confidence when discussing the development of morality in the public sphere. Events of the last century seem to have undermined any robust "faith in progress."[52] It is not my present purpose to

[51] Ignatieff remarks: "Resistance to historical truth is a function of group identity: nations and peoples weave their sense of themselves into narcissistic narratives that strenuously resist correction." *The Warrior's Honor*, p. 185.

[52] For an interesting recent discussion, see P.-A. Taguieff, *Le Sens du Progrès: Une Approche Historique et Philosophique* (Paris: Flammarion, 2004). Also helpful here is A. O. Hirschman's *The Rhetoric of Reaction: Perversity, Futility, Jeopardy* (Cambridge, MA: Harvard

argue for or against a general theory of moral and political progress. I
am however asserting that if political apology is to be defended, a narrative that appeals to the possibility of progress in the limited sense I have
described is indispensable. Were this ideal completely empty, political
apology would become a sort of charade, for its commitments to trustworthiness and cooperation in the future would mean nothing. Political
apology would be reduced to a political stratagem intended to accomplish some momentary objective. Or more likely, it would have no role at
all to play, and the governing narrative would – assuming that wrong-
doing was as pervasive in human life as we know it to be – take the
form of justifications of revenge for never-to-be-forgotten insults and
injuries.

This is not a merely abstract proposition. Ignatieff comments with
reference to the former Yugoslavia, Rwanda, and South Africa:

> ... the past continues to torment because it is *not* past. These places are not living
> in a serial order of time but in a simultaneous one, in which the past and the
> present are a continuous, agglutinated mass of fantasies, distortions, myths, and
> lies. Reporters in the Balkan war often discovered, when they were told atrocity
> stories, that they were uncertain whether these stories had occurred yesterday
> or in 1941 or 1841 or 1441. For the tellers of the tale, yesterday and today were
> the same. Simultaneity, it would seem, is the dream time of vengeance. Crimes
> can never safely be fixed in the historical past; they remain locked in the eternal
> present, crying out for blood.[53]

It is not by accident that we speak of "cycles" of revenge (though "spirals"
would be more accurate); the temporal structure of revenge and counter
revenge may be set out on a linear time line, but seems experienced as
a kind of circle the whole meaning of which is present to the mind with
equal vividness, and without possibility of a non-reiterative future.

The overlap between the ideals of political apology and those guiding
the narrative of forgiveness is only partial. The latter included ideals of
harmony of self, of affection, and of love; these are not ideals required
for the narrative of political apology.

University Press, 1991). I note that by "progress" I do not mean "optimism." W. T. Davis
puts it well: "Optimism, not despair, is the enemy of hope. Optimism blinds us to the
shadow side of life. Optimism wears a forced smile, represses intuitive danger signals, and
projects its own evil onto others. Optimism is a life that denies the truth and therefore
prevents necessary change. Hope then, arises not amid optimism but amid the ruins of
crumbled dreams." *Shattered Dream: America's Search for Its Soul* (Valley Forge, PA: Trinity
Press International, 1994), p. 165.

[53] M. Ignatieff, *The Warrior's Honor*, p. 186.

As was true with respect to forgiveness, however, the backdrop of political apology is the imperfection of the political and social world. Political narrative attempts to respond to that imperfection in ways that allow for emendation but make no promise of comprehensive improvement of the picture as such. Its aim on any particular occasion is quite specific and localized, and its ideals encourage the possibility of that sort of patchwork improvement. To one attempting either to flee the imperfections of the socio-political world, or to mend those imperfections altogether, political apology as I have defined it would seem either irrelevant or unacceptably accommodating.

I argued that forgiveness made interpersonal reconciliation possible in at least the minimal sense of non-interference, and that when it is successful political apology accomplishes something similar. The ideals of political apology include reconciliation, or at least conciliation where only lack of relation or conflict existed before.[54] At a minimum, this means not just non-interference but a willingness to cooperate as members of the same community, as the occasion demands. When one of the parties is the sovereign or government, non-interference without cooperation is unlikely. The dependence of both individuals and political bodies on the government is in practice going to be significant; and in some sense the obverse will ultimately be true as well. By contrast, the relation between individuals who have accomplished forgiveness need not be one of continued dependence, or indeed anything at all beyond non-interference.

Political "reconciliation" in the minimalist sense I have mentioned – non-interference, willingness to cooperate with each other, but not necessarily forgiveness – may seem to be a superficial achievement in comparison with reconciliation understood as deep reunion, love, and harmony. But compared to ongoing violent conflict and ferocious retaliation, it is heaven on earth. Furthermore, the reconciling ideals of political apology are substantive and noble, even though they are not intended to satisfy the soul's deepest yearnings. I have not argued that political apology is

---

54 Everything I have said about "reconciliation" should be taken to apply to conciliation as well; given that the latter term is rarely used, however, I have for the most part avoided it. The assumption that "reconciliation" implies pre-existing relation or harmony leads to statements such as this: "Aboriginal people have never asked for reconciliation, we have never asked for the imposition of white culture or government over us. The term 'reconciliation' is premised on the notion of a pre-existing state of goodwill between the invaders of and Aboriginal people. Such goodwill has never existed." P. Coe, *Voices of Aboriginal Australia*, ed. I. Moores (Sydney: Butterfly Books, 1994), p. 283.

the magic key that unlocks the secrets of reconciliation at the political level, and do not believe that is the case.[55] And yet the part that political apology may play in civic reconciliation is neither trivial nor dispensable, and a community in which it is commended and practiced is an accomplishment as difficult as it is rare.

[55] For a sobering and perceptive discussion of the relation between truth and political reconciliation, see Ignatieff, *The Warrior's Honor*, pp. 164–190. I am obviously in agreement with his concluding point that "reconciliation built on mutual apology accepts that history is not fate, that history is not to blame" (p. 190).

5

Truth, Memory, and Civic Reconciliation without Apology

> Progress, far from consisting in change, depends on retentiveness....
> Those who cannot remember the past are condemned to repeat it.
>
> Santayana[1]

Throughout this study I have argued that interpersonal forgiveness as well as political apology require that the truth be told and heard. Both are therefore committed not only to truth telling, but to the proposition that it is better to remember than to forget. I also argued that both may promote reconciliation within their respective spheres and in their respective senses of the term, which is to say that the reconciliation they afford is built on truth and memory. I did not argue that reconciliation is impossible without forgiveness or apology. In this concluding chapter, I discuss a well known and fascinating candidate for civic reconciliation that is certainly committed to remembering, but is silent on the question of apology and forgiveness, in spite of the fact that its context was that of war and bitter civic discord. I do not offer it as an example of failed apology, but as an intriguing counter-example to the theses I have advanced. What are its successes and failures? What does it teach us about the relationship between truth telling, narrative, memory, political apology, and civic reconciliation (I am not focusing here on international reconciliation)?

A people's memory of itself is expressed in part through its narrative, and that narrative can be and often is presented not just discursively but

---

[1] G. Santayana, *The Life of Reason or the Phases of Human Progress*, 5 vols., 2nd ed. (New York: C. Scribner's Sons, 1936), vol. 1, p. 284.

also in stone, wood, and metal. War memorials are particularly instructive when considered as sites of memory and truth telling. By definition, moral issues of justification, liability, and apology are inseparable from communal remembering of war. These issues become all the more pressing and perplexing in at least two sorts of cases: civil war, and a war in which one suffered defeat. As of this writing, the greatest modern foreign policy catastrophe for the United States was the Vietnam War. The United States not only lost – completely and unequivocally – but waged war at tremendous human, financial, and civic cost. The internal discord, moral hatred, and institutional damage caused by the enterprise was incalculable. For the nation as a whole, the defeat in Vietnam was unprecedented. Civic reconciliation was desperately needed, and it would have to take form in some sort of shared narrative. How is a calamity of this magnitude and character to be remembered?[2]

For several decades, the answer in the United States was – as little as possible. Especially as far as the federal government was concerned, the story was not to be told. And this determined forgetfulness by the collectivity that was keenly felt as an insult, a denial of due recognition for the sacrifices made by those who served their nation in the war. The war's disrepute had devolved upon its soldiers. It is as though the nation first sought to purify itself of its loss by shifting the stain to those it had sent to fight, sending them away again . . . this time into official oblivion. The resentment felt in response added yet another layer to the hatreds engendered by the war.

With the decision to memorialize the war, a chance for reconciliation finally presented itself. The act of civic memory I have in mind is inscribed in the symbolic heart of the capital city of the United States, namely "the Mall" in Washington, DC.[3] But the decision to memorialize the war

---

[2] Other periods and other nations have of course also struggled with the problem of public memory. How did (and how should) the Southern Confederacy of the United States remember its soldiers who died – in vain – in defense of a cause inseparable from the preservation of slavery? To take a very different context, consider S. Friedländer's observation on "what for some Germans seems to be an intractable predicament: the Nazi past is too massive to be forgotten, and too repellent to be integrated into the 'normal' narrative of memory. For the last forty years, Germans belonging to at least two generations have been caught between the impossibility of remembering and the impossibility of forgetting." "Some German Struggles with Memory," in *Bitburg in Moral and Political Context*, ed. G. Hartman, p. 27.

[3] The Mall in its present shape is a fairly recent creation. Taking the White House, Capitol, and the monuments to Lincoln and Jefferson as reference points, the area defined is quadrilateral in shape, or more precisely, trapezoidal. At the west end of the area sits the Lincoln Memorial, and opposite it at the east end, the Capitol. The White House to the

itself ignited a bitter round of controversy – in effect, a conflict over memory. Disputes about memorialization are not unusual, as the history of the other monuments on the nation's Mall show.[4] But this particular dispute centered on an unresolved issue: given that the war ended in total defeat, and that the morality of the cause lay at the heart of the domestic disagreement, should memory valorize the cause and those who served it? Or valorize the one but remain neutral on the other? Or valorize neither? The debate concerns the extent to which a memorial should unite war and politics, though in a peculiar context. The Mall's land is sanctified neither in the sense that Verdun and Gettysburg are, because it is not a battlefield, nor in the sense definitive of the monumental Arlington National Cemetery (which is connected to the Mall by the Arlington Memorial Bridge). No one is buried on the Mall itself (with the exception of Mr. Smithson, who is buried in the Smithsonian Institution's "Castle"). The Mall's memorials connect (and occasionally separate) war and politics on a purely symbolic level.

The answer to the question as to how to remember the Vietnam War was the result of a massive amount of controversy, public commentary, an open competition among proposals, and revisions insisted upon by various governmental authorities. In a real sense it was the result of collective effort, sentiment, thought, and prejudice – as well as of a single individual's brilliant architectural imagination. Amazingly – given the conflict that is at every level the context of the memorial – the designer turned out to be a woman, of Asian extraction, and too young to have had any direct involvement in the war or the domestic turbulence it caused.[5]

north and the Jefferson Memorial to the south bisect the area vertically. For convenience I shall extend the usual nomenclature and refer to this area as the "Mall." For all practical purposes, the center of the Mall is marked by the towering Washington Monument. The area derives its substantive unity not so much from its geometric properties as from its purpose, namely that of memorializing, and from the surprisingly tight set of symbolic connections between the monuments. It has been and continues to be a work in progress, as befits an unfinished narrative.

4 As an example, consider the torturous century-long history of the construction of a monument one would have thought relatively uncontroversial, viz., that dedicated to George Washington. See F. L. Harvey's *History of the Washington National Monument and Washington National Monument Society* (Washington, DC: Government Printing Office, 1903). No controversy about a national memorial has been, so far as I know, as divisive as that surrounding the Vietnam Veterans Memorial; and this is traceable to the unresolved question as to the justice of the war itself.

5 Maya Lin was at the time a twenty-one year old student. The criteria set down for the design competition – themselves the product of, as well as the occasion for conflict and debate – were that the monument (1) be reflective and contemplative in character, (2) be harmonious with its site and surroundings, (3) provide for the inscription of the names

The Vietnam Veterans Memorial (VVM) was dedicated in 1982 and rapidly became the most visited, commented upon, and imitated memorial in the United States. It sparked memorial building not just around the country, but also demands from many constituencies for memorials on the Mall to their heroes, causes, and suffering. To date, a Korean War Memorial, F. D. Roosevelt Memorial, World War II Memorial, and Holocaust Museum have followed the VVM on or near the Mall. More will join an already crowded field. It is a sort of stampede of claims to public memory, sympathy, and recognition, all connected in one way or another to suffering or the triumph over opposition. The VVM has had a profound effect on countless individuals who have visited it, as is shown by the reams of artifacts left at "the wall," as though at a cemetery or site of pilgrimage (the artifacts are carefully collected and preserved by the National Park Service). It is the site of continued, communal remembrance, and has "spoken to" myriad visitors who have, in turn, responded with oceans of emotion, commentary, and what might be characterized as offerings. But what exactly is remembered, and what is forgotten? What truth is grasped, and what not? What is said, and what unsaid?

of those who gave their lives or remain missing, (4) make no political statement about the war, and (5) occupy up to two acres of land. Objections to the Vietnam Veterans Memorial (hereafter VVM) are thus partly objections to the criteria for the competition. The design competition was open to all U.S. citizens over eighteen years of age. The jury of seven internationally known architects and one writer/design critic was selected by the Vietnam Veterans Memorial Fund (VVMF). A total of 1,421 entries were submitted to the competition. They were judged anonymously (identified to the jurors only by number). After deliberating, the jury unanimously recommended Lin's design to the eight directors of the VVMF, who in turn accepted the nomination unanimously. The proposal then went through the lengthy federal approval process. After a rancorous and heated debate between supporters and opponents of the design, it was finally agreed to add a sculpture of three servicemen and, a bit further away, a flagpole to the Memorial site. Realistic statues of three soldiers (two of them white, one black) sculpted by Frederick Hart, and the flagpole were added in the area between the VVM and the Lincoln Memorial (the dedication ceremony was held on Veteran's Day, November 13, 1982), constituting a sort of entrance device for those approaching from the southwestern side. The figures contemplate the names of the dead from a distance. The inscription at its base reads: "This flag represents the service rendered to our country by the veterans of the Vietnam War. The flag affirms the principles of freedom for which they fought and their pride in having served under difficult circumstances." The statues and flagpole add a conventional, representational dimension to the memorializing of the Vietnam veterans. Still later, a sculpture of three nurses (all women) was also added toward the southeastern approach. They strike one as helpless and vulnerable (they seem to be waiting for a "medivac" helicopter), even as they also give care. These clusters are further testimony to the conflictual views about public memory and narration of the war – as well as to the importance attached to public recognition.

It is a truism in empirical psychology that memory is selective and not merely replicative. As the editors of a recent volume on the subject put it, "a virtual consensus now exists among memory researchers that memory is a dynamic medium of experience shaped by expectancies, needs, and beliefs, imbued with emotion, and enriched by the inherently human capacity for narrative creation."[6] This is not to say, of course, that there is no distinction between truly and falsely remembering the past – else the notions of forgiveness and apology would hardly be worth our attention. It is to say that the distinction can become complicated, especially when the truth is that of a *narrative* in the sense of the term I have discussed.

All the more so, indeed, when the sphere is social or political, and the subject is war. We should be even more inclined to think of political narratives as reconstructive recollections of the past whose claim to tell "the truth" is best responded to critically. But we should not infer, to repeat a point, that the narratives are therefore "myths" and "false." Certainly, civic memory is subject to political control, and its control is crucial to the exercise of power.[7] Orwell was on target when he wrote (in the voice of "the Party") that "who controls the past controls the future; who controls the present controls the past."[8] Political power, including in a democracy, can be exercised – at least in the short run – on the basis of the political equivalent of false or partial and distorted memories. Testimony is ample as to the efforts by the powerful to regulate communal memory – often by controlling how that memory is inscribed in public memorials – and correspondingly to extirpate competing memories.[9] Yet the blend of

[6] S. J. Lynn and K. M. McConkey, "Preface" to their edited volume *Truth in Memory* (New York: Guilford Press, 1998), p. ix.

[7] J. E. Young insightfully comments: "the usual aim in any nation's monuments... is not solely to displace memory or to remake it in one's own image: it is also to invite the collaboration of the community in acts of remembrance. To the extent that the myths or ideals embodied in a nation's monuments are the people's own, they are given substance and weight by such reification and will appear natural and true; hence, an inescapable partnership grows between a people and its monuments. It is at precisely this point, however, that a critical approach to memorials might rescue us from a complicity that allows our *icons* of remembrance to harden into *idols* of remembrance.... In effect, there can be no self-critical monuments, only critical viewers." "Memory and Monument," in *Bitburg in Moral and Political Perspective*, ed. G. Hartman, p. 112. As will become evident, I take partial exception to the point that no monument is self-critical.

[8] G. Orwell, *1984* (New York: New American Library, 1961), part 2, ch. 9, p. 248.

[9] For example, consider C. Ugrešić's comment on the bitter violence in the former Yugoslavia: "In the fragmented country both real and psychological wars were waged simultaneously. Mortar shells, psychological and real, wiped out people, houses, cities, children, bridges, memory. In the name of the present, a war was waged for the past; in the name of the future, a war against the present. In the name of a new future, the

truth, memory, and forgetfulness that is inscribed in the VVM is not simply the result of the top-down, or even the bottom-up, exercise of power. So crude a "reading" of the narrative fails to do justice to the complexity of the trauma that shaped the public memory of the war and is reflected in the Memorial.

At the same time, the VVM is the official expression, so to speak, of the nation's sovereign body: it is built on land owned by the federal government, its construction approved by the United States Senate and ultimately the President; its design was vetted by and approved by officially constituted bodies of the government; it is lodged in the symbolic heart of the nation. The Memorial is therefore the nation's statement on the war – primarily to the veterans, secondarily to the citizenry, and finally to the world, including of course the Vietnamese people. As of this writing, it is the only such statement offered by the American people through the proxy of their federal government.

The Memorial not only expresses a view about the war, but teaches how to remember it.[10] The structures on the Washington Mall belong to a particular species of recollective architecture whose symbolic and normative content is prominent. When the subject is war and warriors, memorialization is pedagogy. Matter is put to rhetorical use, made to educate and edify the citizens of the present and form those of the future by persuading them to live out the virtues of the past. It is memory in stone, earth, and water, a patrimony articulated by measured expanses and the interplay of symmetrically arranged symbols. The word "monument" derives from the Latin "monere," which means not just "to remind" but also "to admonish," "warn," "advise," "instruct." "Memorial" derives from "memoria."

My purpose here is to shed further light on the conceptual relation between political apology and reconciliation by examining how civic memory has recorded and recounted to present and future generations

---

war devoured the future. Warriors, the masters of oblivion, the destroyers of the old state and builders of new ones, used every possible strategic method to impose a collective amnesia. The self-proclaimed masters of life and death set up the co-ordinates of right and wrong, black and white, true and false." Trans. C. Hawkesworth, *The Culture of Lies* (London: Phoenix, 1998), p. 6.

[10] To quote Young once again: "Like literary and historical narratives, these memorials [of the Holocaust] recall the national myths, religious archetypes, and ideological paradigms along whose contours a history has been constructed – and perhaps acted upon." And "for *what* is remembered here necessarily depends on *how* it is remembered; and how these events are remembered depends in turn on the icons that do the remembering." "Memory and Monument," p. 105.

the meaning of a conflict whose justice was and is itself a subject of conflict. I shall begin with a brief interpretation of the Memorial, and then turn to an analysis of the conceptual relation.[11]

[i] THE VIETNAM VETERANS MEMORIAL: AN INTERPRETATION

The VVM consists of two walls of polished black granite meeting at a 125 degree, 12 minute angle and tapering off at each end. These tips point like arrowheads to the Washington Monument and Lincoln Memorial. The angle is not, then, just any angle. The Memorial is utterly symmetrical, and neither beautiful nor sublime. When considered in abstraction from the directions they point, its two halves are identical except in the names inscribed and the dates of demise. The wall supports nothing and is not supported by any other structure; there is no internal tension in the design. Especially because its back is against a wall of earth, the Memorial is in no way indifferent to the position of the beholder.

Most of the other memorials on the Mall are either classical in design or have classical antecedents. It is difficult to find any allusion in the VVM to a historical style except by visual incorporation of the Washington Monument and Lincoln Memorial to which it points. Furthermore, unlike all the other memorials on the Mall, this one is invisible from a distance, particularly as one approaches it from the north (the outlines of the Memorial are visible when one reaches the flagpole and statues located between it and the Lincoln Memorial to the southwest). It demands that you enter into its space or miss it altogether.

One comes upon the VVM suddenly, and once there, is led down gently (access to the monument is provided by a path running its length, the grassy area in front being roped off). The observer sees a few names whose order is initially not clear; then more names; then many more. There are no steps. One descends to its heart, precisely where the incline is reversed. The centralizing axis of the monument is horizontal (by contrast, the axis of most other war memorials is vertical). The slowness of exposure to the Memorial is merciful, as then initial surprise turns slowly rather than all at once to shock as one realizes what one is viewing: over

[11] My interpretation of the VVM in section [i] is drawn in part from my "The Vietnam Veterans Memorial and the Washington Mall: Philosophical Thoughts on Political Iconography," *Critical Inquiry* 12 (1986): 688–719. The interpretation of the VVM here departs in a significant way from my earlier discussion.

58,000 names of Americans who died and are missing in action as a result of this war.

Walking down into the embrace of the Memorial, the visitor is engulfed even though the open sky is overhead and a large wide open space faces the monument. The VVM does not close the visitor in, not even in the way that the Lincoln Memorial may be said to do. The walls of the mural-like monument face south to catch the maximum sunlight. The south is the direction of sun, warmth, and life. In the descent toward the center of the monument there may be a delicate allusion to the ancient *tholos* tomb (such as the "tomb of Agamemnon" at Mycenae), buried in the earth and approached by an angled, graded passage downward. Yet this allusion is not strong enough to give the VVM a tomb-like feeling. No doubt the inscription of the names on the polished black granite closely resembles the gravestones in so many American cemeteries, a resemblance accentuated by the presence of flowers and small flags that visitors to the VVM frequently leave at its base. The VVM is to that extent a sort of national gravestone. Further, it possesses complex dimensions of meaning not exhibited by any ordinary gravestone. The suddenness of the visitor's entry into the Memorial's space, the demand that one gives complete attention to it even while remaining in a completely natural setting (without even a roof overhead), the impossibility of avoiding it once there – all these effects would be lost if the Memorial stood on higher ground, in plain view from a distance.

The logical (and chronological) beginning of the monument is neither of the two tips at which one necessarily enters into its space, but rather the point at which the two walls intersect. Starting at the geographic beginning of the Memorial (either of the two tips), one is actually starting part way through the list of names. The rows of names start on the top of the right hand wall (which is at the intersection of the two walls) and follow each other with merciless continuity panel by panel to the eastern tip of that wall (which points to the Washington Monument). The sequence resumes at the western tip, (which points to the Lincoln Memorial) and terminates at the bottom of the left-hand wall.

Thus the list both ends and begins at the center of the monument. Reading halfway through the list all the way to the eastern tip, one's eyes are naturally drawn to the Washington Monument. The visitor who continues to read the names in the proper sequence would be forced to turn and walk to the other end of the Memorial to see the Lincoln Memorial. In other words, reading the names on the VVM is interrupted halfway through by the sight of the two other symbols. The monument invites the visitor to pause midway to consider the significance of the names in the light of memories of Washington and Lincoln. Moreover, in reading the names on the Memorial one is necessarily reading from west to east, from the traditional direction of death to that of resurrection and new life. However, one is forced to double back toward the west in order to finish reading the catalogue of names. The complexity of the monument's directionality goes still deeper, for although the face of the VVM is directed to the south, the Memorial also resembles the tip of an arrow that is pointing north – the region long associated with darkness and mystery.[12]

The peculiar way in which the VVM begins and ends – specifically with the names of the first and last Americans to die in Vietnam – reminds one that the conflict had neither an official start (in sharp contrast, for example, to President Roosevelt's statesman-like appeal for a declaration of war on Japan) nor an official end (there were few celebrations, few parades for the returning veterans, let alone on a national level). The disturbing inarticulateness of the Vietnam War that is in one sense embodied in the organization of the Memorial, is in another sense overcome by the VVM's intricate symbolism and, indeed, simply by the existence of the Memorial on the Mall. One could argue that its very presence there bespeaks national recognition of and respect for the veterans' service, and to that extent articulates a certain settling of accounts. And yet the matter is still more complex.

The list of names both ends and begins at the center of the monument, suggesting that the monument is both open and closed; open physically, at a very wide angle, like a weak "V" for "victory" (a "V" lying on its side, instead of with its arms pointing upward); but closed in substance – the war is over. This simultaneous openness and closure becomes all the more interesting when we realize that the VVM iconically represents a book. The pages are covered with writing, and the book is open partway through. The closure just mentioned is not that of the book but of a chapter in it. The openness indicates that further chapters have yet to be

---

[12] I am indebted to the independent art historian F. V. O'Connor for ideas concerning the symbolic content of the four directions. O'Connor's theory of directional symbolism is developed in "An Iconographic Interpretation of Diego Rivera's *Detroit Industry* Murals in Terms of Their Orientation to the Cardinal Points of the Compass," published in the exhibition catalog *Diego Rivera: A Retrospective* ed. L. B. Downs and C. N. Helms (New York: Founders Society Detroit Institute of Arts, 1986), pp. 215–29.

written, and read. It is important that the back of the monument is to the earth – against earth regarded by its owners as hallowed, as it lies at the symbolic center of the nation's capital. The suggestion that the Vietnam War is but one chapter in the book of American history would be lost if the wall were above ground, backed by thin air. By inviting its viewers to understand the Vietnam War in this context, the VVM not only asks its spectators to remember that war, it admonishes them to write the next chapter thoughtfully and with reflection on the country's values, symbols of which are pointed to by the Memorial itself.

And yet the lessons are deeply unclear, as the metaphor of the "book" suggests in spite of itself. A chronicle of proper names is not a narrative. A book of names, even organized in this brilliantly suggestive way, is a "book" only in name. *What* does this chapter *mean*? The Memorial deliberately leaves the answer underdetermined. We are offered just two short inscriptions, both written at the point where the two arms meet: one at the apex of the right-hand one, after the date "1959" (when the first American was killed), and the other on the bottom of the left-hand one, after the date "1975" (when the last American was killed). The first of these inscriptions reads

IN HONOR OF THE MEN AND WOMEN OF THE ARMED FORCES OF THE UNITED STATES WHO SERVED IN THE VIETNAM WAR. THE NAMES OF THOSE WHO GAVE THEIR LIVES AND OF THOSE WHO REMAIN MISSING ARE INSCRIBED IN THE ORDER THEY WERE TAKEN FROM US.

The second reads

OUR NATION HONORS THE COURAGE, SACRIFICE AND DEVOTION TO DUTY AND COUNTRY OF ITS VIETNAM VETERANS. THIS MEMORIAL WAS BUILT WITH PRIVATE CONTRIBUTIONS FROM THE AMERICAN PEOPLE. NOVEMBER 11, 1982.

Normally, war memorials honor those who died, not all those who fought, and normally they honor the cause as well. The point is emphasized even by the monument's title: it is a memorial to the Vietnam veterans, not the Vietnam war. That it honors everyone who fought there without qualification suggests that they had not previously been honored by the American people. The Memorial seeks to bring about civic reconciliation by correcting the record and through public recognition. And it is clear not only from activities at the VVM but also from the many web sites, publications, and organizations, that the veterans and their families and friends view it as *their* memorial, as a way of proclaiming and redeeming the honor of *their* service to country.[13]

It should be obvious by now that there is nothing heroic about this memorial. It suggests honor without glory. The VVM is not inspiring in the usual way that memorials are. The focus throughout is on individuals. Even the appearance of a mechanical and impersonal order is avoided. Such an order would have arisen if the names were alphabetized or divided into categories according to the branches of the armed forces (the nearby monuments to the Second Division, Seabees, and Marines, by contrast, focus on one of the Armed Services). The chronology of the war is marked by the death of individuals. A visitor searching for a particular name is forced to "read" a number of other names, so paying attention once again to individuals.

It is true that the Memorial speaks first of all of loss and pain. As the Memorial's architect pointed out, it is physically a gash in the earth, a scar only partially healed by the trees and the grass and the polish.[14] The VVM is not a comforting memorial; it is perhaps because of this, rather than in spite of it, that it possesses remarkable therapeutic capacity. When people find on the VVM the name they have been looking for, they touch, even caress it, remembering. It is often followed by another: tracing the name on a piece of paper. Usually the names of individuals who die in a war are listed on a monument in their hometown. The VVM makes the loss of these individuals a matter of national concern. The result is a striking conversion of private grief and public display – a much noted commonplace at the Memorial. The designer of the Memorial wanted it to serve as an occasion for therapeutic catharsis, and in this she succeeded.[15] For

---

[13] A. Danto writes that "we erect monuments so that we shall always remember, and build memorials so that we shall never forget.... Memorials ritualize remembrance and mark the reality of ends." But the continuation of the point about the difference between monuments and memorials does not hold of the VVM: "The memorial is a special precinct, extruded from life, a segregated enclave where we honor the dead. With monuments we honor ourselves." "The Vietnam Veterans Memorial," *The Nation* August 31, 1985, p. 152.

[14] R. Campbell quotes Lin in "An Emotive Place Apart" as saying that "I thought about what death is, what a loss is.... A sharp pain that lessens with time, but can never quite heal over. A scar. The idea occurred to me there on the site. Take a knife and cut open the earth, and with time the grass would heal it. As if you cut open the rock and polished it." *American Institute of Architects Journal*, 72 (1983), p. 151.

[15] Lin is quoted in *U.S. News and World Report* (November 21, 1983, p. 68) as saying that she intended the memorial "to bring out in people the realization of loss and a cathartic healing process." In her statement submitted as part of the design competition, Lin wrote: "Brought to a sharp awareness of such a loss, it is up to each individual to resolve

the visitor, sympathetic resonance with the display of another's emotion is difficult to avoid. Momentarily joining strangers, publicizing private grief; these are among the modulations of civic association the VVM encourages.

By emphasizing the price paid by so many individuals, the VVM asks the onlooker to think about whether the sacrifice was worthwhile and whether it should be made again. It does not take a position as to the answers, but instead implies terrifying questions: Did these individuals die in vain? Was their death in keeping with the nation's best traditions as symbolized by the nearby monuments? For what and when should fellow citizens die in war?

That the person contemplating the monument is implicated in these questions is also emphasized by the fact that its polished black granite functions as a mirror. One cannot help seeing oneself looking at the names, and on a bright day the reflections of the Washington or Lincoln Memorials as well. The dead and living thus meet, and the living are forced to ask whether those names should be on that wall, and whether others should die in similar causes. You are forced to wonder where you were then and what role you played in the war whether by commission or omission; or where you would be and what role you would play if a similar conflict were proposed or engaged. The character of the Memorial is in that respect *interrogative*.

[ii] RECONCILIATION WITHOUT APOLOGY?

The therapeutic and in that sense reconciliatory effect of the Memorial is inseparable from its interrogative character, and that in turn from its neutrality as to the justice of the war. Neutrality on that issue seems intended to make possible the non-neutral proclamation of the honor of the veterans' service in Vietnam, and thus rejection of the suspicion that they acted shamefully by answering their country's call. It would seem that veterans can reconcile their doubts about the conduct and even purposes of the war with their belief that their service was honorable, and non-veterans can retain the same doubts but also affirm the veterans' sacrifice. Public

---

or come to terms with this loss. For death is in the end a personal and private matter and the area contained within this memorial is a quiet place, meant for personal reflection and private reckoning" (from the "Design Competition: Winning Designer's Statement," reproduced by the Vietnam Veterans Memorial Fund, Inc.). As A. Danto says in concluding "The Vietnam Veterans Memorial" (p. 155): "Be prepared to weep. Tears are the universal experience even if you don't know any of the dead."

recognition of the sacrifice rights the wrong of the earlier official oblivion. This is a kind of personal, and civic, resolution of conflict.[16] It is telling that contrary to loud warnings before the fact, the VVM has not become a rallying place for all sorts of "anti-American" groups. It has never been defaced. Nor has it become a rallying place for unreflective or unrestrained exhibitions of a country's self-love. No declarations of war will be made within the arms of this memorial.

The VVM is not, then, therapeutic simply in a "psychological" way (though it is that as well). Its therapy depends on a notion of public recognition as valuable, as well as on the assertion of two specific values – honor in serving one's country, and courage – the latter being the only virtue explicitly mentioned on the Memorial itself. But the striking success of its reconciliatory therapy also depends on its silences. No mention is made of the nearly three million Vietnamese killed in the war. The Memorial does not even hint that reconciliation with the nation's former enemies is in order. The thought would immediately raise the question of the justice of the war, not to mention issues of recognition of the injury done, apology, and perhaps reparations. The sacrifice of those who *refused* to serve for principled reasons, and either went to prison or had to emigrate, is also unmentioned. Above all, the Memorial is silent as to the justification of the decision to go to war. The cost of the war to Americans is brilliantly and movingly recognized; and it is rationalized – insofar as it is rationalized here – by the fact of public recognition embodied in the VVM, and the assertions that the service was both honorable and courageous. The assumption seems to be that as a result, an apology to the veterans for expending life and limb is not due. Differently put, the question of political apology does not arise because the question of the justice of the war, and with it of responsibility for the war, is avoided. One is offered therapeutic reconciliation without apology, reconciliation without a stand on the questions of justice or responsibility (all without a recognition of the horrendous cost imposed on the other side). This

---

[16] For a different interpretation, see W. Hubbard, "A Meaning for Monuments," *Public Interest*, 74 (1984): 17–30. Hubbard does not take into account the therapeutic effect of this memorial. His criticism of the VVM culminates in the following: "Little wonder, then, that the sheer emotional impact of the Vietnam Veterans Memorial satisfies us. Not having the idea that artworks can provide guidance in human dilemmas, we do not sense the absence of such guidance here. We take from the monument not a resolution of our conflicting emotions over the war, but an intensified, vivified version of those emotions" (p. 27). He assimilates the VVM to "modernist" architecture whose purpose is not to be *about* something in the world so much as to *be* a thing in the world (p. 26).

is therapeutic reconciliation built on a blend of truth, minimal assertion (in the form of the two inscriptions), an invitation to reflection, and deliberate silence – one might even say, evasion.

The difficulty with this approach to the problem of civic memory of conflict is, first, that it depends on the thesis that serving one's country in war regardless of the cause is noble. And yet that is an unpersuasive thesis, as any standard counter-example suggests. The cause must be noble if service to it is noble. Secondly, the solution depends on the thesis that the virtues can be separated. It assumes that a claim to be courageous in a war coheres with a claim either to agnosticism about the war's justice or the warranted judgment that the war is unjust. The "therapeutic" power of the VVM has actually depended on the stronger formulation of that proposition – that one can be courageous in the service of an unjust war. Many veterans, and certainly many non-veterans, must surely believe that the cause was not just (and not simply that the war was a failure for strategic reasons). The list of "errors" compiled by Robert McNamara and examined in the preceding chapter would provide ample support for this belief. But this version of the "separation of the virtues" thesis is not defensible. As Plato's Socrates argues in the *Laches* (192c–d), if courage is a virtue – and the VVM obviously assumes that it is – then it is conceptually dependent on being exercised for the sake of an end that is praiseworthy. Injustice does not meet that standard.[17] Courage in the service of wrong is not a virtue, and thus no longer courage proper (it is more like endurance, strong will, and toughness). Would one call a child molester "courageous" in light of his persisting in his activities at great personal risk? "Hate the war, not the warrior" is ultimately no more defensible than St. Augustine's "hate the sin, not the sinner." Conversely, to support the warriors morally is to endorse the war they serve. If warriors cannot avoid the moral taint of a war in which they participated, then another context for apology arises, viz., what is due to those they injured.

Paradoxically, the VVM both invites reflection on the justifiability of the war and reconciles sentiments in such a way as to placate. Indeed, the rules governing the competition among proposed designs for the memorial required that it not take a "political" stand. The result is an unstable compromise, a half remembering and half forgetting, a nagging

---

[17] The point is not that the virtues are "one" in the sense that they are interdefinable (as though to define one virtue is to define them all), but that a person cannot be credited with one virtue while also being credited with the negation of another. I am also arguing here that a virtue such as courage is a "thick" concept in the sense that to call an act courageous is to endorse it.

question and a proud reassurance of honor and courage. Because it attempts reconciliation without either political apology or the denial that any apology is in order, it necessarily sidesteps essential questions. In so doing, it embodies and encourages a national decision to forget them. These are, to repeat, the questions as to whether the war was just in conception and in execution; whether the warriors (and non-warriors as well) are absolved of moral responsibility; and whether or not apology is due on several fronts. My skepticism about the theses that service to one's country in time of war is in and of itself honorable no matter what the war, and that courage can serve injustice, bears on all three of these questions. Even a proponent of the war who thought the cause altogether just must admit that the execution was incompetent, at monumental cost, and if only on those grounds must raise the question of apology.

The unfortunate result of the silences in the official narrative is that these fundamental issues remain unresolved and ever more difficult to raise publicly, especially for a "public figure," especially in a democracy. This is always the result of habituation to silence about essentials. But in the long run, a nation – particularly a democratic one – cannot afford to pass over in uncomfortable silence matters of such grave importance. These are precisely the sorts of hard issues that ought to be addressed through common deliberation. The avoidance of the question of apology in a people's official narrative is the avoidance of full and public discussion of truth and responsibility. The "politically impossible" is politically indispensable, and Santayana's famous line, quoted at the start of this chapter, challenges anyone who denies it. To be sure, taken by itself that line is misleading: for one could remember perfectly and yet wish to repeat the past. One could remember in order to celebrate evil, or to keep resentment and revenge alive. Remembering is not a panacea, but must be accompanied by defensible interpretation and assessment. But forgetting is the path to ignorant repetition, and remembering is a necessary condition of living both wisely and in light of the truth. It may be objected that the truth is in dispute. But then why not determine it by means of a truth commission, or a well-structured dialogue about the moral fundamentals? Without honest assessment of the past, no memory worth having; without honest memory, no present worth living; without apology for injuries done, no future worth hoping for. The errors of the dead and dying repeat themselves, and with them the conflict and moral hatred they engender. This is the nightmare of self-perpetuating violence and revenge that forgiveness and political apology seek to address in their respective spheres.

Civic reconciliation premised on so compromised a moral basis as that reflected by the Vietnam Veterans Memorial is, unfortunately, as brittle as it is unlikely to help the next generation avoid earlier mistakes. The ideals of accountability, responsibility, trustworthiness, self-governance according to justifiable shared norms, the replacement of revenge by due justice, the obligation of the powerful to respect those over whom they rule, and the indispensability of both truth and its public statement – these guide the narrative of political apology. They cannot be ignored or replaced without moral and practical hazard. Consequently, due political apology ought not be evaded. Particularly when the powerful – whether one or many – apologize when apology is due, the earlier flawed civic narrative cannot simply be cited and re-lived, unless amnesia rules the realm. There is no guarantee that the next chapter will be better written when guided by these ideals. But it is certain that it will not be better written if it is blind to them.

Epilogue

Today everybody permits himself the expression of his wish and his dearest thought; hence I, too, shall say what it is that I wish from myself today, and what was the first thought to run across my heart this year – what thought shall be for me the reason, warranty, and sweetness of my life henceforth. I want to learn more and more to see as beautiful what is necessary in things; then I shall be one of those who makes things beautiful. *Amor fati*: let that be my love henceforth! I do not want to wage war against what is ugly. I do not want to accuse; I do not even want to accuse those who accuse. *Looking away* shall be my only negation. And all in all and on the whole: some day I wish to be only a Yes-sayer.

Nietzsche[1]

How are we to respond to the brutal fact that the world is torn by wrong-doing both personal and political? I submit that forgiveness and apology are indispensable. My account of forgiveness and political apology is set against the broad canvas of the ineliminable imperfection of human life and the desirability of reconciliation. I have argued that they respond to that context with varying degrees of success, in a way meaningfully contrasted with several other classical as well as modern responses that I characterized as "perfectionist." Forgiveness is a model virtue for the project of reconciliation with moral wrong-doing – one salient and ongoing feature of the human world's imperfection. Like political apology (the analogue to forgiveness in a political context), forgiveness does not reiterate the past but instead promises renewal without forgetfulness, excuse, or condonation of past wrongs. It rejects the Platonic "narrative

---

[1] F. Nietzsche, *The Gay Science*, par. 276, p. 223.

of nostalgia" – a tale of yearning for another, better, world, accompanied by a determination to flee from this one – and endorses instead a narrative of reconciliation whose elements include both the aspiration to improve the given and the acceptance that this world will always be of mixed character. This narrative articulates a view of ourselves as affective, embodied, vulnerable creatures, of the "good life" to which we aspire, and of the virtues – such as forgiveness – that are constitutive of that life. As a virtue, forgiveness expresses a praiseworthy or excellent way of being responsive to the world, given the sorts of beings we are, and the ideals which guide us.[2]

Responsiveness to the world's moral shortcomings is not, of course, always an unalloyed success. All too often the conditions for forgiveness are not realized as we would wish. The result is a distinction between forgiveness at its best (which I have called the model or paradigmatic case), when all of the relevant conditions are met, and imperfect forgiveness, when only some of the relevant conditions are met (examples include forgiving on behalf of others, unilaterally forgiving the dead or unrepentant, and self-forgiveness). Where none of the conditions is met, the threshold of what will count as forgiveness is not crossed; sadly and painfully, in such cases we are either unforgiven, or unable to forgive. I do not infer that some wrong-doers are *unforgivable*; indeed, I have argued against that notion, as I have against labeling even heinous offenders "monsters."

I hope to have shown that forgiveness is fundamentally an interpersonal process whose success requires actions from both parties. Anything an individual can accomplish here on his or her own regarding forgiveness is less than fully adequate. Consequently, forgiveness should not be understood as a "gift" that may be bestowed at the discretion of the injured party. It also follows from this view that forgiveness is not to be understood primarily as therapy, as a psychologically effective way to "deal with" injury, or simply as the overcoming of anger, however welcome those may be. Genuine forgiveness does not consist simply in a change of attitude or feelings on the part of the would-be forgiver.

Forgiveness does forswear revenge and moderate anger. It commits to overcoming anger altogether. The relevant species of anger is moral hatred, or what I have called, following Bishop Butler, resentment. It is

---

[2] In the first chapter of this book, I noted that properly speaking forgiveness is the expression of the virtue of "forgivingness," but that for ease of reference, I would refer to forgiveness as a virtue.

a complex emotion with both cognitive and affective dimensions; consequently, it is partly but not altogether under the command of will or reason. Even forgiveness at its best, then, takes time.

Revenge and retaliation are commonplace not just between individuals but in the political sphere. Quite understandably, forgiveness is sometimes touted as indispensable to civic reconciliation. I have argued against the notion of "political forgiveness" on conceptual as well as prudential grounds. The analogue to interpersonal forgiveness in the political arena is apology and the acceptance thereof. The notions are related in numerous ways (both seek to address the nightmare of self-perpetuating violence, for example), but they are also distinct, as befits the different areas of human life to which they respond. Political apology is a surprisingly nuanced and subtle notion, and I have articulated its conditions or norms in part through examination of a series of historical examples. Similarly, the forgiveness of debts, political pardon, judicial pardon or clemency by a court of law, and giving up the anger provoked by the gross inequity of the natural and human world, form part of the same family of concepts as forgiveness and political apology, but are significantly different from each other.

Both forgiveness and apology share a commitment to truth and thus to memory; both hold that true reconciliation depends on truth telling. A challenge to this view is offered by the way in which the United States chose to memorialize the Vietnam War. I concluded this book with a critical examination of the way in which the Vietnam Veterans Memorial attempts reconciliation without apology.

I will conclude my effort to answer the leading questions of this book by sketching still others not tackled here. A book framed by the theme of reconciliation with imperfection may perhaps be permitted to acknowledge its own limits, while inviting steps beyond them.

The ideals of responsibility, respect, self-governance, truth, mutual accountability, friendship, and growth that underpin forgiveness require a great deal of elaboration and justification. Why ought we to adopt them? I have argued that they "fit" with forgiveness as a virtue, but have not attempted to show that we are rationally compelled to endorse them. This holds as well on the political front, where the analogue to forgiveness is the acceptance of apology. In its endorsement of honesty, truth telling, accountability, and trustworthiness, apology commits to ideals that overlap with those of interpersonal forgiveness. Its analogue to growth is "progress," and its analogue to responsibility is accountability (especially on the part of those who exercise power). We need to understand not only whether and how the ideals of forgiveness and apology may themselves be justified, but also whether the ideals bear a hierarchical relation to each other.

Much more should be said about the way in which forgiveness and political apology express or exemplify these ideals. For example, what does it mean to strive for an ideal that by definition stands to the mixed world as does the more to the less perfect, without being moved to abandon the less perfect? This blend of emendation and acceptance requires systematic analysis.[3] A secular moral outlook within which forgiveness and apology are commended does not seek to replace this world with one in which there is nothing to forgive, or to flee to a world so perfectly molded as to lack wrong-doing. And yet, as its affirmation of growth and renewal indicate, this outlook is emendatory or progressive rather than resigned or quietist. I have tried to show how it works out in the case of forgiveness and apology, but what I earlier called the "bi-focal" perspective on the world and its potential for emendation deserves elaboration.

What general political theory is most hospitable to apology and reconciliation? This intriguing question leads to another. I have argued that forgiveness is helpfully understood as a virtue, but have not argued that "virtue ethics" is the best general moral theory.[4] Virtues have their place in utilitarian and deontological theories as well. What overarching moral theory best accommodates forgiveness? Many important lines of inquiry beckon.

[3] For helpful discussion of this sort of issue see T. Shapiro's "Compliance, Complicity, and the Nature of Nonideal Conditions," *The Journal of Philosophy* 100 (2003): 329–355.

[4] I owe the distinction between virtue theory and virtue ethics to J. Driver; see her "The Virtues and Human Nature," in Roger Crisp, ed. *How Should One Live?* (Oxford: Oxford University Press, 1996), p. 111, fn. 1.

Bibliography

The bibliography includes all the works and web sites cited in this book, as well as works and sources bearing on forgiveness, political apology, and reconciliation that I have found particularly useful in preparing this study. I have attempted to provide a comprehensive list of philosophical publications and web sources on my central topics, but not a multidisciplinary bibliography of relevant works (for further references, see the web sites mentioned at the end of the bibliography). Web sites cited in this book were valid as of October 8, 2006.

Accatoli, L. 1998. *When a Pope Asks Forgiveness: The Mea Culpa's of John Paul II.* Trans. J. Aumann. Boston: Pauline Books.

Adams, J. E. 1989. *From Forgiven to Forgiving.* Wheaton, IL: Victor Books.

Adams, M. 1991. "Forgiveness: A Christian Model." *Faith and Philosophy* 8: 277–304.

Aetna, Inc. "Aetna Statement on Pre-Civil War Insurance Policies." March 10, 2000. See http://www.aetna.com/news/2000/prtpr_20000310.htm.

Alford, C. 2005. "Hate is the Imitation of Love." In *The Psychology of Hate,* ed. R. Sternberg. Washington, DC: American Psychological Association. Pp. 235–254.

Allen, J. 1999. "Balancing Justice and Social Utility: Political Theory and the Idea of a Truth and Reconciliation Commission." *University of Toronto Law Journal* 49: 315–353.

Allen, T. 2006. *Trial Justice: The International Criminal Court and the Lord's Resistance Army.* London and New York: Zed Books.

Allison, H. 2001. "Reflections on the Banality of (Radical) Evil: A Kantian Analysis." In *Rethinking Evil: Contemporary Perspectives,* ed. M. P. Lara. Berkeley: University of California Press. Pp. 86–100.

Andrews, Molly. 2000. "Forgiveness in Context." *Journal of Moral Education* 29: 75–86.

Améry, J. 1980. *At the Mind's Limits: Contemplations by a Survivor on Auschwitz and Its Realities.* Trans. S. Rosenfeld and S. P. Rosenfeld. Bloomington: Indiana University Press.

215

———. 1994. *On Aging: Revolt and Resignation*. Trans. J. D. Barlow. Bloomington: Indiana University Press.

Annas, J. 1999. *Platonic Ethics, Old and New*. Ithaca, NY: Cornell University Press.

Ansart, P., ed. 2002. *Le ressentiment*. Brussels: Bruylant.

Appleby, R. S. "Truth, Truth Telling and Reconciliation." A speech given on May 19, 2002 at the Institute for Global Engagement's Annual Brandywine Forum. www.globalengagement.org/issues/2002/10/appleby2002-p.htm.

Arendt, H. 1958. *The Human Condition*. Chicago: University of Chicago Press.

———. 1968. "Truth and Politics." In her *Between Past and Future: Eight Exercises in Political Thought*. New York: Viking Press.

Aristotle. 1999. *Nicomachean Ethics*, 2nd ed. Trans. T. H. Irwin. Indianapolis: Hackett.

Atkins, K. 2002. "Friendship, Trust and Forgiveness." *Philosophia* 29: 111–132.

Atkinson, J. 1999. "Truth and Reconciliation the Athenian Way." *Acta Classica* 42: 5–13.

Augsburger, D. 1981. *Caring Enough to Forgive: True Forgiveness*. Ventura, CA: Regal Books.

Augustine, Saint. 1865. *Opera Omnia*, ed. J.-P. Migne, 16 vols. Paris: Bibliothecae Cleri Universae.

———. 1982. *Unfinished Commentary on the Epistle to the Romans*. In *Augustine on Romans*. Text and trans. by P. Fredriksen Landes. Chico, CA: Scholars Press.

Austin, J. L. 1970. "A Plea for Excuses." In *Philosophical Papers*, 2nd ed., ed. J. O. Urmson and G. J. Warnock. Oxford: Oxford University Press. Pp. 175–204.

Bacon, F. 1930. "On Revenge." In F. Bacon, *The Essays*, ed. G. Montgomery. New York: Macmillan Company. Pp. 9–10.

Balázs, Z. 2000. "Forgiveness and Repentance." *Public Affairs Quarterly* 14: 105–127.

Barahone de Brito, A. 2007. "Passion, Constraint, Law, and *Fortuna*: The Human Rights Challenge to Chilean Democracy." In *Burying the Past: Making Peace and Doing Justice after Civil Conflict*, ed. N. Biggar. Washington, DC: Georgetown University Press. Pp. 150–183.

Barnett, M. A. 1990. "Empathy and Related Responses in Children." In *Empathy and Its Development*, ed. N. Eisenberg and J. Strayer. Cambridge: Cambridge University Press. Pp. 146–162.

Barry, R. 1980. "Just War Theory and the Logic of Reconciliation." *New Scholasticism* 54(2): 129–152.

Bavelas, J. 2004. "An Analysis of Formal Apologies by Canadian Churches to First Nations," Occasional Paper #1, Centre for Studies in Religion and Society, University of Victoria, Victoria, Canada. See http://web.uvic.ca/csrs/publications/occasional/apologies.php.

———, with A. Black, C. R. Lemery, and J. Mullett. 1990. "Motor Mimicry as Primitive Empathy." In *Empathy and Its Development*, ed. N. Eisenberg and J. Strayer. Cambridge: Cambridge University Press. Pp. 317–338.

Beardsley, E. 1980. "Understanding and Forgiveness." In *The Philosophy of Brand Blandshard*, ed. P. A. Schilpp. La Salle, IL: Open Court. Pp. 247–258.

Beatty, J. 1970. "Forgiveness." *American Philosophical Quarterly* 7: 246–252.

Benn, P. 1996. "Forgiveness and Loyalty." *Philosophy* 71: 369–384.

Bennett, C. 2002. "The Varieties of Retributive Experience." *Philosophical Quarterly* 52: 145–163.

———. 2003. "Is Amnesty a Collective Act of Forgiveness?" *Contemporary Political Theory* 2: 67–76.

———. 2003. "Personal and Redemptive Forgiveness." *European Journal of Philosophy* 11: 127–144.

Berhend, B. 1999. *Alice Lakwena and the Holy Spirits: War in Northern Uganda 1985–1997.* Trans. M. Cohen. Athens: Ohio University Press.

Bernstein, R. 1988. "Metaphysics, Critque, and Utopia." *Review of Metaphysics* 42: 255–273.

———. 2002. *Radical Evil: A Philosophical Interrogation.* Boston: Polity Press.

Bicknell, J. 1998. "The Individuality in the Deed: Hegel on Forgiveness and Reconciliation." *Bulletin of the Hegel Society of Great Britain* 37–38: Pp. 73–84.

Biggar, N., ed. 2001. *Burying The Past: Making Peace and Doing Justice After Civil Conflict.* Washington, DC: Georgetown University Press.

Bittner, R. 1992. "Is It Reasonable to Regret Things One Did?" *Journal of Philosophy* 89: 262–273.

———. 1994. "Ressentiment." In *Nietzsche, Genealogy, Morality: Essays on Nietzsche's Genealogy of Morals,* ed. R. Schacht. Berkeley: University of California Press. Pp. 127–138.

Blanshard, B. 1961. *Reason and Goodness.* London: George Allen & Unwin Ltd.

Blumenfeld, L. 2002. *Revenge: A Story of Hope.* New York: Simon and Schuster.

Blustein, J. 2000. "On Taking Responsibility for One's Past." *Journal of Applied Philosophy* 17: 1–19.

Bok, S. 1999. *Lying: Moral Choice in Public and Private Life.* New York: Vintage Books.

Boleyn-Fitzgerald, P. 2002. "What Should 'Forgiveness' Mean?" *Journal of Value Inquiry* 36: 483–498.

Boltanski, L. 1999. *Distant Suffering: Morality, Media, and Politics.* Trans. G. Burchell. Cambridge: Cambridge University Press.

Boraine, A. 2000. *A Country Unmasked: Inside South Africa's Truth and Reconciliation Commission.* Oxford: Oxford University Press.

Boss, J. A. 1997. "Throwing Pearls to the Swine: Women, Forgiveness, and the Unrepentant Abuser." In *Philosophical Perspectives on Power and Domination,* ed. L. Kaplan and L. F. Bove. Amsterdam: Rodopi. Pp. 235–247.

Bourdieu, P. 1997. "Marginalia – Some Additional Notes on the Gift." In *The Logic of the Gift: Toward an Ethic of Generosity,* ed. A. D. Schrift. New York: Routledge. Pp. 231–241.

Boyd, R. 2004. "Pity's Pathologies Portrayed: Rousseau and the Limits of Democratic Compassion." *Political Theory* 32: 519–546.

Braithwaite, J. 2000. "Survey Article: Repentance Rituals and Restorative Justice." *Journal of Political Philosophy* 8: 115–131.

Braund, S., and G. W. Most., eds. 2003. *Ancient Anger: Perspectives from Homer to Galen.* Volume 32 of Yale Classical Studies. Cambridge: Cambridge University Press.

Brecke, P. See Long, W.

Brinkmann, K. 2003. "Hegel on Forgiveness." In *Hegel's Phenomenology of Spirit,* ed. A. Denker and M. Vater. Amherst, NY: Humanity Books. Pp. 243–264.

Brison, S. J. 2003. *Aftermath: Violence and the Remaking of a Self.* Princeton, NJ: Princeton University Press.

Bristol, G., and C. McGinnis. 1982. *When it's Hard to Forgive.* Wheaton, IL: Victor Books.

Brooks, R. L., ed. 1999. *When Sorry Isn't Enough: The Controversy Over Apologies and Reparations for Human Injustice.* New York: New York University Press.

Burkle, H. 1989. "Guilt and Its Resolution Outside of the Christian Tradition." *Communio* 6: 172–196.

Burnyeat, M. 1999. "Utopia and Fantasy: The Practicability of Plato's Ideally Just City." In *Plato II*, ed. G. Fine. Oxford: Oxford University Press. Pp. 297–308.

Bush, G., Sr. 1989. "Letter Accompanying Redress Checks." See http://reserve.mg2.org/apology%20events/Civil%20Liberty%20Act%201998.htm.

Butler, J. 1896. Sermon VIII, "Upon Resentment" and Sermon IX, "Upon Forgiveness of Injuries." In *The Works of Joseph Butler*, Vol. 2, ed. W. E. Gladstone. London: Clarendon Press. Pp. 136–167.

Calhoun, C. 1992. "Changing One's Heart." *Ethics* 103: 76–96.

Campbell, R. 1983. "An Emotive Place Apart." *American Institute of Architects Journal* 72: 150–151.

Camus, A. 1955. *The Myth of Sisyphus.* Trans. J. O'Brien. New York: Random House.

Card, C. 1972. "On Mercy." *Philosophical Review* 81: 182–207.

_____. 2002. *The Atrocity Paradigm: A Theory of Evil.* Oxford: Oxford University Press.

CBS News. "Aetna Issues Apology for Slave Policies." March 10th, 2000. See http://www.cbsnews.com/stories/2000/03/10/null/main170356.shtml.

Chatterjee, D. K., ed. 2004. *The Ethics of Assistance: Morality and the Distant Needy.* Cambridge: Cambridge University Press.

"Civil Liberties Act of 1988." See http://www.children-of-the-camps.org/history/civilact.html.

Christie, K. 2000. *The South African Truth Commission.* New York: Palgrave.

Christodoulidis, E., and S. Veitch, eds. 2001. *Lethe's Law: Justice, Law and Ethics in Reconciliation.* Oxford: Oxford University Press.

Clinton, W. "Presidential Letter of Apology." October 1, 1993. See http://www.children-of-the-camps.org/history/clinton.html.

Coe, P. 1994. *Voices of Aboriginal Australia*, ed. I. Moores. Sydney: Butterfly Books.

Convey, E. 2003. "Payout Is no Relief for Abuse Victims." *Boston Sunday Herald* December 21. P. 8.

Cose, E. 2004. *Bone to Pick: of Forgiveness, Reconciliation, and Revenge.* New York: Atria Books.

Crocker, D. 1999. "Reckoning with Past Wrongs: A Normative Framework." *Ethics & International Affairs* 13: 43–64.

_____. 2000. "Retribution and Reconciliation." *Philosophy and Public Policy Quarterly* 20: 1–6.

_____. 2000. "Truth Commissions and Transitional Justice." *Report from the Institute of Philosophy and Public Policy* 20(4): 23–31.

Cunliffe, Christopher, ed. 1992. *Joseph Butler's Moral and Religious Thought.* Oxford: Clarendon Press.

Cunningham, M. 1999. "Saying Sorry: The Politics of Apology." *Political Quarterly* 70: 285–294.

Currie, G., and I. Ravenscroft. 2002. *Recreative Minds: Imagination in Philosophy and Psychology.* Oxford: Oxford University Press.

Dahl, R. 1976. *Modern Political Analysis,* 3rd ed. Englewood Cliffs, NJ: Prentice Hall.

Danto, A. 1985. "The Vietnam Veterans Memorial." *The Nation,* August 31. Pp. 152–155.

Darwall, S. 1977. "Two Kinds of Respect." *Ethics* 88: 36–49.

———. 1999. "Sympathetic Liberalism: Recent Work on Adam Smith." *Philosophy and Public Affairs* 28: 139–164.

———. 2002. *Welfare and Rational Care.* Princeton, NJ: Princeton University Press.

———. 2006. *The Second-Person Standpoint: Morality, Respect, and Accountability.* Cambridge, MA: Harvard University Press.

Davis, W. T. 1994. *Shattered Dream: America's Search for Its Soul.* Valley Forge, PA: Trinity Press International.

Deigh, John. 1995. "Empathy and Universalizibility." *Ethics* 105(4): 743–763.

De Kock, E., and J. Gordin. 1998. *A Long Night's Damage: Working for the Apartheid State.* Saxonwold, South Africa: Contra Press.

DeLancey, C. 2002. *Passionate Engines: What Emotions Reveal about Mind and Artificial Intelligence.* Oxford: Oxford University Press.

Derrida, J. 1997. *Cosmopolitanism and Forgiveness.* Trans. M. Dooley and R. Kearney. London and New York: Routledge.

Diderot, D. 2007. "Ressentiment." In *Encyclopédie: ou Dictionnaire Raisonné des Sciences, des Arts et des Métiers,* ed. D. Diderot and J. D'Alembert. 14: 186. See http://www.lib.uchicago.edu/efts/ARTFL/projects/encyc/.

Digeser, P. E. 2001. *Political Forgiveness.* Ithaca, NY: Cornell University Press.

———. 2004. "Forgiveness, the Unforgivable and International Relations." *International Relations* 18: 480–497.

Dillon, R. S. 2001. "Self-Forgiveness and Self-Respect." *Ethics* 112: 53–83.

Dobel, J. P. 1980. "The Vietnam War: Is it Time to Forgive and Forget? Three Views." *Worldview* 23: 13–16.

Dover, K. J. 1974. *Greek Popular Morality in the Time of Plato and Aristotle.* Berkeley and Los Angeles: University of California Press.

Downie, R. S. 1965. "Forgiveness." *Philosophical Quarterly* 15: 128–134.

Driver, J. 1996. "The Virtues and Human Nature." In *How Should One Live?,* ed. R. Crisp. Oxford: Oxford University Press. Pp. 111–130.

Dwyer, S. 1999. "Reconciliation for Realists." *Ethics and International Affairs* 13: 81–98.

Eisikovits, N. 2004. "Forget Forgiveness: On the Benefits of Sympathy for Political Reconciliation." *Theoria* 52: 31–63.

Eizenstat, S. 2003. *Imperfect Justice: Looted Assets, Slave Labor, and the Unfinished Business of World War II.* Foreword by E. Wiesel. New York: Public Affairs.

Eliot, G. 2003. *Middlemarch.* London: Penguin.

Eliot, T. S. 1962. *The Complete Poems and Plays.* New York: Harcourt Brace Jovanovich.

Elshtain, J. B. 2001. "Politics and Forgiveness." In *Burying the Past*, ed. N. Biggar. Washington, DC: Georgetown University Press. Pp. 40–56.

Elster, J., ed. 2006. *Retribution and Reparation in the Transition to Democracy*. New York: Cambridge University Press.

Emerson, J. G. 1964. *The Dynamics of Forgiveness*. Philadelphia: Westminster.

English, B. "Why Do They Forgive Us?" *Boston Globe*, April 23, 2003. Pp. C1, C4.

Enright, R. D, and J., North, eds. 1998. *Exploring Forgiveness*. Foreword by D. Tutu. Madison: University of Wisconsin Press.

Fehr, E., and B. Rockenbach. 2003. "Detrimental Effects of Sanctions on Human Altruism." *Nature* 422: 137–140.

Finley, M. 1967. "Utopianism Ancient and Modern." In *The Critical Spirit: Essays in Honor of H. Marcuse*, ed. K. H. Wolff and B. Moore. Boston: Beacon Press. Pp. 3–20.

Flanigan, B. 1992. *Forgiving the Unforgivable*. New York: Macmillan.

———. 1996. *Forgiving Yourself*. New York: Macmillan.

Flew, N. 1934. *The Idea of Perfection in Christian Theology*. Oxford: Oxford University Press.

Flood, C. 1996. *Political Myth: A Theoretical Introduction*. New York: Garland.

Foss, M. 1946. *The Idea of Perfection in the Western World*. Princeton, NJ: Princeton University Press.

Fow, N. R. 1996. "The Phenomenology of Forgiveness and Reconciliation." *Journal of Phenomenological Psychology* 27: 219–233.

Frei, N. 2002. *Adenauer's Germany and the Nazi Past: The Politics of Amnesty and Integration*. Trans. J. Golb. New York: Columbia University Press.

Friedländer, S. 1986. "Some German Struggles with Memory." In *Bitburg in Moral and Political Perspective*, ed. G. Hartman. Bloomington: Indiana University Press. Pp. 27–42.

Fuchs-Burnett, T. 2002. "Mass Public Corporate Apology." *Dispute Resolution Journal* 57: 27–32, 82–84. See http://www.findarticles.com/p/articles/mi_qa3923/is_200205/ai_n9060883.

Garrard, E. 2003. "Forgiveness and the Holocaust." In *Moral Philosophy and the Holocaust*, ed. E. Garrard and G. Scarre. Aldershot: Ashgate. Pp. 231–245.

———, and D. McNaughton. 2003. "In Defence of Unconditional Forgiveness." *Proceedings of the Aristotelian Society* 104: 39–60.

Gellman, B. "Hussein, on His Knees, Begs Forgiveness for Massacre; Jordanian King Visits Families of Slain Israeli Girls." *The Washington Post*, March 17, 1997. P. A1.

Gill, K. 2000. "The Moral Functions of an Apology." *The Philosophical Forum* 31: 11–27.

Gingell, J. 1974. "Forgiveness and Power." *Analysis* 34: 180–183.

Gobodo-Madikizela, P. 2003. *A Human Being Died that Night*. New York: Houghton Mifflin.

Goldie, P. 2000. *The Emotions: A Philosophical Exploration*. Oxford: Clarendon Press.

———. 2003. "Narrative and Perspective; Values and Appropriate Emotions." In *Philosophy and the Emotions*, ed. A. Hatzimoysis. Cambridge: Cambridge University Press. Pp. 201–220.

_____. 2003. "One's Remembered Past: Narrative Thinking, Emotion, and the External Perspective." *Philosophical Papers* 32: 301–319.

Golding, M. 1984–85. "Forgiveness and Regret." *Philosophical Forum* 6: 121–137.

Goldman, A. 1995. "Simulation and Interpersonal Utility." *Ethics* 105: 709–726.

Gordon, J. See de Kock, E.

Gordon, R. 1995. "Sympathy, Simulation, and the Impartial Spectator." *Ethics* 105: 727–742.

Govier, T. 1999. "Forgiveness and the Unforgivable." *American Philosophical Quarterly* 36: 59–75.

_____. 2002. *Forgiveness and Revenge.* New York: Routledge.

Graybill, L. S. 2002. *Truth and Reconciliation in South Africa: Miracle or Model?* London: Lynne Rienner.

Griffiths, P. E. 1997. *What Emotions Really Are: The Problem of Psychological Categories.* Chicago: University of Chicago Press.

_____. 2004. "Towards a 'Machiavellian' Theory of Emotional Appraisal." In *Emotion, Evolution, and Rationality,* ed. D. Evans and P. Cruse. Oxford: Oxford University Press. Pp. 89–105.

Griswold, C. 1986. "The Vietnam Veterans Memorial and the Washington Mall: Philosophical Thoughts on Political Iconography." *Critical Inquiry* 12: 688–719.

_____. 1996. *Self-Knowledge in Plato's Phaedrus.* Rpt. University Park: Pennsylvania State University Press.

_____. 1999a. *Adam Smith and the Virtues of the Enlightenment.* Cambridge: Cambridge University Press.

_____. 1999b. "Relying on Your Own Voice: An Unsettled Rivalry of Moral Ideals in Plato's *Protagoras.*" *Review of Metaphysics* 53: 533–557.

_____ 2003. "Longing for the Best: Plato on Reconciliation with Imperfection." *Arion* 11: 101–136.

Haber, J. G. 1991. *Forgiveness.* Lanham, MD: Rowman and Littlefield.

_____. 1998. "Forgiveness and Feminism." In *Norms and Values: Essays on the Work of Virginia Held,* ed. J. Haber and M. Halfon. Lanham, MD: Rowman and Littlefield. Pp. 141–150.

Habermas, J. 1995. "Reconciliation Through the Public Use of Reason: Remarks on John Rawls' Political Liberalism." *Journal of Philosophy* 92: 109–131.

Hamber, B. 2001. "Does the Truth Heal? A Psychological Perspective on Political Strategies for Dealing with the Legacy of Political Violence." In *Burying the Past,* ed. N. Biggar. Washington, DC: Georgetown University Press. Pp. 131–148.

Hampton, J. See J. G. Murphy.

Hardimon, M. O. 1994. *Hegel's Social Philosophy: The Project of Reconciliation.* Cambridge: Cambridge University Press.

Harris, W. 2001. *Restraining Rage: The Ideology of Anger Control in Classical Antiquity.* Cambridge, MA: Harvard University Press.

Hartman, G., ed. 1986. *Bitburg in Moral and Political Perspective.* Bloomington: Indiana University Press.

Harvey, F. L. 1903. *History of the Washington National Monument and Washington National Monument Society.* Washington, DC: Government Printing Office.

Harvey, J. 1993. "Forgiveness as an Obligation of the Moral Life." *International Journal of Moral and Social Studies* 8: 211–221.

Havel, V. 1986. *Living in Truth.* Trans. P. Wilson. London: Faber and Faber.

———. 1997. *The Art of the Impossible: Politics and Morality in Practice.* Trans. P. Wilson et al. New York: Knopf.

Haybron, D. 2002. "Moral Monsters and Saints." *The Monist* 85: 260–284.

Hayner, P. 1994. "Fifteen Truth Commissions – 1974 to 1994: A Comparative Study." *Human Rights Quarterly* 16(4): 597–655.

———. 2002. *Unspeakable Truths: Facing the Challenge of Truth Commissions.* New York: Routledge.

Hegel, G. W. F. 1977. "Conscience: The 'Beautiful Soul,' Evil, and Its Forgiveness." In *Phenomenology of Spirit*, trans. A. V. Miller. Oxford: Oxford University Press. Pp. 383–409.

Helmick, R., and R. Petersen, eds. 2002. *Forgiveness and Reconciliation.* Philadelphia: Templeton Foundation Press.

Henderson, M. 2003. *Forgiveness: Breaking the Chain of Hate.* Portland, OR: Arnica Publishing.

Hestevold, H. S. 1985. "Justice to Mercy." *Philosophy and Phenomenological Research* 46: 281–291.

Heyd, D. 1982. *Supererogation: Its Status in Ethical Theory.* Cambridge: Cambridge University Press.

Hieronymi, P. 2001. "Articulating an Uncompromising Forgiveness." *Philosophy and Phenomenological Research* 62: 529–555.

Himmelfarb, G. 1991. *Poverty and Compassion.* New York: Alfred A. Knopf, Inc.

———. 2004. *The Roads to Modernity.* New York: Alfred A. Knopf, Inc.

Hirschman, A. O. 1991. *The Rhetoric of Reaction: Perversity, Futility, Jeopardy.* Cambridge, MA: Harvard University Press.

Holmgren, M. R. 1993. "Forgiveness and the Intrinsic Value of Persons." *American Philosophical Quarterly* 30: 341–352.

———. 1998. "Self-Forgiveness and Responsible Moral Agency." *Journal of Value Inquiry* 32: 75–91.

Homer. *The Iliad.* 1961. Trans. R. Lattimore. Chicago: University of Chicago Press.

Horsburgh, H. J. 1974. "Forgiveness." *Canadian Journal of Philosophy* 4: 269–289.

Hubbard, W. 1984. "A Meaning for Monuments." *Public Interest* 74: 17–30.

Hughes, M. 1975. "Forgiveness." *Analysis* 35: 113–117.

Hughes, P. M. 1995. "Moral Anger, Forgiving, and Condoning." *Journal of Social Philosophy* 26: 103–118.

———. 1997. "What Is Involved in Forgiving?" *Philosophia* 25: 33–49.

Hume, D. 1990. *Enquiries Concerning Human Understanding and Concerning the Principles of Morals.* Ed. P. H. Nidditch. Oxford: Oxford University Press.

———. 2000. *A Treatise of Human Nature.* Ed. D. F. Norton and M. J. Norton. Oxford: Oxford University Press.

Hurka, T. 1993. *Perfectionism.* Oxford: Oxford University Press.

Ignatieff, M. 1998. *The Warrior's Honor: Ethnic War and the Modern Conscience.* London: Chatto and Windus.

Interview, "Linda Biehl and Easy Nofemela." The Forgiveness Project. http://www.theforgivenessproject.com/stories/linda-biehl-easy-nofemela.

Inwood, B., and Gerson, L. P. 1997. *Hellenistic Philosophy*, 2nd ed. Indianapolis, IN: Hackett.

Jacoby, S. 1976. *Wild Justice: The Evolution of Revenge.* New York: Harper and Row.

James, W. 1998. "What Makes a Life Significant." In *Talks to Teachers on Psychology; and to Students on Some of Life's Ideals.* London: Longmans, Green, and Co. Pp. 292–294.

Jankélévitch, V. 1998. "Le Pardon." In *Philosophie Morale.* Paris: Flammarion. Pp. 993–1149.

Johnson, M. 2004. "Faculty Senate Meeting: The University of Alabama Senate: Approved Minutes." See http://facultysenate.ua.edu/04-05/mn042004.html

Jones, L. G. 1995. *Embodying Forgiveness: A Theological Analysis.* Grand Rapids, MI: W. B. Eerdmans.

Kamtekar, R. 1998. "Imperfect Virtue." *Ancient Philosophy* 18: 315–339.

Kant, I. 1991. *The Metaphysics of Morals.* Trans. and Introduction by M. Gregor. Cambridge: Cambridge University Press.

———. 2004. *Religion within the Boundaries of Mere Reason.* Trans. and ed. A. Wood and G. di Giovanni. Cambridge: Cambridge University Press.

Kestenbaum, V. 2002. *The Grace and the Severity of the Ideal: John Dewey and the Transcendental.* Chicago: University of Chicago Press.

Kierkegaard, S. 1938. *Purity of Heart.* New York: Hayes and Brothers.

Kogler, H. H., and K. R. Stueber, eds. 2000. *Empathy, Agency, and the Problem of Understanding in the Human Sciences.* Boulder, CO: Westview Press.

Kolnai, A. 1973–74. "Forgiveness." *Proceedings of the Aristotelian Society N.S. 74.* Pp. 91–106.

———. 1999. "The Utopian Mind." In *Privilege and Liberty and Other Essays in Political Philosophy,* ed. Daniel J. Mahoney. Lanham, MD: Lexington Books. Pp. 121–132.

Konstan, D. 1996. "Friendship, Frankness, and Flattery." In *Friendship, Flattery, and Frankness of Speech: Studies on Friendship in the New Testament World,* ed. J. Fitzgerald. New York: E. J. Brill. Pp. 7–19.

———. 2001. *Pity Transformed.* London: Duckworth Press.

———. 2002. "Ressentiment Ancien et Ressentiment Moderne." In *Le Ressentiment,* ed. P. Ansart. Brussels: Bruylant. Pp. 259–276.

———. 2006. *The Emotions of the Ancient Greeks: Studies in Aristotle and Classical Literature.* Toronto: University of Toronto Press.

Konstan, D., et al. 1998. *Philodemus: On Frank Criticism.* Atlanta, GA: Scholars Press.

Kort, L. F. 1975. "What Is an Apology?" *Philosophy Research Archives* 1: 80–87.

Krašovec, J. 1999. *Reward, Punishment, and Forgiveness: The Thinking and Beliefs of Ancient Israel in the Light of Greek and Modern Views.* Supplements to Vetus Testamentum 78. Leiden: Brill.

Kristeva, J. 2002. "Forgiveness: An Interview with A. Rice." *Publications of the Modern Language Association of America* 117: 278–295.

Krog, A. 1999. *Country of My Skull: Guilt, Sorrow, and Limits of Forgiveness in the New South Africa.* New York: Three Rivers Press.

Krondorfer, B. 1995. *Remembrance and Reconciliation; Encounters between Young Jews and Germans.* New Haven, CT: Yale University Press.

Lambert, J. C. 1985. *The Human Action of Forgiving.* New York: University Press of America.

Lang, B. 1994. "Forgiveness." *American Philosophical Quarterly* 31: 105–117.

Lara, M. P., ed. 2001. *Rethinking Evil: Contemporary Perspectives.* Berkeley: University of California Press.

Laub, D. 1991. "Truth and Testimony: The Process and the Struggle." *American Imago: Studies in Psychoanalysis and Culture* 48: 75–91.

Lauritzen, P. 1987. "Forgiveness: Moral Prerogative or Religious Duty?" *Journal of Religious Ethics* 15: 141–154.

Lazare, A. 2004. *On Apology.* Oxford: Oxford University Press.

Levi, P. 1989. *The Drowned and the Saved.* Trans. R. Rosenthal. New York: Vintage Books.

———. 1995. *The Reawakening.* New York: Touchstone.

Levi, P. 2001. "Interview with Primo Levi (1979)." Conducted by G. Segrè. In *The Voice of Memory: Interviews 1961–1987,* ed. M. Belpoliti and R. Gordon. Trans. R. Gordon. New York: The New Press. Pp. 266–271.

Lewis, M. 1980. "On Forgiveness." *Philosophical Quarterly* 30: 236–245.

Liddell, H. G., R. Scott, H. S. Jones. 1968. *A Greek-English Lexicon.* Oxford: Clarendon Press.

Lieberman, M. S. 1998. *Commitment, Value, and Moral Realism.* Cambridge: Cambridge University Press.

Lilla, M. 2001. "Hegel and the Political Theology of Reconciliation." *Review of Metaphysics* 54: 859–900.

Linder, D. 1996. "Juror Empathy and Race," *Tennessee Law Review* 63: 887.

Little, D. 1999. "A Different Kind of Justice: Dealing with Human Rights Violations in Transitional Societies." *Ethics and International Affairs* 13: 65–80.

Loewen, J. A. 1970. "Four Kinds of Forgiveness." *Practical Anthropology* 11: 153–168.

———. 1976. "The Social Context of Guilt and Forgiveness." *Practical Anthropology* 17: 80–96.

Lomax, E. 1995. *The Railway Man: A True Story of War, Remembrance, and Forgiveness.* New York: Random House.

Long, W., and P. Brecke. 2003. *War and Reconciliation: Reason and Emotion in Conflict Resolution.* Cambridge, MA: MIT Press.

Lynn, S. J., and McConkey, K. M., eds. 1998. *Truth in Memory.* New York: Guilford Press.

Lyons, D. 2004. "Corrective Justice, Equal Opportunity, and the Legacy of Slavery and Jim Crow." *Boston University Law Review* 84: 1375–1404.

Mabbott, J. D. 1949. "Punishment." *Mind* 48: 152–167.

MacIntyre, A. 1984. *After Virtue.* Notre Dame, IN: University of Notre Dame Press.

———. 1999. *Dependent Rational Animals.* Notre Dame, IN: University of Notre Dame.

Mandela, N. 1995. *Long Walk to Freedom.* New York: Little, Brown, and Company.

Margalit, A. 2002. *The Ethics of Memory.* Cambridge, MA: Harvard University Press.

McConkey, K. M., see Lynn, S. J.

McEwan, I. 2001. *Atonement.* New York: Random House.

McGary, H. 1989. "Forgiveness." *American Philosophical Quarterly* 26: 343–351.

———. 1992. "Forgiveness and Slavery." In *Between Slavery and Freedom: Philosophy and American Slavery,* eds. H. McGary and B. Lawson. Bloomington: Indiana University Press. Pp. 90–128.

McGinn, B. 1985. *The Calabrian Abbot: Joachim of Fiore in the History of Western Thought.* New York: Macmillian Publishing Company.

McGinn, C. 1997. *Ethics, Evil and Fiction.* Oxford: Oxford University Press.

McNaughton, D. See Garrard, E.

Meister, R. 2002. "Human Rights and the Politics of Victimhood." *Ethics and International Affairs* 16: 91–108.

Mendez, J. E. 2001. "National Reconciliation, Transitional Justice, and the International Criminal Court." *Ethics and International Affairs* 15(1): 25–44.

Metzler, K. 1991. *Die griechische Begriff des Verzeihens: Untersuch am Wortstamm syngnome von den ersten Belegen bis zum vierten Jahrhundert n. Chr.* Wissenschaftliche Untersuchungen zum Neuen Testament, Zweite Reihe, 44. Tübingen: J. C. B. Mohr.

Meyer, L. R. 2000. "Forgiveness and Public Trust." *Fordham Urban Law Journal* 27: 1515–1540.

Midgley, M. 1984. *Wickedness: A Philosophical Essay.* New York: Routledge.

Mill, J. S. 1992. "Speech on Perfectibility." In *The Autobiography of John Stuart Mill,* ed. A. O. J. Cockshut. Halifax, England: Ryburn Publishing.

Miller, I. W. *Eye for an Eye.* Cambridge: Cambridge University Press, 2006.

Mills, J. 1995. "On Self-Forgiveness and Moral Self-Representation." *Journal of Value Inquiry* 29: 405–406.

Minas, A. 1975. "God and Forgiveness." *Philosophical Quarterly* 25: 138–150.

Minow, M. 1998. *Between Vengeance and Forgiveness.* Boston: Beacon Press.

Moellendorf, D. 2002. *Cosmopolitan Justice.* Boulder, CO: Westview Press.

Moeller, R. G. 2001. *War Stories: The Search for a Usable Past in the Federal Republic of Germany.* Berkeley: The University of California Press.

Moore, K. 1989. *Pardons: Justice, Mercy, and the Public Interest.* Oxford: Oxford University Press.

Morton, A. 2004. *On Evil.* London: Routledge.

Muellner, L. 1996. *The Anger of Achilles: Mênis in Greek Epic.* Ithaca, NY: Cornell University Press.

Murdoch, I. 2003. *The Sovereignty of the Good.* New York: Routledge.

Murphy, J. G. 1982. "Forgiveness and Resentment." *Midwest Studies in Philosophy* 7: 503–516.

———. 1988. "Forgiveness, Mercy, and the Retributive Emotions." *Criminal Justice Ethics* 7: 3–15.

———. 2003. *Getting Even: Forgiveness and Its Limits.* Oxford: Oxford University Press.

Murphy, J. G., and J. Hampton. 1988. *Forgiveness and Mercy.* Cambridge: Cambridge University Press.

Nagel, T. 1988. "Moral Luck." In *Mortal Questions.* Cambridge: Cambridge University Press. Pp. 24–38.

Narayan, U. 1997. "Forgiveness, Moral Reassessment and Reconciliation." In *Explorations of Value,* ed. T. Magnell. Rodopi: Amsterdam. Pp. 169–178.

Neblett, W. R. 1974. "Forgiveness and Ideals." *Mind* 83: 269–275.

The New King James Bible. 1979. New York: T. Nelson Publishers.

Newberry, P. A. 2001. "Joseph Butler on Forgiveness: A Presupposed Theory of Emotion." *Journal of the History of Ideas* 62: 233–244.

Nieman, S. 2002. *Evil in Modern Thought*. Princeton, NJ: Princeton University Press.

Nietzsche, F. W. 1976. *Thus Spoke Zarathustra*. In *The Portable Nietzsche*, ed. and trans. W. Kaufmann. New York: Penguin.

———. 1997. *Twilight of the Idols*. Trans. R. Polt. Indianapolis, IN: Hackett.

———. 1998. *On the Genealogy of Morality*. Trans. M. Clark and A. J. Swensen. Indianapolis, IN: Hackett.

Nixon, R. "Richard Nixon/Frank Gannon Interviews." June 10, 1983. See http://www.libs.uga.edu/media/collections/nixon/nixonday7.html.

North, J. 1987. "Wrongdoing and Forgiveness." *Philosophy* 62: 499–508.

Norton, D. 1974. "Rawls's Theory of Justice: A 'Perfectionist' Rejoinder." *Ethics* 85: 50–57.

Norval, A. 1998. "Memory, Identity, and the Impossibility of Reconciliation: The Work of the Truth and Reconciliation Commission in South Africa." *Constellations* 5(2): 250–265.

Novitz, D. 1998. "Forgiveness and Self-Respect." *Philosophy and Phenomenological Research* 58: 299–315.

Nussbaum, M. 1990. "'By Words not Arms': Lucretius on Gentleness in an Unsafe World." In *The Poetics of Therapy*, ed. M. Nussbaum. Edmonton, Alberta: Academic Printing and Publishing. Pp. 41–90.

———. 1998. "Equity and Mercy." In *Literature and Legal Problem Solving: Law and Literature as Ethical Discourse*, ed. P. J. Heald. Durham, NC: Carolina Academic Press. Pp. 15–54.

O'Connor, F. V. 1986. "An Iconographic Interpretation of Diego Rivera's *Detriot Industry* Murals in Terms of Their Orientation to the Cardinal Points of the Compass." In *Diego Rivera: A Retrospective*, ed. L. B. Downs and C. N. Helms. New York: Founders Society Detriot Institute of Arts. Pp. 215–229.

Oliver, K. 2004. "Revolt, Singularity, and Forgiveness." In *The Colonization of Psychoanalytic Space: A Psychoanalytic Social Theory of Oppression*. Minneapolis: University of Minnesota Press. Pp. 155–194.

O'Neill, B. 1999. *Honor, Symbols, and War*. Ann Arbor: University of Michigan Press.

Orwell, G. 1961. *1984*. New York: New American Library.

Owen, H. P. 1972. "Perfection." *Encyclopedia of Philosophy* 5: 87–88.

Passmore, J. 2000. *The Perfectibility of Man*. 3rd ed. Rpt. Indianapolis, IN: Liberty Press.

Perada, C. 2001. "Forgiveness and Oblivion." In *Rethinking Evil*, ed. M. P. Lara. Berkeley: University of California Press. Pp. 210–222.

Pettigrove, G. 2004. "The Forgiveness We Speak: The Illocutinary Force of Forgiving." *The Southern Journal of Philosophy* 42: 371–392.

———. 2004. "Unapologetic Forgiveness." *American Philosophical Quarterly* 41: 187–204.

Pippin, R. 1979. "The Rose and the Owl: Some Remarks on the Theory-Practice Problem in Hegel." *Independent Journal of Philosophy* 3: 7–16.

———. 1997. *Idealism as Modernism*. Cambridge: Cambridge University Press.

———. 1999. *Modernism as a Philosophical Problem*. New York: Routledge.

Plato. 1997. *Complete Works*, ed. J. M. Cooper and D. S. Hutchinson. Indianapolis, IN: Hackett.

Popkin, M., and B. Nehal. 1999. "Latin American Amnesties in Comparative Perspective: Can the Past Be Buried?" *Ethics and International Affairs* 13: 99–122.

Potter, N. 2001. "Is Refusing to Forgive a Vice?" In *Feminists Doing Ethics*, ed. P. DesAutels and J. Waugh. Lanham, MD: Rowman and Littlefield. Pp. 135–150.

Radzik, L. 2004. "Making Amends." *American Pholosophical Quarterly* 41, 141–154.

Reagan, R. "Remarks on Signing the Bill Providing Restitution for the Wartime Internment of Japanese-American Civilians." August 10, 1988. See http://facstaff.uww.edu/mohanp/ethnic7b.html.

Reeves, J. "An Apology for Slavery." *The Decatur Daily*, April 21, 2004. P. C1.

Regan, D. T., and J. Totten. 1975. "Empathy and Attribution: Turning Observers into Actors." *Journal of Personality and Social Psychology* 32: 850–856.

Richards, N. 1988. "Forgiveness." *Ethics* 99: 77–97.

Ricoeur, P. 1967. *The Symbolism of Evil.* Trans. E. Buchanan. New York: Harper and Row.

———. 1992. *Oneself as Another.* Trans. K. Blamey. Chicago: University of Chicago Press.

———. 1995. "Sanction, Réhabilitation, Pardon." In *Le Juste*, Vol. 1. Paris: Editions Esprit. Pp. 193–208.

Robbennolt, J. K. 2003. "Apologies and Legal Settlement: An Empirical Examination." *Michigan Law Review* 102: 460–516.

Roberts, R. C. 1995. "Forgivingness." *American Philosophical Quarterly* 32: 289–306.

Romilly, de. Jacqueline. 1995. *Tragedies Grecques Au Fil des Ans.* Paris: Les Belles Lettres.

———. 1995. "Indulgence et Pardon dans la Tragédie Grecque." In *Tragedies Grecques au Fil des Ans.* Paris: Les Belles Lettres. Pp. 62–77.

Roochnik, D. 2007. "Aristotle's Account of the Vicious: A Forgivable Inconsistency." *History of Philosophy Quarterly*, 24: 207–220.

Rorty, A. O. 2000. "The Dramas of Resentment." *The Yale Review* 88: 89–100.

Rorty, A. O., ed. 2001. *The Many Faces of Evil: Historical Perspectives.* New York: Routledge.

Rotberg, R., and Thompson, D., eds. 2000. *Truth v. Justice.* Princeton, NJ: Princeton University Press.

Runciman, W. G. 1969. *Social Science and Political Theory.* Cambridge: Cambridge University Press.

Ryle, G. 1963. *The Concept of Mind.* London: Hutchinson & Co.

Sanford, D. 1972. "Degrees of Perfection." *Encyclopedia of Philosophy* 2: 324–326.

Santayana, G. 1936. *The Life of Reason or the Phases of Human Progress*, 5 vols., 2nd ed. New York: C. Scribner's Sons.

Sarat, A., and Hussain, N., eds. 2007. *Forgiveness, Mercy, and Clemency.* Stanford, CA: Stanford University Press.

Saunders, T. J. 2001. "*Epieikeia*: Plato and the Controversial Virtue of the Greeks." In *Plato's Laws and Its Historical Significance*, ed. F. L. Lisi. Sankt Augustin: Academia Verlag. Pp. 65–93.

Scheffler, S. 2001. *Boundaries and Allegiances: Problems of Justice and Responsibility in Liberal Thought*. Oxford: Oxford University Press.

Scheler, M. 1954. *The Nature of Sympathy*. Trans. P. Heath. London: Routledge & Kegan Paul.

———. 1992. "Negative Feelings and the Destruction of Values: *Ressentiment*." Trans. W. W. Holdheim. In *On Feeling, Knowing, and Valuing*, ed. H. J. Bershady. Chicago: University of Chicago Press. Pp. 116–143.

Schimmel, S. 2002. *Wounds Not Healed by Time: The Power of Repentance and Forgiveness*. Oxford: Oxford University Press.

Schopenhauer, A. 1891. *The World as Will and Idea*. London: Kegan Paul, Trench, Trubner and Co.

———. 1995. *On the Basis of Morality*. Providence, RI: Berghahn Books.

Seneca. 1995. *Moral and Political Essays*, ed. J. Cooper and J. F. Procopé. Cambridge: Cambridge University Press.

Shaftesbury, A. A. C. 1999. *Characteristics of Men, Manners, Opinions, Times*, ed. L. E. Klein. Cambridge: Cambridge University Press.

Shapiro, T. 2003. "Compliance, Complicity, and the Nature of Nonideal Conditions." *The Journal of Philosophy* 100: 329–355.

Shay, J. 2003. *Achilles in Vietnam: Combat Trauma and the Undoing of Character*. New York: Scribner.

Shea, D. 2000. *The South African Truth Commission: The Politics of Reconciliation*. Washington, DC: United States Institute of Peace.

Sherman, N. 1998. "Empathy, Respect and Humanitarian Intervention." *Ethics and International Affairs* 12: 103–120.

Shklar, J. 1957. *After Utopia: The Decline of Political Faith*. Princeton, NJ: Princeton University Press.

Shriver, D. W. 1995. *An Ethic for Enemies: Forgiveness in Politics*. Oxford: Oxford University Press.

———. 2001. "Where and When in Political Life is Justice Served by Forgiveness?" In *Burying the Past*, ed. N. Biggar. Washington, DC: Georgetown University Press. Pp. 23–39.

Silber, J. R. 1960. "The Ethical Significance of Kant's *Religion*." In I. Kant's *Religion within the Limits of Reason Alone*. Trans. T. M. Greene and H. H. Hudson. New York: Harper and Row. Pp. 78–142.

Smedes, L. B. 1996. *The Art of Forgiving*. Nashville, IN: Morrings.

Smith, A. 1982. *The Theory of Moral Sentiments*. Ed. D. D. Raphael and A. L. Macfie. Rpt. Indianapolis, IN: Liberty Press.

Smith, C. F. 1988. *Thucydides*, vol. 2. Cambridge, MA: Harvard University Press.

Smith, T. 1997. "Tolerance and Forgiveness: Virtues or Vices?" *Journal of Applied Philosophy* 14: 31–42.

Snow, N. 1993. "Self-Forgiveness." *Journal of Value Inquiry* 27: 75–80.

Solomon, R. 2003. *Not Passion's Slave: Emotions and Choice*. Oxford: Oxford University Press.

Sontag, S. 2003. *Regarding the Pain of Others*. New York: Farrar, Straus and Giroux.

Sophocles. 1969. *Ajax*. Trans. J. Moore, in *Sophocles II*, ed. D. Grene and R. Lattimore. Chicago: University of Chicago Press.

———. 1969. *The Women of Trachis*. Trans. M. Jameson, in *Sophocles II*, ed. D. Grene and R. Lattimore. Chicago: University of Chicago Press.

Speight, A. 2005. "Butler and Hegel on Forgiveness and Agency." *Southern Journal of Philosophy* 43: 299–316.

Stein, E. 1989. *On the Problem of Empathy*. Trans. W. Stein. Washington, DC: ICS Publications.

Stockdale, J. 1995. *Thoughts of a Philosophical Fighter Pilot*. Stanford, CA: Hoover Institution Press.

Stockdale, J., and S. Stockdale 1984. *In Love and War*. New York: Harper and Row.

Stolberg, S. G. "Senate Issues Apology Over Failure on Antilynching Law." *New York Times*, June 14, 2005. P. A1.

Strauss, B. 1985. "Ritual, Social Drama and Politics in Classical Athens." *American Journal of Ancient History* 10: 67–83.

Strawson, P. F. 1980. *Freedom and Resentment, and Other Essays*. New York: Methuen.

Strazzabosco, J. 1996. *Learning about Forgiveness from the Life of Nelson Mandela*. New York: Rosen Publishing Group.

Stueber, K. R., see Kogler, H. H.

Sugarman, R. 1980. *Rancor Against Time: The Phenomenology of 'Ressentiment.'* Hamburg: Felix Meiner Verlag.

Sussman, D. 2005. "Kantian Forgiveness." *Kant-Studien* 96: 85–107.

Swanton, C. 2003. *Virtue Ethics: A Pluralistic View*. Oxford: Oxford University Press.

Swinburne, R. 1989. *Responsibility and Atonement*. Oxford: Clarendon Press.

Taguieff, P.-A. 2004. *Le Sens du Progrès: Une Approche Historique et Philosophique*. Paris: Flammarion.

Tavuchis, N. 1991. *Mea Culpa: A Sociology of Apology and Reconciliation*. Stanford, CA: Stanford University Press.

Tilly, C. 2002. *Stories, Identities, and Political Change*. New York: Rowman and Littlefield Publishers.

Todorov, T. 2002. *Imperfect Garden: The Legacy of Humanism*. Trans. C. Cosman. Princeton, NJ: Princeton University Press.

Torpey, J. 2001. "'Making Whole What Has Been Smashed: Reflections and Reparations.'" *Journal of Modern History* 73: 333–358.

Totten, J., see Regan, D. T.

Tutu, D. 1999. *No Future without Forgiveness*. New York: Random House.

Twambley, P. 1976. "Mercy and Forgiveness." *Analysis* 36: 84–90.

Ugrešić, D. 1998. *The Culture of Lies: Antipolitical Essays*. Trans. C. Hawkesworth. London: Phoenix House.

Unamuno, M. de. 1954. *Tragic Sense of Life*. Trans. Crawford Flitch. New York: Dover Publications.

United States Senate Resolution 39 IS of February 7, 2005 (an apology to victims of lynching). See http://thomas.loc.gov/home/c109query.html (Library of Congress website).

Usener, H. 1977. *Glossarium Epicureum*. Edendum curaverunt M. et W. Schmid. Rome: Edizioni dell'Ateneo & Bizzarri.

VanDeMark, B. 1995. *In Retrospect: The Tragedy and Lessons of Vietnam*. New York: Vintage Books.

Van Vugt, W. E., and Cloete, G. D., eds. 2000. *Race and Reconciliation in South Africa: A Multicultural Dialogue in Comparative Perspective.* Lanham, MD: Lexington Books.

Velleman, D. J. 2003. "Narrative Explanation." *Philosophical Review* 112: 1–26.

———. 2006. *Self to Self.* Cambridge: Cambridge University Press.

Waldron, J. 1992. "Superseding Historical Injustice." *Ethics* 103(1): 4–28.

Walker, M. 2006. *Moral Repair: Reconstructing Moral Relations after Wrongdoing.* Cambridge: Cambridge University Press.

Wallace, R. J. 1994. *Responsibility and the Moral Sentiments.* Cambridge, MA: Harvard University Press.

Warner, R. 1987. *Thucydides: History of the Peloponnesian War.* New York: Penguin.

Watkins, J. 2005. "Forgiveness and Its Place in Ethics." *Theoria* 71: 59–77.

Watson, G. 1987. "Responsibility and the Limits of Evil." In *Responsibility, Character, and the Emotions: New Essays in Moral Psychology,* ed. F. Schoeman. New York: Cambridge University Press. Pp. 256–286.

Weizsäcker, R. von. 1986. "Speech by Richard von Weizsäcker, President of the Federal Republic of Germany, in the Bundestag during the Ceremony Commemorating the 40th Anniversary of the End of the War in Europe and of National Socialist Tyranny, May 8, 1985." In *Bitburg in Moral and Political Perspective,* ed. G. Hartman. Bloomington: Indiana University Press. Pp. 262–273.

Wells, H. G. 1967. *A Modern Utopia.* Lincoln: University of Nebraska Press.

Wiesenthal, S. 1969. *The Sunflower.* New York: Schocken Books.

Williams, B. 1993. "Moral Luck." In *Moral Luck.* Cambridge: Cambridge University Press. Pp. 20–39. First published in the *Proceedings of the Aristotelian Society* S.V. 50 (1976): 115–130.

———. 1993. *Shame and Necessity.* Berkeley: University of California Press.

———. 1995. *Making Sense of Humanity.* Cambridge: Cambridge University Press.

———. 2002. *Truth and Truthfulness: An Essay in Genealogy.* Princeton, NJ: Princeton University Press.

Wilson, J. 1988. "Why Forgiveness Requires Repentance." *Philosophy* 63: 534–535.

Wilson, R. 2003. "Justice and Retribution in Postconflict Settings." *Public Culture* 15: 187–190.

Wispé, L. 1990. "History of the Concept of Empathy." In *Empathy and Its Development,* ed. N. Eisenberg and J. Strayer. Cambridge: Cambridge University Press. Pp. 17–37.

———. 1991. *The Psychology of Sympathy.* New York: Plenum Press.

Wittgenstein, L. 2001. *Philosophical Investigations,* 3rd ed. Trans. G. E. M. Anscombe. Oxford: Blackwell.

Wollheim, R. 1984. *The Thread of Life.* New Haven, CT: Yale University Press.

Woodruff, P. 1993. *Thucydides: On Justice, Power, and Human Nature.* Indianapolis, IN: Hackett.

Woodruff, P., and H. Wilmer, eds. 1988. *Facing Evil: Confronting the Dreadful Power Behind Genocide, Terrorism and Cruelty.* Chicago: Open Court Publishing.

Worthington, E. L., Jr., ed. 1998. *Dimensions of Forgiveness. Psychological Research and Theological Perspectives.* Philadelphia: Templeton Foundation Press.

Wright, F. 2006. *God's Silence.* New York: Random House.

Young, J. E. 1986. "Memory and Monument." In *Bitburg in Moral and Political Perspective*, ed. G. Hartman. Bloomington: Indiana University Press. Pp. 103–113.

Zawadski, P. 2002. "Le Ressentiment et l'Égalité: Contribution à Une Anthropologie Philosophique de la Démocratie." In *Le Ressentiment*, ed. P. Ansart. Brussels: Bruylant. Pp. 31–56.

Also cited: on-line bibliographies and web resources on forgiveness:
www.brandonhamber.com/resources_forgiveness.htm
www.forgiving.org
www.forgivenessweb.com/RdgRm/Bibliography.html
www.learningtoforgive.com
The "Kentucky Forgiveness Collective," at http://www.geocities.com/forgivenessresearch/latest.htm

A selected list of Truth Commission reports available in English:

From Madness to Hope: The 12-Year War in El Salvador: Report of the Commission on the Truth for El Salvador. 1993. United Nations: UN Doc. S/25500/Annex. Available at http://www.usip.org/library/tc/doc/reports/el_salvador/tc_es_03151993_toc.html.

Guatemala. Memory of Silence: Report of the Commission for Historical Clarification. 1999. The main conclusions and recommendations of this report are available in English at http://shr.aaas.org/guatemala/ceh/report/english/toc.html.

Nunca Mas: Report of the Argentine National Commission on the Disappeared. 1986. New York: Farrar Straus & Giroux. The full report in English and Spanish can be found at www.nuncamas.org/index.htm.

Report of the Chilean National Commission on Truth and Reconciliation, 2 vols. 1993. Trans. P. E. Berryman. Notre Dame and London: University of Notre Dame Press. The full report in English can also be found at http://www.usip.org/library/tc/doc/reports/chile/chile_1993_toc.html; and in Spanish, at http://www.derechos.org/koaga/iii/1/cuya.html (along with information about other Truth Commissions in Latin America).

Truth and Reconciliation Commission of South Africa Report. 5 vols. 1998–99. Cape Town: Juta & Co. and New York: Grove's Dictionaries. The full report can also be found at http://www.doj.gov.za/trc/. I refer in this book to the transcript of the 1997 hearings of Amy Biehl's killers, at http://www.doj.gov.za/trc/hrvtrans/index.htm.

Numerous papers that evaluate and comment on the South African Truth and Reconciliation Commission can be found on the website of the Centre for the Study of Violence and Reconciliation: http://www.csvr.org.za/

Index